D1707233

OVER THE TOP JUDAISM

*Precedents and Trends in the Depiction of Jewish
Beliefs and Observances in Film and Television*

Elliot B. Gertel

University Press of America,® Inc.
Lanham · Boulder · New York · Toronto · Oxford

University Press of America,® Inc.
4501 Forbes Boulevard
Suite 200
Lanham, Maryland 20706
UPA Acquisitions Department (301) 459-3366

PO Box 317
Oxford
OX2 9RU, UK

ISBN 0-7618-2624-6 (paperback : alk. ppr.)

CONTENTS

PART THREE
GLIMMERS OF SANCTITY ON BIG AND SMALL SCREEN:
ADMIRABLE AND INSIGHTFUL PRODUCTION EFFORTS

PREFACE

These pages are intended to open new discussion by giving attention to television episodes in the context of series and by pointing to cross-fertilization of themes and motifs between big and small screens in their depiction of Judaism and of Jewish life. This book is intended for students of film and television and for the general, interested reader, as well as for writers and producers who may want to consider the possible ramifications of their work. I have made every effort to name the writers of all television episodes and films analyzed here.

I have dealt mainly with productions of the 1980s through the early 2000s. Trends in film have already been documented in two thorough volumes,[1] and handy overviews of the Jewish image in television have begun to appear.[2] I have made the Eighties my starting point because, as I will argue in the Introduction, approaches that influence current film and television more directly were added in that decade to longstanding trends. I have, however, examined in detail, and with oral histories, some earlier,

---

1. See the Lester Friedman and Patricia Erens volumes cited in the Introduction. See, also, David Desser and Lester D. Friedman, *American-Jewish Filmmakers: Traditions and Trends* (Urbana and Chicago: University of Illinois, 1993).

2. The most complete survey to date is Jonathan Pearl and Judith Pearl, *The Chosen Image: Television's Portrayal of Jewish Themes and Characters* (Jefferson, North Carolina: McFarland and Company, Inc., 1999). The book does yeoman service. I disagree strongly, however, with the authors' commentary on many of the episodes, and with their overall suggestion that the featuring of Jewish characters and themes on television is in and of itself a positive indication.

classic productions that demand attention in any discussion of television and film writing about Judaism.

These chapters grow out of more than twenty years of reviewing film and television for the *National Jewish Post and Opinion*, based in Indianapolis, Indiana. In 1977, Gabriel Cohen, the tireless and courageous founder and editor of that newspaper, asked me to do a review column of film and television. He had seen an article I wrote in *The Reconstructionist* about a bad television adaptation of Harry Kemelman's novel, *Friday The Rabbi Slept Late* (1964).[3] At first I turned him down. I was in graduate rabbinical school with a full load of courses and other jobs. Some months later, I saw something else on television that got my goat, and sent him a column.[4] It was published on July 27, 1979. My reviews were originally called, "An Occasional Column," as I never imagined how filmic ideas, and, especially, television representations of Jews and Judaism would proliferate. I have been writing a regular column for the *Post* ever since, though, over the last decade, there have been some years with more than forty reviews in what came to be called "Media Watch." I shall always be most grateful to Gabriel for his resolve, verve and kind interest in me and in his other columnists. I owe a great debt to the staff of the *Post* for all their help through the years, including Gregg Birnbaum, David Edy , and, especially, Ed Stattmann. Ed Stattmann's total dedication to the newspaper, until late into the night, has inspired me with the importance of getting my columns in as frequently as possible, even when I have been overwhelmed by other commitments. I am indebted, as well, to the readers of the *National Jewish Post and Opinion* who have communicated with me through the years.

I am also thankful to Rabbi Ira Eisenstein, who published that first TV review in *The Reconstructionist*, and to Dr. Trude Weiss-Rosmarin, brilliant scholar and legendary editor of *Jewish Spectator*, who began to publish my writing when I was fifteen. At first, Dr. Weiss-Rosmarin regarded my film and TV review columns in the *Jewish Post and Opinion* as time stolen from more serious writing. But I believe she recognized the importance of media criticism when she asked me to review the first major

---

3.   See "Lanigan's Rabbi," *The Reconstructionist* (*March 1977*).
4.   The film was *Summer of My German Soldier*. I was appalled at the way that a Jewish father was depicted as cruel in comparison with a kind young Nazi prisoner of war.

volume on filmic treatment of Judaism, *Hollywood's Image of the Jew* (1982), by Lester Friedman, even though, at first, she was adamant that "we don't write on films (or records) and the other media which are supposed to be 'the message.'"[5] In recent years, Robert Bleiweiss, Dr. Weiss-Rosmarin's hand-picked successor at *Jewish Spectator*, brought talent, thoughtfulness, grace, and his own visionary insights to the magazine, as she knew he would, and continued her tradition of encouraging many writers on Jewish themes, including me. His son, Rabbi Mark Bleiweiss, followed in that tradition during his term as editor. The chapters on *Naked City* and *Route Sixty-Six* originally appeared in *Jewish Spectator* in different form. I also thank Vida Bleiweiss for her friendship and support.

I am most thankful to Rabbi Benjamin Jolkovsky, dedicated and pioneering editor of the internet magazine, *Jewish World Review*. He prodded me for permission in 1998, when launching the *Review*, to reprint some of my columns, thus giving them exposure to a large audience on the World Wide Web. Gabriel Cohen was kind to encourage this, as well as the reprinting of columns in the Albany *Jewish World*, beginning in 1998, at the request of Sam Clevenson, the editor of that newspaper, who has thus disseminated my media reviews.

I am deeply grateful to the men and women and children of Congregation Rodfei Zedek in Chicago, and before that, Congregation Beth El-Keser Israel in New Haven, for their support and interest. They knew that I had a "double life" as a TV and film critic, and have been most understanding and helpful. I particularly acknowledge synagogue and auxiliary presidents who have been most encouraging, knowing that I came with an unusual "side line": Norman Sider, Harry Moskow, Shirley Holbrook, Edward Hamburg, Sara Segal Loevy, Louis Winer, Joseph J. Abbell, Arnold Newberger, Harold Dray, Irving Paley, Joseph Pinkert, Mendl Siegel and Jules Levinstein, Jane Melnick-Stengel, Sharon R. Glick and Cass Friedberg, in Chicago; and Herbert Etkind, Dr. Alan Gelbert, Adele Tyson, Stephen Alderman, David Sagerman, Morris Oppenheim and Paul Goodwin in New Haven. Rev. Louis Friedman, Ethel Goldberg Epstein, Thea Crook and Etty Dolgin have been considerate, understanding and supportive as

---

5   In a personal letter to me, September 7, 1976. The review appeared in *Jewish Spectator* (Spring 1983). In 1985 she sent me a gift of Patricia Erens' book, "not for review. I thought you'd like to have it." (March 17, 1985). Obviously, she still maintained some quota on articles about film.

synagogue staff members with whom I worked closely during my years in these respective congregations. Thanks, also, to Rose Solomon and Leatrice Berman for kind assistance. I am also grateful for the support and kindness of Rabbi Larry Heimer and Rabbi Ralph Simon and, most recently, of Cantor Julius Solomon. I thank Ethel Goldberg Epstein for typing some early drafts of chapters in this book, and David Crook for typing most of the manuscript onto computer diskette.

I owe special thanks to Rodfei Zedek volunteers who have graciously boosted my writings: Pam Spitzner, bulletin editor; Ammiel Prochovnick, webmaster; and Carol Gittler, Vivian Handel, Carol Schneider, Helen Tyson and Gloria Williams of the Irving and Dorothy Nelson Gift Shop.

Special thanks to my longtime dear friends, Rabbi Robert and Deborah Slosberg for encouraging and inspiring me in many ways, and for inviting me to their congregation, Adath Jeshurun in Louisville, to speak over a weekend on film and television, giving me the opportunity on that and other occasions, over twenty years, to witness the intelligence, grace, and good humor that they bring to the synagogue, day school, and to the entire community, as well as to the Conservative Movement in American Judaism.

Special thanks, also, to Rabbi Stuart Federow, who has always been an active booster of the column, and to Rabbi Reuven Frankel (Deerfield, Illinois) and Dr. Frederick Dietz (Rockford, Illinois), for arranging for me to speak on the media, and to Cantor Alan Smolen of Elgin, Illinois, who has alerted me to programs that he wanted me to review. Aviva Silberman of Highland Park, Illinois was a most thoughtful reader who often called media matters to my attention. Raymond and Betty Epstein have also been avid readers of the *Post*, always with a good word. Other column readers who have provided much encouragement through the years include Rabbi Robert A. Alper, Rabbi Jacob Chinitz, Sid Cohen, Rabbi Wayne Dosick, Rabbi Samuel H. Dresner, Dr. Lawrence J. Epstein, Dr. Harry Essrig, Milton Fromer, Hannah Grad Goodman, Elliot H. Gertel and Jamie Morris, Dr. Judith Weinstein Klein, Rabbi Simeon Kolko, Gertrude Left, Dr. Jacob R. Marcus, Dr. Harry Orlinsky, Dr. Marc Lee Raphael, Rabbi Bernard S. Raskas, Chana Rosen, Morris U. Schappes, Ida Cohen Selaven, Rabbi David Saperstein, Cantor Morton Shames, Gene Siskel, Albert Smolover, Dr. Alfred Sofer, Bob Spodick, Rabbi Alex and Bella Weisfogel, Susan Winkelstein, Dr. Jeffrey S. Winter, Prof. Walter P. Zenner, and Cantor Paul Zim. Rabbis Mark Diamond, Richard Leibovitz, Stuart Lipson, Joel

Newman, and Benjamin Scolnic have been most encouraging toward my media columns since our student days.

I am most grateful to Rabbis Mordecai Simon and Ira Youdovin of the Chicago Board of Rabbis, and to Lydia Talbott of the Broadcast Ministries of Chicago, and Joe Loughlin, of the broadcasting office of Archdiocese of Chicago, who were so helpful to me in my role as chairman of the Joint Commission on Broadcasting of the Chicago Jewish Federation and the Chicago Board of Rabbis. They also prodded me to be on television programs, including a "prime time" Sunday noon panel arguing about films with Protestant and Catholic critics.

I respectfully acknowledge my teachers in the public schools of Springfield, Massachusetts who taught me to think and to interpret various media critically, especially Olive Beverly, Alvin Brown, Ruth Dickerman, David Douglas, Robert Heon, David Margeson, Justin O'Connor, Laurie Pieterse, and William Young. I am most grateful to my rabbi, Dr. Samuel H. Dresner, of blessed memory, who taught me at a young age the importance of critiques, from a rabbinic point of view, of literature and film. As a result of summer discussions with Professor George A. Panichas in the Springfield Public Library during my high school, college and seminary years, I learned of D. H. Lawrence's observation that "the critic, like the good beadle, should rap the public on its knuckles and make it attend during divine service."

I learned much from television writers, producers and directors who were kind enough to allow me to take their oral histories and recollections of certain series and personalities, and I acknowledge them here: Art Baer, Orin Borsten, Oliver Crawford, Sam Denoff, Abram S. Ginnes, Nate Esformes, Irvin Kershner, Ernest Kinoy, Chester Krumholz, Herbert B. Leonard, John Meredyth Lucas, Sam Manners, Michael McGreevey, Stanley Leslie Neufield, Barry Oringer, Bill Persky, David Noel Rich, Howard Rodman Jr., Alvin Sargent, Hal Sitowitz, Peter Tauber, Mort Thaw, Shimon Wincelberg, and Paul Wolff. Thanks also to Professor Jay Dratler Jr. for his reminiscences and to Bernard Lechowick for engaging in dialogue with me.

I acknowledge the encouragement and efficient assistance of the Screen Writers Guild of America, particularly Karen Pederson and Adam Kersh of the James R. Webb Memorial Library.

I thank staff and former staff members of the University Press of America for their interest in this project, especially Beverly Baum, Nicole Coviello, Diana Lavery, Lois Raimond, and Stephen Ryan. I also thank Dr.

Over the Top Judaism

Gerhard Falk of Buffalo, New York, for introducing me to the University Press, and Jane Jordan Browne and Scott Mendel for advising me on contract matters. I am exceedingly grateful to Edmond Vadnais of Ibex Indexing Service, and to his associate, my excellent proofreader, Genevieve E. Miller, for their fine eye and helpful pointers. This project could not have been completed without the reassuring and competent services of Susan Peabody, who, from a distant coast, did the camera-ready work, assisted in the proofreading, and recommended Edmond and Gen, whose fine work complemented hers. Any errors that remain are solely my responsibility.

This book was made possible through a generous gift from The Rabbi Solomon Goldman Foundation and its directors Gayola Goldman Epstein and Albert Zemel. My research into Rabbi Goldman's life and insights has inspired and enlightened more than I can express. I was not surprised to find in the correspondence of this titan scholar, intellectual and community leader, a 1939 letter to Barney Balaban of Paramount Pictures, encouraging the motion picture industry to showcase the achievements of the Jewish community in Palestine, "one of the most glorious achievements of the modern age."[6]

As always, I am most grateful to my parents, William and Sylvia Gertel, for their love, help and support, and for teaching me to appreciate fine art, comedy and dramatics, but to take in all media critically and with a grain of salt. I am thankful to Ted and Joan Gertel for their support and encouragement, and I hope that Alex, Aaron, Jason and Diana enjoy this book.

This book is dedicated to the memory of my maternal grandparents, Hyman and Diana Rubin. They were always totally supportive of me and of my writing. Immigrants to this country, they had an intelligent and heartfelt feel for the blessings of American life and for the best in American pop culture. They were among the first in Springfield, Massachusetts to own a television set, and made time to enjoy the great movies of the thirties and forties. Though observant of the Sabbath, they made special arrangements to attend Saturday matinees with their children by arranging for purchase of tickets before the Sabbath. I admire their effort to accom-

---

6.   Rabbi Solomon Goldman to Barney Balaban, March 21, 1939. Dr. Goldman added: "The film industry owes this to itself, to America, as well as to the Jewish People." Cited with permission of the American Jewish Archives.

modate the American culture of their time within the framework of synagogue attendance and home observances.

Elliot B. Gertel
Chicago, Illinois
November 25, 2002

INTRODUCTION

F or more than a quarter of a century, a lot of movies and TV programs have been obsessed with Judaism. One can argue that many American Jews were infatuated first with film and then, simultaneously, with television. The movies, and then television, have imposed standards, aesthetics, values, and even vocabulary that American culture, including American Jewish culture, had to engage, whether in imitation, protest, or adaptation. Yet such engagement, for all of its occasional valor, has not been without distortion of Judaism, of Jewish teachings and observances.

At first these seductive media mesmerized Jews. But Judaism was left alone. It was kept off stage, to the side, as a precious relic or heirloom. One thinks of the 1950 film, *Molly*, originally entitled *The Goldbergs*, and based on the famous television series of that name. Gertrude Berg assumed her classic TV role as Molly Goldberg, beloved Jewish matriarch. Most of the film came across as a rather general nostalgia for European parents, not much different from the *I Remember Mama* genre. Toward the end one sees covered *challah* rolls and Shabbat candles, though the actual rituals are only suggested and not performed.

It was a bold statement in the 1950s just to show *challah* and Shabbat candles at a time when the name of the film had to be changed from *The Goldbergs* to *Molly*.[1] For most of the Jewish audience, the immigrant experience and the close-knit family were still realities, and there was no need to translate or to fill in between the lines. Likewise, the presence of ritual objects in the homes of parents was still widely taken for granted. (By the 1970s, ritual objects in film and TV began to be more the domain of

---

1. See Patricia Erens, *The Jew in American Cinema* (Bloomington: Indiana University Press, 1984), p. 229.

immigrant grandparents.) Just the image of a Sabbath table spoke volumes more than any dialogue.

In the 1960s and 1970s, however, depiction of Jews and of Jewish practices became more aggressive, more pointed. There was a determined and concerted effort to stand up for Jewish identity and to throw Jewish practices back into the face of a film culture that had ignored them or shunted them aside. The irony was that the "film culture" consisted of many Jews who had been embarrassed about delving into their heritage, but now sanctioned, with a vengeance, an explosion of Jewish references, associations, and even ambivalences.

All of this came to a head in the 1973 film, *The Way We Were*, starring Barbra Streisand and directed by Sidney Pollock. The well-known singer/actress was taking her stand that ethnic women with a not-so-typically-Hollywood screen look, in this case Jewish women, can successfully chase after matinee-idol Gentile men.[2]

Whatever one thinks of Streisand's "cause," it should be noted that *The Way We Were* was one of the first portents that Judaism would not go untouched or unscathed in the process of the new Jewish self-determination, even self-infatuation, in filmmaking. In one scene in *The Way We Were*, Streisand's character presents her Gentile lover (played by Robert Redford) with a typewriter and calls it a "Rosh Hashanah present." One can imagine Gentile viewers wondering at the time whether Rosh Hashanah, the Jewish New Year, was a time when they should be sending gifts to Jewish friends. One can safely assume that at the time, Jewish viewers were savvy enough to realize that Streisand and Company were inventing this gift as an inside joke to make the point that the public ought to realize that Jews have holidays other than Chanukah. This was their way of "opening up" Judaism. Little did they know that they were starting a trend that would become widespread and shameless—namely, the concoction, or, more often, the corruption, of Jewish customs and observances under the rubric of "creative media writing." A chapter in this volume is devoted to such innovations in Jewish Law, and another chapter, which reviews an episode of the series,

---

2.   In all fairness to Streisand it must be pointed out that in these earlier films, the point was made that interfaith relationships did not lead very far. The couples split up. In *The Way We Were*, Streisand's character ends up marrying a nice Jewish man named Cohen, and being reasonably contented, even after running into Robert Redford once more.

In The Heat of the Night, points to the fabrication of a tradition that Alexander the Great held a Torah scroll in a synagogue.

Paradoxically, such retreading of Judaism, even when misleading, represented the height of comfort with Judaism in the general culture, on the part of both Jewish and non-Jewish writers and producers. It also revealed an antipathy on their part toward religious Jews that rivaled and even exceeded early Hollywood denigration of Jews as ridiculous or embarrassing.[3]

The acceptance, in the 1980s, of Judaism as a prominent theme in television and in the movies did not come without baggage or cost. The new emphasis on "interpreting" Jewish ritual practices provoked both caricature or censure of Judaism.

The treatment of Hasidim on both screens became an important indicator of attitudes toward Jews and Judaism in general, even as courtroom dramas became television's most convenient forum for scrutinizing conventional values, mores and behaviors, including religious traditions. In the early 1990s, the law firm-based series, *Civil Wars*, paraded Hasidim to such an extent that several of them literally fell out of a door when it was opened. The episode dealt with a dispute between synagogues over willed property. Writers M. Finkelstein, Channy Gibson and Charles H. Englee had attorney Eli Levinson (Alan Rosenberg) arbitrating between members of two congregations who argued the relative merits of the deceased having worshipped in one place on Rosh Hashanah and the other on Yom Kippur. Note the use of the names of Jewish holidays, an easy peg for TV or movie "Judaism" since *The Way We Were*.

The Hasidim in this episode require Eli's counsel just to have a rational discussion (even about the wishes of their own *rebbe* or rabbi). Yet they dismiss Eli as unfit to arbitrate because he does not know Yiddish. He has little in common with them, personally or spiritually. Nor do they show him any respect or recognition as a co-religionist. Tellingly, this was the episode on *Civil Wars* in which Eli had a transformational experience, a kind of revelation or epiphany, by visiting a client at a mental institution and in the process finding and giving courage to triumph over mental illness. The Hasidim, representing Judaism, were a foil and embarrassment

---

3.   See Erens, pp. 91 ff., and Lester D. Friedman, *Hollywood's Image of the Jew* (New York: Frederick Ungar Publishing Company, 1982).

in marked contrast with the spiritual insight that came from mental illness itself.

The parade of Hasidim on *Civil Wars* was actually the culmination of a long march that continued throughout the Eighties, beginning with a 1981 episode of the sitcom, *Barney Miller*, set at a police precinct and starring Hal Linden. On that particular episode, the Hasidim run wild. They complain that their neighborhood is not sufficiently patrolled by the police, and then decide to wage war on the police station, smashing windows, injuring cops. Their behavior appalls both the Jewish and non-Jewish officers.

The Hasidim in *Barney Miller* came across as violent, hot-headed and fool-hardy savages. Worse still, they seem to have been intended as proof that traditional Jewish communities are laughable and without substance. When a Hasid tries to account for the riot with a Talmudic saying, a cop tells him to stick it back into his hat. Another Hasid quotes the Talmud twice, and the two quotations obviously contradict one another. The implication here is that Judaism, at least Orthodox Judaism, has no standards, and sanctions whatever ethics or beliefs one chooses at the moment. The writers make their point well when they arrange that the Hasidim are "booked" at the same time as reactionary survivalists, caught hiding in the city sewers with firearms. The bunching together of the two groups sends a clear message.

Such denigration of the Hasidim as both silly and contemptible, on *Barney Miller* and on *Civil Wars*, continued a trend set by Woody Allen who could simply show a character standing between Hasidim, whether in *Annie Hall* (1977) or in *Zelig* (1984), and make his audience roar with laughter. The trend may have begun with a French film, *The Mad Adventures of "Rabbi" Jacob* (1974). Hasidic garb was still exploited for an easy laugh in the 2002 film, *Welcome to Collinwood*.

In similar fashion, the courtroom drama, *L.A. Law*, showed unrestrained contempt for observant Jews in what has become for many TV series, particularly sitcoms, a requisite show about a *mohel* or ritual circumciser. The writers could not resist ridiculing an elderly rabbi for snipping "a little too much," and being sued. The firm takes the case because the rabbi (Nehemiah Persoff) is one of the "dearest friends" of a senior partner's father. (Often in television dramas, rabbis are parents' friends and never friends of the principals.) Stuart Markowitz (Michael Tucker) volunteers to defend the *mohel* because he is the Jewish partner in the firm and "knows the subject matter." In the course of the trial, interestingly, the plantiff, the baby's father, refers to Markowitz (who is intermarried) as a "self-hating Jew."

The writers use Jewish identity and Jewish rituals as an excuse for *mohel* jokes. They even mock the Yiddish accent of the *mohel*, who keeps protesting that his error was only a "*neeke*," that is, a nick. But the *mohel* admits to having said "oops." So the jokes run. In Stuart's final argument he observes that since, in Orthodox Judaism, there is no sex before marriage, disfigurement of the penis would not affect "social life." The judge decides that the *mohel* should not practice any longer because of age and "loss of ability."

Aside from reflecting a rampant disdain in the entertainment industry for older people (especially among younger writers and producers), this episode of *L.A. Law* was somewhat of a milestone in that, taken together with the *Civil Wars* segments previously cited, it bespeaks the ambivalences which both animate and obstruct most television and film writing about Jews and Judaism. The voices of traditional Judaism (which is often dismissed as for "Orthodox" Jews only) condemn and alienate Jewish characters who are not really that involved in Judaism or committed to it, anyway. These Jewish characters then witness (as a kind of justification for distancing themselves?) the exposure of crass and/or nonsensical "Jewish" practices and behaviors.

Television in the 1980s also utilized Hasidim in a more "positive" light, to revive the old Hollywood ideal that "Love Conquers All" (or at least should). This motif has remained strong and consistent in big screen productions since the 1920s,[4] and also became a stock-in-trade of the small screen. A 1987 episode of *The Days and Nights of Molly Dodd* highlights Molly's (Blair Brown) attraction to a Hasidic widower whose charming and witty message on her answering machine intrigues her and who actually visits her apartment to take piano lessons. When Molly asks a Jewish girlfriend about the Hasidim, the latter answers that while she doesn't know much about Hasidim or Judaism, she is certain that Molly's Hasidic friend has broken all the rules just by talking to her on the telephone, let alone visiting her apartment.

As if to confirm and to explain the Hasid's anomalous behavior, writer Wendy Kout has the screenplay chirp some platitudes about his being a widower, being lonely, and looking to get some "song" back into his life.

---

4.   See the Friedman and Erens surveys of films of the 1920s.

But Hasidim usually visit their *rebbe* when they are troubled, are supported by their community which believes in timely remarriage after loss of a spouse, and regard song and dance as basic to their religious expression.

In the awkwardness of their first encounter, Molly apologizes to the Hasid for joking about her Irish mother being a "Jewish mother" who keeps nagging her, now divorced, to remarry. A few piano lessons lead to the Hasid's kissing Molly passionately on the lips and then sighing, "I'm sorry. This isn't right. I can't do it. It's not fair. I can't see you again." Then he says: "You brought music back into my life." In the last segment of the half-hour episode, Molly dreams that she is lying in bed naked, with the Hasid lying naked on the other half of a TV screen. They sing a duet, in bed, and then suddenly spring onto a stage, dressed like Fred Astaire and Ginger Rogers, dancing and singing up a storm along with nuns and Hasidic men who break into choreography reminiscent of Busby Berkeley, complete with a Statue of Liberty prop. It would seem that in the 1980s, depicting the fantasy of melting pot romance became even more romantic than showing an actual affair. Even so, the adherence to strict religious practices had to be broken down at least a little bit—not a Rosh Hashanah present perhaps, but the loosening of traditional strictures regarding sexual contact.

Why all the attention to Hasidim? One is reminded of the old joke about an American Jewish woman who is seated in a bus next to a Hasid. She cannot control her contempt and regales him: "You Hasidim live in the Middle Ages. Your practices are primitive and silly. You're an embarrassment to us." The man replies: "I'm sorry, madam, I'm Amish, and I'm proud of my religion." The woman then apologizes profusely, saying how much she admires the Amish resolve to cling to their tradition and mores in a confused and confusing world.

That old joke still applied in the 1980s even as Jewish practices and expressions became more pronounced in TV and film writing. Its point is illustrated, to some degree or another, in much of the material documented and analyzed in this book. The key to spotting the message behind most of these productions is the rhetoric or behavior of the Jewish character, where there is a principal Jewish persona. Does that character distance himself or herself from observant or at least involved Jews on the grounds that their practices and "tribalism" are silly or embarrassing or outright immoral? Whether or not there are major Jewish characters, is there a use of

"Judaism" to promote other values and ideas or to praise and promote skills other than Jewish learning or ritual?[5]

What, for example, is *Roseanne* or *The Nanny* promoting in episodes about bar mitzvah and seder ceremonies? What is *Seinfeld* or *Northern Exposure* saying about a Jewish protagonist?

The purpose of this book is to explore trends and patterns in the depiction of Jewish beliefs and observances in film and television. The material is organized to focus on various themes such as life cycle events, religious festivals, aspects of Jewish beliefs and behaviors ("usages"), even conversion to Judaism. It then highlights in great detail bizarre or inappropriate spins on Jewish teachings, concerns and practices.

The last section showcases thoughtful and affecting productions that have successfully broken from longstanding formulas and are promising in their creative and heartfelt approaches to Judaism and to Jewish life. The outstanding productions in Part Three represent a hope and model for meaningful future depiction of Judaism in both media.

Significantly, the third episode of the HBO series, *The Sopranos*, broadcast in January 1999, concentrated on the very themes of Hasidim and circumcision and combined them in a promising, if vexing, approach to depicting Jews and Judaism on television.[6]

It seems that a wealthy Hasidic man, Shlomo Teitelbaum, wants gangster Tony Soprano (James Gandolfini) to "convince" his son-in-law Ariel to stop withholding a Jewish divorce from Teitelbaum's daughter.[7]

---

5. An emerging trend in film and television, especially since 1990, is either assault upon or distortion of Jewish beliefs and practices by films and TV episodes that glorify New Age concepts and worldviews. These I hope to explore in another book. Among the films that started this trend are *White Palace* (1990), *Shine* (1996), Hallmark's crass "melting pot" musical, *Mrs. Santa Claus* (1996), *A Price Above Rubies* (1998) and *Tuesdays With Morrie* (1999). Some of the television series explored in this book, like *Beverly Hills 90210*, *Northern Exposure*, *The Nanny*, *thirtysomething*, and *Dharma and Greg* have contributed immensely to this trend. Yet there are also films and television programs that are challenging it.

6. I am grateful to my brother, Dr. Ted Gertel, for telling me about this episode and for providing me with a videotape of it.

7. On the problem of traditional Jewish divorce being in the hands of the husband, see Elliot B. Gertel, "Jewish Views on Divorce," in *The Jewish Family and Jewish Continuity*, ed. Steven Bayme and Gladys Rosen

"He's not only harming my daughter," Teitelbaum says, "but he's mocking our laws of marriage." We're told that there was once a "rabbis' goon squad" to persuade recalcitrant husbands (by beating them, when necessary, if I get the implication), but that it was "put out of business by the D.A.'s office."

Soprano wants twenty-five per cent of Teitelbaum's business in order to intimidate Ariel, who has been demanding fifty per cent to grant his wife a divorce, on the grounds that he has worked himself to the bone for his father-in-law. Soprano's men are impressed that Ariel, though a smaller man, is "strong as a bull" when they try to push him around, and stands up for his rights even when threatened with death. "If we don't kill him, we should put him to work," they say. Ariel tells the mobsters about Masada, where 900 Jews held off 15,000 Roman soldiers for 20 years. "You're looking at Romans," the gangsters tell him. Finally, Soprano and his goons convince Ariel to give his wife the *get* (divorce document) when they promise to "act like a *mohel*" and "finish his *bris* (covenantal circumcision) if he refuses.

It is noteworthy that in this episode, a Jewish confidant of the mobsters, Herman (Hesh) Rabkin (the name almost suggests "rabbi"), played by Jerry Adler, warns his friends, after no initial protest against their dealing with the Hasidim, to keep away from "those fanatics." When, at first, an Italian makes a pun about Hasidim ("I seed 'em but I don't believe 'em") we expect the familiar mocking motifs that were established during the Eighties. Yet Hesh quotes the Talmudic dictum that "the altar sheds tears" when a "Jew gets a divorce" (exact wording: "when a man divorces the wife of his youth"). Tony Soprano tells his psychiatrist that he is impressed that "these Hasids, they have their beliefs; they're not afraid of death."

Even so, the hour, while breaking some stereotypical molds (and at least as problematic in its treatment of Italians as of Hasidim), is not without its gibes. Tony's psychiatrist questions the motivation for the Hasidim's faith: "Maybe they have the belief because they are afraid." Shlomo Teitelbaum tells the mobsters that he does not want Ariel killed, but he knows the perils of dealing with gangsters and still tries to bargain them down. He tries (unsuccessfully) to renege on his deal with Soprano, and quotes his son's warning, in (bad) Yiddish, that calling in the gangsters would be like creating a *golem* (a Frankenstein monster). The comparison

(Hoboken, N.J.: Ktav, 1994).

to a *golem* makes such an impression on Tony that he mentions it at his therapy session.

Here, in one fell swoop, at the end of the twentieth century, writer Saraceni introduces the stock *mohel* joke and parading of Hasidim, but in an entirely different context, if not exactly admiring, then one that takes Jews more seriously. There is, at least, an effort to think outside the box, though it is undermined by the lingering suggestion that Jews cannot be trusted to keep the mafia code.[8]

In this context, that is a nasty and dangerous suggestion, but only, I suppose, if one respects the counsel of thieves and murderers. Still, the Jewish character who would distance himself from the Hasidim and put them down is not allowed to have the last word. The Hasidim are presented as rather complex people, not simply butts of one-liners.

For the most part, however, the productions examined in this book force me to expose transformation of Judaism into a joke or a school for dispassionate wisecracking; exploitation of religious festivals in order to act out any number of agendas and ambivalences; employment of Jewish rituals and usages in the glorification of behaviors destructive of Jewish teachings and values, whether or not inappropriate behaviors are condemned in the script or teleplay; hijacking of transitional rites of passage—whether for birth, marriage, conversion or for death—for purposes of obfuscating Jewish beliefs and mocking Jewish parents and community.

That such trends exist and are prominent in television and film will come as no surprise to students of these media.

---

8. The theme of Jews as untrustworthy among thieves also began in the 1980s and early 1990s with films like *Goodfellas* and *Miller's Crossing* (both 1990).

PART ONE
FROM THE SUBLIME TO THE RIDICULOUS: DISTORTION OF JEWISH OBSERVANCES

ഇരു

1

MISDIRECTED LIFE-CYCLE EVENTS

ℰℭℜ

Brit Milah and Bar Mitzvah in Homage to Insult: "Cheers," "Roseanne"

I f a series is on long enough to go for the easy laugh, it will feature a *brit milah* (covenant of circumcision) episode. Hence, the episode on "Cheers" in 1989, scripted by David Pollock and Elias Davis.

Frasier (Kelsey Grammer), the lovable egghead who frequents the Cheers bar, is nervous about the *"bris"* ceremony that is very important to his wife, Lilith (Bebe Neuwirth). It seems that Frasier, who is not Jewish, keeps having cold feet about the ceremony, and brings the baby into the bar for sanctuary at least one time, and smuggles in the baby one time, in order to protect the newborn from what he obviously considers a fate worse than birth.

Nowhere in this episode is there the slightest attempt to explain the meaning of the word *bris* or *brit* (covenant), or to give the baby a Hebrew name or to discuss any of the attendant rituals intelligently. Indeed, the only Hebrew name that turns up here is that of the mother, Lilith. That this is the name of the she-devil of Jewish lore will fortunately be lost on the general audience, whom the events put out of sympathy with the mother's strange ritual inclinations, anyway. Frasier offers an opening disclaimer about being raised without a religious tradition and being determined that his son will not be "similarly deprived." He expresses gratitude to Lilith "and her Jewish faith for providing Frederick a heritage of spirituality." But these premature words are not taken seriously by anyone, including Lilith, who, it is suggested, will do what she wants, anyway.

Likewise, writers Pollock and Davis are determined to portray this first-time Jewish mother as pushy and domineering, especially in her imposition of her religious rituals on her husband and his friends, and to show the same woman being carried out after the ritual, in a terrible state, because she, too, could not tolerate witnessing it. Don't we get at least a strong suggestion here that the ceremony is barbaric? The concern over the *bris* is exaggerated to the point not only of mockery, but of contempt.

If all this were not bad enough, the crowning offensiveness of this episode is the introduction of the one performing the circumcision, a Dr. Levinson. So we have here, as well, the perpetuation of a trend, which is offensive to Jewish tradition—namely, that medical circumcision is sufficient, without any effort to find a *mohel*, a person of special piety and training, to perform the rite of circumcision.

My sense is that the writers actually concocted the *bris* scenario in order to make Lilith more "sympathetic," more vulnerable, and thus, in an offbeat way, to transfer to her the affection that the audience had for her husband, Frasier (who later got his own Lilith-free series, anyway). It would seem that, far from regarding Lilith as overbearing, her acid-tongue and unalterable will are presented as admirable defense mechanisms in the wise-cracking and self-serving Cheers milieu. This became clear in a later episode in which Frasier enters the Boston bar all upset that his nasty mother-in-law is visiting to torment him on his fifth wedding anniversary. Frasier describes his mother-in-law as "demanding, unreasonable, cold, sadistic, nothing is to her liking, ever." He laments that he is not the way his mother-in-law would like him to be—namely, dead. He says that he is not the only one who cannot get along with this woman, that there is "unrelenting tension between Lilith and her mother."

What we have here is a very unflattering portrait of a Jewish mother, to say the least. What is interesting, if not reassuring, is that we do not have the wholesale put-down a la Philip Roth novels and 1960s and 1970s avant-garde cinema. For the verbal intimidation and nasty tongue of this woman are actually glorified and admired. She proves to be more than a match for the Cheers waitress who is the acid-tongued favorite, Carla (Rhea Perlman). So the nasty Jewish mother-in-law emerges as the champion wise-cracker in an environment in which this is the most admired or at least the most formidable quality. She beats Carla, who is not Jewish, at her own game. She can even be regarded as an authentic and sincere vicious tongue, for she does not talk that way only to one-up Carla. That is the way she normally treats her daughter, son-in-law, and everyone else. She does not discriminate or put on an act. So in this episode of *Cheers* we get a new twist on the nasty, manipulative, domineering, Jewish mother persona of the big or little screen. She is considered the height of wit and formidability!

I'm not so sure that this is such a compliment, though Marilyn Cooper holds her own well enough in her role as Lilith's domineering mom. For all the perverse admiration still suggests a rather twisted admiree, and a not-altogether-funny dysfunctional (Jewish) family. Writers keep reminding us that the family is "Jewish," with references to the *bris* and with a *chuppah* strangely out of place at the "renewal of wedding vows" ceremony—on the Sabbath, yet—which Mom has insisted that the children have, even though there has never been a reference to conversion to Judaism on Frasier's part. For "comic relief," Frasier physically pushes his mother-in-law around a few times. The issue of physical harassment aside, don't such shoves suggest that the queen of the wisecracks is unloved or even unlovable and that one more nasty TV Jewish mother deserves to be pushed away?

Jewish matrons as mistresses of the insult were also featured in a fall 1995 episode of *Roseanne* in which Roseanne (Barr) and Dan (John Goodman) crash a bar mitzvah party. Close to term in her midlife pregnancy and fretting about "baby jail," Roseanne insists on a Saturday night fling with Dan at a nearby hotel, whose crowded scheduling delays her dinner and retards her relaxation plans. Tired of waiting for the restaurant, she finds that she can steal a few hors d'oeuvres from a bar mitzvah, and then the ethnic jokes abound as she pulls Dan into the party. "Wow," she says, "Jewish people in their natural habitat."

The Rabbi (Bob Nickman) greets the couple almost as they enter (not exactly his duty according to Emily Post or Helen Latner) and immediately asks them the name of their temple. "Beth Midler," Roseanne improvises, just after teaching Dan that he doesn't have to bow every time he says "shalom." Writers Eric Gilliland and Daniel Palladino make a point of showing that at a bar mitzvah wise-cracking Roseanne will not always get the last word. When the band leader asks for requests, she bids for something from *Jesus Christ Superstar* and the moderator shrugs her off with the perennial line, "There's one in every crowd," inviting her to offer the first toast for the family that we know she doesn't know.

Once the start of dinner is announced, there is a shameless stampede toward the smorgasbord table (a scene that, admittedly, is not rare in synagogues). Dan says, "Look at them grab at the food," and Roseanne, in admiration of the *fressing* (*stuffing* of food), says, "These are our people." A spoof on eavesdropping and pushy Jewish professionals (mostly legal and medical) is, of course, included.

In this brief exchange, we may well have the Baby Boomers' take on *Goodbye, Columbus*. Philip Roth saw himself as rebelling against vulgarity in the Jewish community with his own concoction of artistic, literary vulgarity—the higher vulgarity, if you will. This episode of *Roseanne* argues for the sacredness of the 1990s residue of the 1960s vulgarity: the atmosphere and characters at the typical bar mitzvah celebration are to be extolled as the model for the bad manners, insults and belligerent warmth—in that order—which are the trademark of *Roseanne* and of most sitcoms of the moment. Roseanne and Dan even find a "biblical" basis for this contention: "They ate way better in the Old Testament."

Even two self-indulgent and super-critical young Jewish matrons are extolled as superior practitioners of the art of insulting Roseanne herself, whose prowess at vicious ridicule is being analyzed by her daughters, over gin, in the episode's subplot. In some ways, ironically, the stereotype of the "Jewish Princess" as outcast is reversed, whether consciously or subconsciously, so that the whining complainers become the patron saints of nasty one-liners. Note what is sanctified in the process as "the Jewish Way." As Roseanne says, "Man, the people are completely rude for no reason. I love it here!"

The lovable but manipulative Uncle Saul, who seeks adulation and homage so much that he is willing to pretend to recognize faces and to stuff hundred dollar bills in everyone's pocket, represents more than what Roseanne calls the "rich uncle." He becomes the Patriarchs-according-to-the-Baby-Boomer-sitcom, the old reliable who is really so insecure emotionally that he must always declare his love for family members through incessant gift-giving, and who, a widower once or twice, finds less reason to marry within the faith. The suggested demeanor of elderly Jewish women may well be an explanation for a desire to marry outside the fold. The rabbi's mother is, after all, depicted as a nasty-mouthed old lady who is always *schnorring* cigarettes.

One wonders whether writers compare notes across networks on stereotypes and common one-liners. On *The Nanny*, the Jewish grandmother is depicted in the same manner, and one has heard many times the same joke, "Man, I though they [Jews] only liked Chinese food."

One would think that such worship of vulgarity is not enough of a theme to sustain either a generation, a genre, or a sitcom, though in the cases of *Cheers* and *Roseanne*, it worked for a long time.

Brit Milah and *Seder* as Sacred Joke: "The Nanny"

The Nanny (1993-1999) could be on target as social commentary on the vulgarities of American Jewry. The series sometimes offered disarming allusion to the awkwardness that growing numbers of American Jews feel with respect to simply keeping straight the holidays and their respective importance and dates (as synagogue answering machines attest to congregants confusing festivals with business days). When a friend of Fran's unexpectedly appears—and quite dressed up, Fran frets, "Don't tell me it's a holy day and I didn't go to temple. God will punish me." There was even a knowing reference to the lengths that religious schools will go to keep the interest of the kids: "You look just like when our Hebrew school did *The Best Little Whore House in Texas.*"

The purpose of the joke was not to defend the sacredness of Jewish traditions and values, though one-liners about Jews and Judaism abounded in this spoof about a Jewish woman from Queens (Fran Drescher) who ends up being the nanny for the children of a Broadway producer from London. The first real treatment of Jewish ritual was not until the third season. Not surprisingly for TV Jewish fare, the occasion chosen was a *brit milah* (or *bris*), a circumcision.

Unlike other series, which mock the *brit* itself, *The Nanny* manages to mock only Jewish and Gentile reactions to the ceremony. Writer Frank Lombardi depicts Fran's mother, Sylvia, as obsessed with making the refreshments a success because "future freeloading in Florida depends on the party." Young Brighton, the nanny's ward of roughly bar mitzvah age whom she engages to videotape the event, believes that he has been engaged to film a "brisket" until he catches an eyeful of what is actually transpiring, much to his own shock. The *mohel* (ritual circumciser) waves at the camera, but is not made the fool.

This first foray into Jewish ceremonies (a Passover *seder* would follow) is rather quickly overshadowed by a "safari" in Hollywood made possible by young Brighton's video. Like most *Nanny* episodes (until the final season), the requisite bad taste is held in check. The Freudian one-liners are hurled in clusters with the obvious hope that they will catapult over the heads of the younger viewers and keep their parents amused. The expected *brit* jokes are here, but they are restrained, and even the nanny's comment about the tastelessness of "serving miniature franks at a *bris*" is far less risqué than most of the double entendres toward which the program is prone.

Sometimes the satire can get too personal, and unfairly so. In another Lombardi episode about the enmity between Fran's mother and her sister-in-law, Brighton quips that if his older sister Maggie is getting a sweet sixteen party, he'd like a bar mitzvah. When his dad reminds him that he's not Jewish, Nanny Fine observes, "You know, a sizeable donation to Temple Emanu-El could take care of that." While compromise of synagogue standards is fair game for TV sarcasm, this gratuitous jab at New York's largest synagogue is nasty.

Such lines are particularly stinging in view of the one thing that the series depicted as sacred to Fran—namely, not crossing a picket line. She tells her boss, who has suffered bad publicity because of her refusal to do so: "It's against our religion. Like eating pork." When he reminds her that she "most certainly" eats bacon, she responds that she does so "only if it's very crispy or on a club sandwich." When she adds, "But don't tell my grandmother," he reminds her that Yetta eats bacon, as well. "All right," she says, "we all do." She will not cross a picket line because her aunt would roll over in her grave, "which was paid for by her union." The writers are more than conscious that for some Jews certain social stances replaced religion (though in Judaism justice for the worker was among many religious commandments).

Not even Fran's reverence for workers' rights is associated with religious teachings. Viewers are therefore given the suggestion that Jews just seem to "know better" about social issues and other matters. The writing suggests that Fran and her mother believe in some kind of inherent Jewish superiority. Hence, a joke in an episode by Caryn Lucas about Fran's possibly being switched at birth in the hospital, in which Fran is horrified to learn that she was born on Rosh Hashanah because that would mean that most of the Jewish staff, the competent ones, were in temple.

To really understand the mindset of *The Nanny*, one must turn not to Jewish teachings, or to Yiddishisms (which were plentiful but quickly exhausted in the first episodes), but to self-deprecating Jewish jokes of the

1960s. For *The Nanny* is nothing more or less than homage to such "humor" which is the real sacred text of the series.

Consider the use of Holocaust associations for "humor" about the romantic relationship between the nanny and her boss. In expressing her hurt feelings regarding her boss's "taking back" a declaration of love made while the two of them were facing a plane crash, Fran responds to Mr. Sheffield's disclaimer that "friends...don't dwell on the past": "Our people might have enjoyed *Hogan's Heroes* [a comedy about American prisoners of war to the Germans], but that doesn't mean that we are going to go out and drive a Mercedes. All right, we may drive a Mercedes, but it doesn't mean we're going to fly Lufthansa—unless we have mileage." This line by writers Nastaran Dibai and Jeffrey B. Hodes is, of course, intended to be self-mockery of the inconsistency of Jews who trade principle for status. It trivializes the concept of forgiveness by drawing on old jokes about Jewish bargain-hunting which are presumed to be tasteful because of their "sacredness" at having been around.

The same reverence of "sacred" old Jewish jokes permeated an episode by Rick Shaw which was *The Nanny's* "deepest" foray into Jewish ritual—namely, the 1997 Passover episode. Mr. Sheffield asks the butler, "Now is this the holiday Miss Fein said you can't eat all day, then stuff yourself, or the one when you light candles, then stuff yourself, or the one when you build a straw hut, then stuff yourself?" "No," the butler responds, "I believe it's the one when you hide crackers from small children, then stuff yourself." This motif continues throughout the episode. It is, of course, based upon the old joke about the maid describing the strange rituals of her Jewish employers who eat in the dining room but smoke in the bathroom on Shabbat, smoke in the dining room but eat in the bathroom on Tish'a B'Av, and both eat and smoke in the bathroom on Yom Kippur.

Like the episode that gently treats *brit* jokes in general, the *seder* segment adopts an old joke in a creative way. For one brief moment during the *seder*, when the youngest of Fran's wards asks the four questions, there is almost an interlude of reverence, despite all the sideplots, including Fran's mother sticking the butler, an invited guest, with all the cooking and serving. (We are told that cheesecake, which is not kosher for Passover, is the dessert of choice.) The writer undermines his own reverent moment by having Sylvia add a "fifth question" about when Sheffield will marry the nanny (the notion that interfaith marriage is *beshert* or destined) and then having the nanny dash out to seek her "messiah" (or Elijah?), Barbra

Streisand, even though Fran has succeeded in attracting her young wards to the warmth and ritual of the *seder* table.

If there had just been silence at the end of the *seder* scene, this could have been one of the most touching presentations of Judaism on TV. Maybe old jokes, while not sacred scripture, can convey something sacred if combined with effective moments of silence. Unfortunately, *The Nanny* never rose to the challenge of demonstrating this.

Brit Milah and *Kashrut* as "Common" Judaism: "Seinfeld"

It seems that every successful sitcom must have a requisite *brit* or *bris* sequence. Yet the way that this is handled is indicative of the culture and attitude of the particular series. This is especially true of an October 1993 episode of *Seinfeld*. First, there is the comedy of the everyday. So a *bris* (circumcision), being a milestone event, must become a subplot to other things—in this case, a lot of hospital and mental ward humor, and a lot of dark humor to boot. Then, there must be the muffed or side-swiped mission—in this case, Elaine (Julia Louis-Dreyfus), choosing the most bizarre possible *mohel*. Then, there are the formula denials of Jewishness (as per the *Seinfeld* tradition). Elaine asks what a *mohel* is; Jerry explains in his most objective, Gentile tones. Jerry (Seinfeld) asks his friend George: "Ever seen one?"—namely, a circumcised male. George responds, "Yea, my roommate in college." Jerry asks: "Yea, what did you think?" George: "I got used to it."

After keeping the family and guests waiting for several tense minutes, the script sees that the tension is broken, or rather exacerbated, by the most neurotic *mohel* one can imagine, who himself shares his morbid ruminations about being mugged and then spit at in this neighborhood, who can't bear a baby's cries, who shares the most rambling anxieties about what can go wrong if a glass is out of place, and tops off the tumult he causes with the confession, "I could have been a kosher butcher like my brother. The money's good. He's got a union with benefits. And cows don't have families. You make a mistake with a cow, you move on with your life."

The only one who matches the *mohel's* neurosis and stand-up mannerisms is Jerry, who pays dearly for flinching in his role as the baby's godfather, not, happily, in a way that injures the baby or that affects Jerry in the worst-case scenario of such a sequence. As if to add insult to injury (and it is the tradition of *brit milah*, the sacred covenant of circumcision, that is injured most in this episode, with the exception of one dead body), the salvation of the ceremony turns out to be none other than the eccentric Kramer (Michael Richards), who mocks circumcision as a barbaric ritual, comparing it to the sacrifice of virgins, and who is rewarded with replacing Jerry and Elaine as the child's godparent, because, as the parents say, he is the only one who cared about the baby.

So we have, all in good fun, of course, the wholesale parody of a sacred Jewish tradition for no other reason than to distance the main characters from it, to free them from any obligations as Jewish godparents, and to give them forum for denial of knowing anything about Jewish traditions and beliefs. Is this the logical conclusion of the *Seinfeld* brand of comedy that so savors everyday mishaps that it can't appreciate events and rituals that offer spiritual transcendence and maybe a bit of holiness?

One thinks of a 1992 *Seinfeld* episode by Larry Charles in which Elaine is disappointed to hear that the only meal available is a kosher meal. "A kosher meal?" she cries. "I don't want a kosher meal. I don't even know what a kosher meal is." This leads to a discussion among passengers seated near-by about what "kosher" means. ("When a rabbi inspects it," says one. "The way they kill the pig," suggests another.) But why bring up "kosher" if one does not have a witty one-liner to explain it meaningfully? Furthermore, as it turns out, Elaine's meal was taken by a passenger who ordered a kosher meal weeks ago, but "forgot." So much for the convictions of Jews. The TV audience is led to believe that people who keep kosher have no consistency or principle in their observances.

Another major "Jewish" episode, written by Seinfeld with Larry David, Tom Gammill and Max Pross, aired in the 1993-1994 season. Seinfeld and his Jewish girlfriend, Rachel (Melanie Smith), went to see *Schindler's List* (the Holocaust film!) in order to find a dark place to make out while his parents were visiting. Realizing that the couple didn't even notice the film was in black and white because of their behavior, Jerry's parents are scandalized that he would behave that way during a film about a person who did so much good. (That it depicts the martyrdom of the victims is not mentioned.)

In a subsequent episode, Jerry's friend Elaine is surprised to learn that he is seeing Rachel again, for she had heard that, after the *Schindler's List* incident, Rachel's dad had asked his daughter not to see Seinfeld. Yet Jerry responds, "I gave him some kishke."

So there we have it, I thought to myself, *Seinfeld* gets around the poor taste of using *Schindler's List* for gratuitous laughs by suggesting that a devoted Jew can be bought off by an ethnic dish, even where his daughter is concerned.

This episode shadowed Jerry and Rachel and their circle of friends to the Hamptons for a weekend with relatives. There, Rachel announces to the group that she doesn't eat lobster because she is kosher.

So I think to myself, again: What am I complaining about? Here, the *Seinfeld* program, which only six months before was waffling on whether or not to say that Jerry is Jewish, now offers the only scenario in TV memory of a Jewish man dating an attractive and engaging Jewish woman—and one who keeps kosher to boot! Kramer, the beloved off-beat character of the series whose comments get the most attention on the show, offers one of the most sincere and touching paeans to Jewish piety I have ever seen on any TV drama, let alone sitcom: "You're so pious.... When you die, you're going to get some special attention." Believe me, in the context of the episode, it is both funny and a heartfelt tribute by an off-the-wall character.

Then there is a scene in which Rachel comes down to the kitchen late at night, tempted by all the talk about the marvelous taste of the lobster. As she is about to sneak a taste, Kramer dissuades her, and she thanks him for it.

So now the pious Jewish woman is depicted as being obsessed with forbidden foods? Then again, I think, temptation is what in fact makes piety so impressive. Everyone is curious and tempted. What is unique and even praiseworthy here is that a regular on a popular series can encourage a Jewish woman to live her faith.

The episode concludes with another character putting the lobster into Rachel's breakfast eggs in order to get even with her when she tells his would-be-girlfriend about something she witnessed about him. It wasn't nice of her to tell, and it was unconscionable of him to defile her food. She is obviously very shaken by his actions.

So, I think to myself, *Seinfeld* is suggesting that just because you keep kosher, you're not immune to telling tales that boomerang back in retribution by assault on your rituals? Then again, it was just innocent and rather universal gossip among friends that Rachel is guilty of, even though Judaism prohibits talebearing and gossip and destroying another's reputation with almost as much detail as dietary laws which are supposed to foster a sense of reverence for life. Rachel is, I suppose, just being human. Did the writers, Peter Mehlman and Carol Leifer, highlight her human foibles in order to render greater praise to her lofty principles and practices, or to indicate that those principles and practices don't help much or amount to much, anyway?

A lot about the *bris* and kosher food episodes was explained in a *Seinfeld* episode about Elaine "prompting" Jewish males to renounce their faith. The episode was shown before Yom Kippur, 1997, in an obvious ploy to provoke rabbis to mention it and thus give the show publicity.

In this bizarre half-hour offering by Steve Koren, Elaine is kissed by a Jewish teen and then, when she goes to discuss the incident with his father, the father kisses her as well. George (the "Italian" played by Jewish actor Jason Alexander) explains to Elaine, "You've got *shiksa* appeal. Jewish men love the idea of kissing a woman that's not like their mother." Convinced by this bit of advice, Elaine again confronts the father, and tells him, "The only reason you like me is because I'm a *shiksa*. If I weren't a *shiksa* you wouldn't be interested in me." Immediately, he declares, "I renounce Judaism." Elaine then goes to the rabbi after complaining, "This *shiksa* thing is totally out of control. What is it with you people?" The rabbi responds that the "*shiksa*" thing is a myth, but then indicates that he'd like to go to Myrtle Beach with Elaine after the High Holidays.

That's it. That is the entire "theme" and "context." Now Seinfeld and crew have explained and even boasted that their specialty is "nothing"—namely, an artful absence of theme and context; that they claim no other perspective or commentary save an ensemble of characters who are basically selfish and immature and shallow. That is not, however, the message they get across or even, I dare say, the agenda of the show. For the program definitely emits a subliminal signal that these offbeat, selfish and nasty people have some kind of perspective that all the world's "other people" do not have. In their bungling and boggling way, they provide human truths that other pundits, including the bizarre rabbi, can barely perceive. That is the byproduct of their "coolness," which may not be virtue, but is certainly their drawing card and the key to the fascination with them.

On *Seinfeld*, there is no distinction between Jew and Gentile, rabbi and stalker. There is only a distinction between Our Gang of ingratiating anti-heroes and the rest of the world. Our Gang happens to consist of the Jewish protagonist who, well into the series, referred to his Jewishness; another Jewish actor who plays an Italian to show that Jewish shtick can be universal; and another Jewish player who portrays the Consummate Joker and therefore represents transcendent funniness; and a protagonist with some Jewish background who plays the quintessential *shiksa*.

Seinfeld's real "theme" is that you don't have to be Jewish to be a cool antihero and to make fun of Jews *and* Gentiles, but it helps. Only four Jews and Gentiles are enlightened, and the rest of the world, Jew or Gentile, is expected to affirm this with every laugh.

Bar Mitzvah as Graduation from Judaism: "Route 66"

I have been watching television all my life, but few TV episodes have haunted me and challenged me like a 1962 episode of *Route 66*, entitled, "Shoulder The Sky, My Lad." I first saw it as a rerun in the late 1980s.

The TV series was about two carefree buddies cruising the country in a 1960 Corvette, taking odd jobs and helping people with their problems. Martin Milner and George Maharis played the principals, Todd Stiles and Buzz Murdock. The series was beautifully written and produced and dramatically effective, and was enhanced by Nelson Riddle's original and impressive music.

In this particular episode, the two men find themselves in Phoenix and take a job in a factory. There, they are befriended by a co-worker who shows them the ropes. The man, Carl Selman, is played by a young Ed Asner in his most affable characterization ever. Selman finds the drifters lodging at a motel near his home, and invites them to dinner. As it happens, it is a Friday night, so the visitors experience a bit of Shabbat at Carl's home. Carl's mother, Annie (Lili Darvas) lights the Shabbat candles and his son, Davey (Mike McGreevey) announces proudly, "I'm being bar mitzvahed." (The verb may be incorrect, but the sentiment of pride and earnestness gets across.) After dinner, while the guests return home, Dad goes out for a newspaper and is mugged, stabbed and killed. Stiles and Murdock rush over from their room when they see Carl dying in a pool of his own blood, having made his way back to his doorstep. His last words to his son are a request to take care of Annie.

In the next scene we see Buzz covering the mirrors in Carl's home, and explaining to Todd that he learned from Jewish friends that this custom teaches that "if you look at yourself, you're thinking of yourself and not life or death." Buzz gets to explain Judaism more than the rabbi, who has one rather unpleasant visit. In his grief, Davey has become withdrawn and hostile to his bar mitzvah teacher. Rabbi Herz, young and clean-shaven, representing the advent of "Americanized" suburban Judaism, declares to Davey: "I'm not going to try and tell you that pain like this goes away soon. But nothing's all black, not even sorrow." He adds, thoughtfully: "Remember some of the things we've studied? They can come in handy now if you'll think about them." Yet Davey rejects any help from the rabbi, even in arranging the funeral. The boy says that he knows where to find the cemetery deed, and will handle such matters himself. "I'll be at the temple tomorrow," the rabbi says while leaving. "If you want me, Davey, say the word."

The dialogue is respectful to the rabbi, but it is the principals who prove to be more helpful to the boy and more connected with him. Perhaps this is because they are, after all, the stars. The writing would suggest that because Todd and Buzz are closer in age and not identified with the God who has "taken" Davey's father, the thirteen-year-old can identify more with them. Todd offers the most disarming words: "Davey, you can't reason it. You'll only tear out your heart trying. It didn't make me any less of a man to cry when I lost my father, and I was much older." When Davey protests that the visitors are putting themselves out too much, Todd responds, "Friendship is not a bother, Davey. It's a privilege. We know you can handle things, but do us a favor. Make us feel useful." All of the good lines about community and spirituality go to the principals.

It is interesting, however, that our road psychologists do not agree among themselves as to how to help Davey live through his grief. Todd insists that life somehow evens itself out—"the blessings, the affliction." Buzz does not argue that point. After all, it echoes what the rabbi said, or at least almost said. But the two argue strategies, ways of helping and healing that are, at least for now, beyond the reach of the rabbi. Buzz is against interference: "There are some agonies you don't share. They're private. It's up to you, nobody else." Todd advocates intervention: " I read it different. In my book it says, 'I'm my brother's keeper.'"

Yet despite the debates and strategies, Davey chooses to confide his question and anger to the person closest to his heart, his girlfriend, Rosie. "Is it all right if I come to the funeral tomorrow?" Rosie asks. "I mean, there isn't a law against Catholics, is there?" Angrily, Davey responds that if there were such a law, it would not be like a "police law." It would be "just religion." But Rosie comes immediately to the defense of religion. "Religion is God. Rabbis and priests know. They hear God's calling. They become holy men." When Davey protests, "It don't make sense," Rosie waxes theological: "There are reasons. Everything means something. Maybe if we think."

Davey declares with contempt that priests and rabbis think that they know all the answers. He denounces clergy for having "so many books." If they really "knew," he says, they wouldn't have to study so much and could make miracles. By the time of the funeral, his anger and disdain have built up so much that he refuses to repeat the Kaddish prayer after the rabbi. He says that he wants to forget.

A few days after the funeral, Davey comes home to find the rabbi comforting his grandmother as they sit at the table. Is it a *shiva* call or was the rabbi waiting to give Davey a bar mitzvah lesson? Davey bitterly declares that he does not want to study for his bar mitzvah. With understanding, the rabbi tells him that he doesn't have to. Emboldened by the indulgence and sympathy, Davey announces that he does not want a bar mitzvah ceremony, and that he doesn't believe in God. He then baits the rabbi: "What are you going to say now, Rabbi? 'All right, Davey, you don't have to.' 'God gives and God takes away.' Right, Rabbi? Well, I don't believe in God. He let my father die. I don't believe in Him." It is at this point that Davey runs away. Todd and Buzz arrive on the scene on time to barely miss running over David with their famous Corvette.

Though Buzz joins Todd in chasing Davey until he eludes them, Buzz is still reluctant to pursue the lad and suggests that they call the police. "Do you know what to say to a kid with an emptiness a mile deep?" he asks. Todd responds, "No, I'll worry about that when the time comes." Buzz grows more impatient. "When the time comes, what are you going to say, 'Hey, kid, believe in God, hah?' What are you going to do? Clobber him over the head and bring him back to his grandmother? Do you think that's going to solve anything?"

As if to underscore Buzz's concerns, the camera follows Davey in his tortured wanderings, and we see him wincing when he encounters fathers walking with their little boys on the street and when he sees photographs of dads and sons in store windows. These scenes are most effective, and are among the best early uses of television as a visual art.

Buzz does come around, however, realizing that his refusal to seek Davey is the result of a failure on his part to face pain in his own life. He suggests that they check another, different "kind of real estate" (to use Todd's or, rather, the writer's witty term)—namely, the cemetery. Viewers are provided with a glimpse at the Beth Israel Cemetery as it looked in

Phoenix in the early sixties, and also with a fine musical interlude by Riddle based on Jewish folk melodies.

In the cemetery, Buzz has to tackle Davey, who wrestles and punches in order to act out his grief and frustration. (The scene is reminiscent of the biblical account of Jacob's wrestling with the angel—a reluctant but knowing angel, in Buzz's case.) Buzz lets Davey hit him, and then, with his nobly gotten bloody nose, he chides, "Go ahead. Take off, run. Don't let yourself stand in one place. This patsy's not coming after you anymore." When Davey asks why Buzz did come, Buzz both scolds and inspires him: "What do you think? You got the market on misery? You think you're the only kid that ever had it tough? Well, let me tell you, I never had a father. I don't even have any memories. I was raised by strangers…I was always alone. I remember one Sunday when I was shining shoes and all the rest of the kids were all dressed up to go to church, and I hated them and hated their parents and I hated the whole world. And I'll tell you something: I would have hated God, too, Davey, except, well, I didn't believe in God anymore. He was like Santa Claus, only for kids and fools. That same night I was sitting on the roof of the tenement where I lived, and there was no stars and no moon, only a red, red sky. And I remember thinking that the sky was red maybe because God was crying for me and all of a sudden I wasn't scared anymore, and I didn't feel lost or alone. And from that second on I never felt alone because I'm not. Nobody is."

In the next and final scene, we witness moments from Davey's bar mitzvah. The *sefer Torah* is removed from the ark, the *Shema* is recited, and David chants some blessings. Todd, the road philosopher par excellence, offers the closing narration: "We've seen a boy starting to become a man, building on a solid foundation, a rich heritage and faith in his Creator."

So went the episode that haunts me. It remains one of the most moving television hours that I ever experienced. The writing by Mort Thaw is fine and memorable, even stirring. The principals and guest stars, notably twelve-year-old Mike McGreevey, acted their roles in a most affecting manner. All aspects of the production, including the filming on location in Phoenix, Riddle's music, the direction by David Lowell Rich, were striking.

Writer Mort Thaw dealt with issues of death and mourning, with stages and expressions of grief, in a perceptive and therapeutic manner only later embraced and understood in society at large and in its educational and healing institutions. He honored Jewish values and traditions by focusing on a fine, if tormented, Jewish family. He made it possible for Jews to represent the proverbial "everyman," and therefore for every person to identify with Jews and with the bar mitzvah ceremony.

From a Jewish point of view, however, the drama is by no means perfect. There are troubling aspects here. The implication seems to be that while both Davey and Rosie can build on the "solid foundation" of their rich heritages and faith in the Creator, their respective religious traditions are just that—"foundations," that help to shape character and to provide a general sense of God, but that also prepare a Jewish boy and Catholic girl to find one another, if that is where life leads them. Neither the synagogue nor the rabbi nor the bar mitzvah ceremony can function or continue to provide ethical and spiritual nurturing without the intervention of an outsider who can speak in almost Constitutional terms of "the Creator." True, instead of the Deist underpinnings of the Bill of Rights, we do get a notion of the Creator who weeps with us, the "God of pathos," as Abraham Heschel described the God of the Hebrew Prophets in works translated at around that time. God had already been described in this way by popular American preachers of all faiths in sermons of the Fifties and early Sixties on the problem of evil and suffering. There is no effort here, as there had been in a contemporaneous episode of *Ben Casey* on a cantor's arguments with God, to place such questioning in the context of Jewish tradition. (That *Ben Casey* episode, "A Nightingale Named Nathan," had been written a few years later by Chester Krumholz and Arthur Dales, and was reminiscent of Levi Yitzhak's famous *din Torah* or "lawsuit" with God.)

In this episode of *Route 66*, there is no sense of Covenant (*brit*), of a sacred agreement within and beyond family, between Jews and their God, that Jews must remain Jews. No one ever challenges Davey's notion that a Jew can simply run away and forget. David's grandmother is depicted as sweet and dignified, but as totally unequipped to be any kind of centering force in his life. She recites the Kaddish prayer better than the actor who plays the rabbi, but gives Davey no sense of connection to her and to her community, or of a filial duty to say Kaddish. True, the writer suggests that the loss of a father requires some male interventions and perspectives, but one wonders what help, if any, the synagogue or the grandmother could have provided to Davey had the Corvette not pulled into town and almost run him down.

There is also something anti-clerical about the episode. We rabbis, I admit, are sensitive to that; it sets off our radar. Davey does, after all, complain about the "many books" in which clergy bury themselves.

Ultimately, he finds comfort not in old sacred words, but in Buzz's image of a weeping sky. The sky is not restricted by any sect or authority or hierarchy—or by Covenant or religious law. But ultimately, to speak about the heart and soul of a "rich heritage" is to have to deal with these things.

Still, the rabbi—and the cantor—are respectfully highlighted in a religious service at the end of the hour. That was certainly a source of pride to Jewish audiences of the early Sixties who were heartened by Will Herberg's description of American religion as "Protestant-Catholic-Jew." What overall effect do such mixed signals provide, both then and now?

At this turn of the century I felt compelled to seek some answers. I make it a point never to interview writers, producers and actors for my weekly columns on current TV and film. Somehow, I have always sensed that personal contact can color one's reviews and thus ruin objectivity. One tends to empathize with the point of view of those who share their time and aspirations. Yet, after thirty years, I regarded myself as mandated to look back at how the creators of classic television fashioned and slanted this moving but provocative fare.

I turned first to the writer, Mort Thaw, a soft spoken and thoughtful man raised in the Brownsville section of Brooklyn by parents who were children of Jewish immigrants from White Russia (Minsk), Poland and the Ukraine. (His father was born in Europe.) Thaw recalls that Yiddish was spoken in his grandparents' home, though his own parents were rather secular in orientation. He did not think that my queries about his Jewish background were relevant to the subject of the episode, though he did tell me that he regretted not having learned Yiddish and Hebrew in his childhood. He remembers always thinking that Yiddish was a "beautiful language." He said that this script for *Route 66* grew out of his own background and experience as a Jew, including his recollections of mourning and bar mitzvah rituals. Interestingly, he did not remember that the boy's girlfriend was Catholic. He went on to write an episode of the *Ironside* series about a stolen Torah scroll. Apparently, Thaw retained some fascination with Jewish themes. He says that the *Route 66* episode was written "on speculation" as a concept he proposed for the series, having followed some of its episodes; the same, he attests, was true of his work for *Ironside*. He had always wanted some connection to show business and came to California in the Fifties. "I had no trade and no money," he reminisces, "and decided to take a shot at writing." It is no surprise that his innate skills and perceptiveness made him a sought-after and distinguished writer for television.

Later, I spoke to the producer of *Route 66* (and of *Naked City, Rin Tin Tin* and other classic television), Herbert B. Leonard, a reflective and resolute individual, whose pleasant but dynamic personality bespeaks the purposefulness and kindness that distinguished his show and won the loyalty and admiration of co-workers and audiences alike. Leonard had been raised in Manhattan. His Jewish education, like Thaw's, was minimal. Through the intervention of his maternal grandmother, he got a job after World War II with an independent Hollywood producer. All of 23 or 24 years old, he was running the studio within two years. He was soon in demand by other producers. In the early Sixties, he created *Route 66*, which was based on his own cross country trip to California in his early twenties with a more socially privileged friend. Maharis's character paralleled Leonard's odyssey to California as a poor kid from a rough neighborhood, and the wealthy pal with whom he traveled was the model for Milner's more patrician persona.

Herbert B. Leonard went on to produce such fine films as *Breaking Away* and *Popi.* He says he treated each episode of his various series as a "little movie." That pride in craftsmanship and in storytelling is apparent in everything he has produced. He regards "Shoulder The Sky, My Lad" as possessing a rare "nobility" of principles, morals and ideals in its depiction of American youth. He is not wrong. But does any of that "nobility" derive from Jewish beliefs and practices?

Michael McGreevey, who played Davey when he was twelve years of age, is now a respected television writer and at forty-something is a seasoned and insightful observer of the television industry. His father, John McGreevey, is a writer's writer, and the two have collaborated on projects including a TV movie, *Ruby and Oswald* and *The Waltons*. Michael wrote for *Fame* and *Quincy*, among other shows. He was raised in Roman Catholic schools and, after falling away from the church in his college years at UCLA, he returned in his mid-twenties through the influence of his wife and devoted Catholic friends, including a thoughtful priest. He has vivid memories of the *Route 66* episode, and is still amazed and thankful that he was given the part of Davey though his background was Catholic. He was a student at Francis de Sales Catholic School when the episode was made, and reminisces that one of his teachers, a nun, asked the class to watch it and complimented him on being such a fine actor to be able to play a Jew. She used the opportunity to comment on the Ecumenical Council and on the positive portrayal of a Catholic girl helping a friend to find God. The nun saw the program as a call for cooperation despite differences in religion. (I would say that Rosie represented a childlike and unthinking attachment to religious authority which builds character and provides noble foundation until one can "grow" into Buzz's concept of the universal Concerned Creator, more vividly conveyed by the red skies than by churches or synagogues.)

McGreevey recalls with amusement that Susan Gordon, who played Rosie, was Jewish, and showed him how to wear his *yarmulke* correctly, while he instructed her in the proper way to make the sign of the cross. He regards the emphasis on Davey's and Rosie's different religious back-grounds as a dramatic device for "contrast" rather than a call for assimilation. To him, the strength of the episode was its honesty in conveying a sense of loss with which any 12 or 13-year old could identify. He remembers being so moved by the script's "emotional content" that he cried the entire day that the scene with Davey and Buzz in the cemetery was filmed. His sense of the program's theme, at that time and since, was that Davey was fortunate that he had people to comfort him and help him to understand that he could find his best comfort in God, Who was not the reason for his father's death. By "people," I'm sure that McGreevey meant Buzz and Todd and Rosie, but what about Davey's grandmother, rabbi and congregation?

The episode's director, David Lowell Rich, had similar memories and impressions of the theme. Now living in the South, where he had received aviation training during World War II and where he resolved to spend his retirement because he "enjoyed the people," Rich was raised in Queens, New York and in Michigan, and comes from a "long line of Methodists." He has over 40 years of television and feature film directing to his credit, including *Route 66, Naked City* and the movie, *Madame X*, starring Lana Turner. "It seemed to me," Rich observes, "that we were not dealing with any particular denominational theme. It seemed to me that we were dealing with a universal theme."—namely, "the story of a young boy and his tribulations," of the boy's "becoming one with the spirit." The message, he adds, was that "No man stands alone. He is one of many. We all go through some kind of bath of purity, as it were, to reach maturity." When I asked Rich what he meant by "bath of purity," he said: "An exposure to something more powerful than ourselves."

The tragedy of this unforgettable and poignant episode of *Route 66* was, in many ways, the story of much vintage television and of its makers, most of whom were Jewish: No one ever considered the dramatic possibilities of the old biblical proposition that Jews are a blessing to themselves and others when they recognize in their own heritage a continuous and precious "exposure to something more powerful than ourselves," which they have a sacred obligation to uphold and to explore. Without some emphasis on the obligation, the exploration becomes little more than a backdrop.

Talking Bar Mitzvah to Death: "The Discovery"

In 1989, the Jewish Theological Seminary of America offered an hour-long program exploring the meaning of bar mitzvah and, indeed, of Jewish life through the eyes of a bar mitzvah student (well-played by Josh Saviano of *Wonder Years* fame). This thirteen-year-old protests that his questions about Jewish beliefs and practices are not receiving adequate response or serious attention from his parents. The film, called *Discovery*, is intended to use his concerns and struggles to teach both Jewish viewers and a general audience everything from A to Z about various Jewish beliefs and observances and even about the Holocaust.

Unfortunately, writer/director James Gordon's ploys to lecture and to exhort the audience are all too obvious. A visit to the room of a cousin who just had his bar mitzvah becomes, for example, an opportunity for the latter to rattle off some basic facts about the *Shema* prayer and the *mezuzah*. An encounter with the rabbi in the sanctuary becomes occasion for the rabbi to offer some basic lessons in what is found in a synagogue sanctuary and in the contents and making of Torah scrolls. When I showed the film to a bar/bat mitzvah class and to a post-bar/bat mitzvah class, the reaction to these scenes was the same: Isn't it a bit late to learn the significance of the *Shema* and the Torah and the Sanctuary at age twelve or thirteen? In order to instruct the audience the film insulted the intelligence of those around bar/bat mitzvah age and demeaned Jewish education to boot!

Not only are the plot and dramatic effect sorely lacking, but the "explanations" are deficient, as well, a major sin for a video produced by a theological seminary. Early in the video, the boy bolts from the car because he feels that his father and mother and sister do not respect or even tolerate his questions about how the Torah was written down. Later on, after only a few words from the rabbi (well-"played," by the way, by real-life Rabbi Samuel Chiel, who takes well to the medium), the boy becomes convinced that what he regarded as evasions on the part of his father are satisfactory theories of "revelation." We never quite learn how the rabbi has "satisfied" the boy. Worse still, in another scene with the cantor, the boy presses for an explanation of the "chosen people" concept. The cantor replies quite matter-of-factly that while at one time Jews believed themselves to be "spiritual supermen called upon to do holy deeds," nowadays " most people reject that idea and say that all great religions of the world have something to contribute." Then the cantor adds: "But other Jews still accept the chosen people idea."

No Hebrew Bible that I have ever seen describes the Jews as "supermen." The whole point of bar mitzvah and of Jewish living is that you don't have to be a "superman" to perform the *mitzvot* or commandments; that is what human beings are put into the world for. Mordecai Kaplan's Reconstructionist Judaism rejected the "chosen people" concept for the reasons mentioned by the cantor in this "drama." The last time I looked, the concept was as basic to Conservative Judaism as to Orthodox and Reform Judaism. Classical Judaism maintains that God entered into a Covenant with the Jewish People, providing them with certain teachings and perspectives on God and human beings that they must preserve in their way of life, in behalf of all humanity. That is the whole point of bar/bat mitzvah. A film on bar/bat mitzvah that fails to get across this point is fatally flawed. Furthermore, it does not enhance the image of cantors to have a cantor trivialize a basic concept like the "chosen people." Did the writer purposely spare the rabbi such dialogue?

Worse even than the dramatic flaws in this film and than vague information or misinformation is the shameless exploitation of Holocaust themes to "convince" the bar mitzvah boy of the "value" of Jewishness. Thus, a scene where the boy visits his grandmother and helps her clean up the attic is clearly a device to have him "discover" some letters of his grandfather who wrote of his impressions of the concentration camps and their impact on his own sense of Jewish identity. The scene is completely trivialized by melodramatic music and over-directing, but it does manage to get across its point: The bar mitzvah boy must remain Jewish because of what his heroic grandfather witnessed.

No one can deny that the Holocaust has important, even crucial ramifications for Jewish identity and belief, but it is utterly counterproductive to urge someone to accept beliefs and responsibilities because of other people's experiences or emotions. In another scene the rabbi sends the boy on a fishing trip with a Holocaust survivor who was never able to have a bar mitzvah because his family was killed. Again, the exaggerated music and over-directing. Again, the implication that Jewishness is identification with someone else's impressions or grief. Solomon Schechter said that you can't love God with your father's heart. Likewise, you cannot make a commitment to Judaism through someone else's suffering, no matter how important or significant or worthy of sharing.

The impression left by the film is that no one in the present enjoys or finds meaning in Judaism except for educational purposes. Grandmother's tender reminiscences of her wedding are merely excuses to explain the Jewish wedding ceremony. A Friday night dinner is intended to serve as the prop for a discourse on the Sabbath to guests invited to dinner. There is no sense of relationships or spirituality here, only of ongoing lectures. The program is also not sure how to depict the Jewish family. The parents seem "normal," bright and competent enough, but they become testy and inarticulate only when it comes to discussing the bar mitzvah. Is this intended to show parent/adolescent conflict? It certainly suggests that Jewish parents lack the ability to communicate Jewish values without grandparents (distinguished from parents by a foreign accent) and without Holocaust survivors and Holocaust memorabilia. Also, it seems that the parents cannot keep their cool in front of the rabbi. The father curtly asks him at one point to get to the point. Children and teenagers to whom I showed this film responded immediately and with shock to the rude way the rabbi was addressed by the father. The writers and producers seem to take in stride these lapses in civility and respect for clergy.

Not much can save *Discovery* as drama or as educational tool, I am afraid. But one scene was effective, and this is what future writers about bar mitzvah should build on. In that scene the boy discusses the meaning of bar mitzvah with his cousin. The latter observes that he felt part of things when he was finally able to become part of the *shiva minyan* and so bring the comfort of a service to a bereaved relative. That sense of becoming part of a spiritual community and of being able to perform *mitzvot* that make a difference in one's life and in the community—these are touching and interesting experiences which should have been elaborated upon.

Discovery is a noble effort flawed by the best of motives: to teach Jewish beliefs and practices, to remember the Holocaust, to reach out to a new generation of Jews—and to many generations of Jews and Gen-tiles—in order to foster an appreciation of Judaism. It fails because it tries to do many things at once that ought not and cannot be done at the same time without oversimplification, trivialization, and lack of dramatic effect.

Bar Mitzvah as Rejection of Parents: "Bronx Zoo"

If I were to give an award to the TV show with the corniest and least original treatment of a "Jewish" theme, it would have to go to a 1988 episode (the last) of the short-lived series, *Bronx Zoo*, a daily-life-at-the-high-school potpourri, starring Ed Asner. Even the title was offensive.

In this particular episode, whose "Jewish" component is all too derivative of Chaim Potok's novel, *My Name Is Asher Lev* (1972), a Hasidic boy, who is at the high school to assist his exterminator father, can't understand how "anything as wonderful as art can be a sin." While his father thinks he's studying Torah with buddies, the son is secretly taking Sunday afternoon art lessons with a teacher he meets in the school. She is a devout Catholic, and fears that she is "corrupting" him by teaching him art.

The episode offers an assortment of unmemorable, melodramatic, scenes. In one of these, the young artist's father finds his pictures behind furnaces in the high school basement. When the father expresses his displeasure at the drawings his son responds: "We have song and dance. Why not art?" The father asks: "Why do you break God's heart? God loves you even more than I do." The bad dialogue is matched by the bad theology. Though ready to throw the pictures into the furnace, the father finds he cannot destroy his son's art. It's too bad no one put the teleplay by Patricia Jones and Donald Reiker, and the story by Bruce Helford, into the furnace.

In another scene, the father visits the teacher to confront her regarding the art lessons she is giving his son. He tells her that the boy will "come apart" if he is ostracized by the community for drawing. "I'm not so sure you're right," she says. "Are you so sure I'm wrong?" he replies. The only thing anyone can be sure of is how inane this dialogue is. What's more, anyone not familiar with Hasidim or with Jewish tradition would have to regard the Jews as at least as clueless as the dialogue. No one bothers to explain that it is not *drawing* as such that bothers Hasidim, whether of portraits or of still lifes, but certain drawings that may be regarded as obscene or sacrilegious. A Jewish teacher does explain to the art instructor that more "liberal" Hasidim have art galleries, but that the young man risks being shunned by the family. Still, the premise of the show is rather silly because it is doubtful that either father or son would communicate so intimately with a strange woman. In the Hasidic world, such laxity in sexual mores would be a far greater break with tradition than drawing pictures. The father says that the rabbi (rebbe?) will know what the boy wants, "and it won't be art." In *My Name Is Asher Lev* (which should be acknowledged, by the way, as the obvious inspiration for this episode), however, the rebbe does in fact find Asher Lev an alternative career in art, at least for a time.

There are some scenes here that are not terrible, and that may even be regarded as good. The Hasidic father does show warmth to his son. The teacher confesses to her priest that she feels she is sinning by "corrupting" the boy by giving him art lessons. The priest responds that what she is doing is not technically "sin" as defined by the Church, but adds that he won't give her absolution for it, either, since she must work it out with her own conscience. One can't help being touched by her piety. But, then again, one must ask why the Hasidic boy does not show similar piety or, at least, soul-searching. Does the show want to suggest that Hasidism and, by implication, Jewish teachings in general are so narrow that they are little more than traps which stifle creativity?

True, the episode does attempt to have the young Hasid express some pious feelings. When asked by his art teacher whether art is important enough to him to give up his religion, he responds: "It's when I feel closest to God." Is the insinuation that the laws and teachings of Judaism somehow stifle one's sense of God's Presence? Couldn't the young Hasid have been written in such a way as to acknowledge other avenues to the Divine Presence in Jewish tradition? The only use that this episode has for Jewish tradition is as an excuse for the son's breaking loose from the father. Thus, for example, when the teacher suggests to her pupil that his father may never forgive him, the latter replies: "I love my father with all my heart and soul. But maybe he asks too much. By the laws of the Torah I'm a man. I'm bar-mitzvahed. My grandfather left Russia when he was fourteen....He made a decision. I have a decision to make, too." In other words, bar mitzvah, like an aptitude for art, becomes a precedent for breaking with a parent and with religious tradition.

Inappropriate Bar/Bat Mitzvah Gifts:
"Square Pegs," "Diff'rent Strokes,"
"Good Advice," "Caroline in the City"

Vulgar depiction of bar/bat mitzvah devolved, in four TV series of the 1980s and 1990s, around the theme of bar mitzvah gifts. These episodes comprise a study in stock television mockery of religious sensibilities and practices. I treat them in chronological order.

Square Pegs (1982-1983), though short-lived, showed signs of becoming an intelligent and engaging show, with much insight into teenage life. Yet soon after premiering, it offered its token "Jewish" episode, and an offensive one at that.

It seems that the high school's self-centered girl is having her bat mitzvah party —a year late, for she has already had her service in a Chinese synagogue while on a spiritual quest with her parents. She is celebrating the event with a famous "new wave" rock group. She invites everyone in the class except the show's four principals, whom she regards as social outcasts. Yet the bat mitzvah girl finally relents because she requires the services of one of them, begrudgingly allowing the other three (one of whom is Jewish) to attend, albeit under demeaning and degrading conditions.

It's impressive—in a perverse sort of way, of course—how a half hour sitcom can synthesize old stereotypes of Jewish overindulgence a la Philip Roth with "new wave" assaults on the Jewish image. One sees a *Goodbye, Columbus* table spread juxtaposed with teenagers of the 1980s with alcohol in hand, joined in their dances—and in their values—by the Jewish grandparents! The honorific Yiddish title, *bubbe*, for Jewish grandmothers no longer applies. The "Jewish" grandmother here is dressed more like the kids than like their parents, refers to her grandchildren as "little fascists," and tries to pick up a high school rock singer with the line, "Do you get into the city much?"

One almost wishes for the 1970s stereotypes of the European *bubbe* and the food-pushing Jewish mother. Here, food-pushing is left to the caterer, boy-chasing to the grandmother, drinking to the teenagers, and religious experiences to the "new wave." The rabbi makes a brief appearance, but only to be told about the trendiness of *Star Wars* bar mitzvah parties and to be shown with lipstick splotches on his face.

Bat mitzvah is supposed to mark a young woman's entrance into a Jewish womanhood characterized since biblical times by grace, kindness and compassion. Thanks to writers Rosie Shuster and Margaret Oberman, the viewer comes away from this bat mitzvah with an image of the teenage Jewish girl as an insensitive conspicuous little consumer who is perpetuating a family tradition of moral laxity, fickleness, and just plain showing off.

The overall impression given in a cute-bordering-on-the-cutesy 1984 episode of *Diff'rent Strokes* is not much better. Arnold (Gary Coleman), an African American lad adopted by Caucasian parents, explores the possibility of becoming a bar mitzvah. It seems that Arnold's parents (both Christian) suddenly decide that religion is "important" and that the children (two already in their teens) should choose a religion that appeals to them. Arnold happens to attend a bar mitzvah, and decides that he'd like to be Jewish because of all the attention and gifts and food that a bar mitzvah boy gets.

Arnold's folks then summon the local neighborhood rabbi, played by Milton Berle, who tells him that bar mitzvah means not just gifts and food, but long years of Hebrew School, too. Scared off by the thought of having to learn Hebrew, Arnold returns to the Harlem church of his deceased mother, and decides that the church of his childhood memories is the best fit.

Writer Daniel Harmon was comfortable depicting religion as something children should select. True, Arnold opts for the church of his earliest years, but that, too, is presented as a matter of personal preference and of aversion to study (a stereotype of African American children?). The writer never lets his wise-cracking rabbi tell us that Judaism means something beyond the catered food and gifts on the one hand, and the Hebrew School regimen on the other. Without somehow broaching the topic of Covenant, he presents Judaism as both too indulgent and too demanding.

The two nastiest bar/bat mitzvah treatments of the 1990s take up the *Square Pegs* precedent of deprecating the Jewish elderly. The short-lived series, *Good Advice* (1993-1994) could not wait to pursue the bat mitzvah theme. The program starred *Cheers* veteran Shelley Long as a marriage counselor/best selling author trying to survive the breakup of her own marriage by surrounding herself with eccentric characters in the workplace, including potential love interest Treat Williams. The first-rate cast was done in by obnoxious writing which hit bottom in the bat mitzvah episode.

The Jewish father (George Wyner), a colleague of Long's character, begins the half hour with complaints about seating relatives at the affair, lamenting that no one likes his Aunt Sadie and no one wants to sit with her. When Aunt Sadie calls a few moments later, he closes the phone conversation with the words, "See you tomorrow. Buy a gift."

To make matters worse, the grandmother (Estelle Harris), who also works in the office as a receptionist, refuses to attend the bat mitzvah. Her son tells her that it is written in the "Old Testament" that she must attend. Her response is that she has never read the Old Testament, but that she is familiar with the guest list, and is appalled that her son has invited her ex-husband.

Lamenting the disorganized planning at the eleventh hour, the bat mitzvah girl's father meditates on the pitfalls of planning a *simchah*, and then pauses to explain to the Treat Williams character that "*simchah*" is "Hebrew for happy event. My mother is known as anti-*simchah*." Indeed, Mother makes it clear that she hasn't spoken to her ex for eighteen years, and has no intention of doing so. Her son replies that he's not asking her to speak to the man, only to show up. Mother inquires whether his "nymphette is coming with him." Her son responds: "Ma, it's his fiancée. I had to invite her. Sometimes I think Oedipus killed the wrong parents."

Writer Gary H. Miller, who belabors even more the mother-son tensions, does not bring much pathos to the situation. Convincing Ma to attend is put on a par with other major challenges, like trying to decide between crab and beef at the bat mitzvah dinner. The crisis reaches its pinnacle when Uncle Joseph (the only one qualified?) refuses to do the blessing over the wine (the *Kiddush* or sanctification of the Sabbath Day) because he is back at Alcoholics Anonymous. This line gets a lot of laughs. No one explains that *halachah* (Jewish religious Law) allows for the recitation of *Kiddush* over grapejuice or even bread by those who cannot, for whatever reason, drink wine. The lesson in flexibility would have been more valuable than the cheap laugh.

After watching this episode of *Good Advice*, one could conclude that there was no religious component whatsoever to bat mitzvah. There was no effort to suggest a religious meaning. The point was made quite well that this Jewish grandmother bears grudges, this Jewish grandfather is a lecher, and this bat mitzvah and her father live for the gifts of friends and relatives, especially cash. The only biblical reference here is a crack that Grandma makes about her ex's fiancée: "I knew you had a Sarah. I didn't know it was the one from the Bible."

At one point a Gentile friend tells the father, "This should be joy not agony." To which Dad responds: "You don't understand. For my people joy *is* agony." Actually, to religiously observant Jewish people, *simchah* is a spiritual joy that comes through serving God and delighting in sacred celebration and texts. The "bat mitzvah" ceremony here is no *simchah,* nor is it satire or social commentary. It's a bad joke.

Television can also be coarse and disparaging of the elderly in its depiction of an "adult" bar mitzvah. In a disjointed 1998 episode of *Caroline in the City* (1995-1999), written by Jason Strouse, thirty-something Richard Karinsky (Malcolm Gets), Jewish associate and later love interest of cartoonist Caroline Duffy (Leah Thompson), considers going through with a bar mitzvah ceremony. The series, *Caroline in the City,* always gave the impression of being spawned from a Jeckyl and Hyde struggle between equally powerful, opposing inclinations toward intelligence, thoughtfulness and humor on the one hand, and toward the silly, the insipid, and the cheap laugh on the other. The character who is always belittled in the process is Richard.

Richard's Aunt Frieda (Carol Locatell) nags him to have a bar mitzvah ceremony because he is the only one in the family of his generation who "never went through with it." The suggestion is that bar mitzvah is an ordeal to be endured. The aunt offers Richard a bribe of five thousand dollars if he will have a bar mitzvah ceremony in a temple.

Since Richard wants the money, he hastens to see the rabbi with whom he studied for bar mitzvah as a thirteen-year-old. It seems that twenty years before, the rabbi (Barry Gordon) had warned Richard that if he didn't go through with his bar mitzvah, he would condemn himself to life in a godless universe, devoid of all hope. Richard chose to walk away before his bar mitzvah because, as he tells his aunt, that godless world "sounded good to me then and it sounds good to me now."

In order to get a quick ceremony and the bribe, Richard tells the rabbi that his aunt has a terminal illness. Actually, the writer informs us, she is about to move to Palm Beach and wants Richard to be "bar-mitzvahed" before she moves. Aunt Frieda, who is rude and tactless and insensitive in addition to being manipulative with her money, spills the news about Richard's bar mitzvah to Caroline and friends, along with details of his schoolboy humiliations.

When Caroline worries that Richard might go to hell for having such a bogus religious ceremony, he quips that Jews have no hell and only one place to spend eternity, Miami Beach. He also suggests that it is a religious tradition in his family to observe Judaism by bribery. He recalls a cousin's husband who "got circumcised for a VCR." The writer tries to mitigate

Richard's materialism by having him confess that he is motivated by embarrassment at not being able to pick up the tab on most of his dates with Caroline.

In the end, Richard refuses to go through with the sham ceremony. For a brief, moving moment, we get the impression that he has too much respect for Jewish tradition and for the integrity of its faith and practices to accept his aunt's bizarre terms. Yet that illusion is quickly shattered by a side plot involving a co-worker's overly tight suits and indecent exposure in the synagogue sanctuary.

Especially annoying is the all-too-common TV theme of the Jewish man whose only role model for integrity is his nominally Christian girlfriend. There is also a slap here at the current generation of bar mitzvah boys and their motivations and pack-like behavior. Blame is placed upon the rabbi's severe rhetoric for feeding into Richard's fascination with godlessness.

No one tells Richard that he automatically became a bar mitzvah, a son of the commandments, at age thirteen, even without the ceremony. (For girls the age of religious maturity is twelve.) Responsibility to one's heritage and family, and accountability for one's actions, should not depend on a ceremony. Richard was never even afforded the gumption to make a spirited (and witty) response to the rabbi's counterproductive rhetoric of twenty years before.

Whenever one becomes a bar or bat mitzvah, commitment to the Jewish people, and to grapple with the faith and texts, with the God, of Judaism, is a given. *Caroline in the City* could have risen above its usual, predictable tugs and strains by tackling these issues with humor, wit and artistry. That is true of the other series that have chosen to obsess on the gifts rather than on the challenge of bar or bat mitzvah.

Bar Mitzvah as Formula Spirituality: "The Education of Max Bickford"

The short-lived, but memorable, series, *The Education of Max Bickford* (2001-2002), was full of surprises. Viewers expecting that Richard Dreyfuss's Bickford was just another generic White Anglo Saxon professor at a prestigious old women's college were, after a couple of episodes, to learn that he is Jewish and not at all reluctant to discuss it, except perhaps with his own son.

At the end of an October episode in which Bickford protests an alumnus award to a woman who assisted Roosevelt's secretary of state, Breckenridge Long, in closing U.S. borders to Jews fleeing Nazi horrors, the theme of bar mitzvah comes up, seemingly out of the blue. Apparently, writer Jan Oxenberg was given the assignment of depicting a burst of Jewish identity on the part of Max's eleven-year-old son, Lester (Eric Ian Goldberg). Lester recalls that his mother, who was a convert to Judaism, took him to temple: "because you wouldn't go," as he reminds his dad. (We learn in a later episode that Bickford's wife was killed by a drunk driver.) Lester remembers that a man gave him a candy apple on a stick and a flag, and that everybody danced around. Max is able to tell Lester that the holiday was Simchat Torah, the Festival of Rejoicing in the Torah (though Dreyfuss does not pronounce it well).

Oxenberg enables Lester to ask his father some penetrating and difficult questions that lead to not a little uneasiness. He wants to know whether his mother was "made" to convert by Max or by Max's father (Lester's Jewish grandpa). Max answers that "She took a class because she wanted to learn, and she felt at home." Lester then contrasts his father's indifference to Judaism with his mother's embrace of it: "Mom was more Jewish because she wasn't Jewish [to begin with] and you're less Jewish because you were always Jewish?" On further reflection, Lester adds: "When something is always there, you don't think about it [that is, appreciate it]." Even the children in Oxenberg's script are profound.

Sure enough, the next episode of *The Education of Max Bickford* took up the theme of Lester's Jewish awakening. Producers Dawn Prestwich and Nicole Yorkin penned this one. Like Oxenberg, they did their best work to date on Jewish themes in this episode; but their best work was not as good as Oxenberg's episode. It was slick. The dialogue was good, but the bar mitzvah episode was formulaic.

Lester decides that he wants a bar mitzvah. He has already checked out the pre-bar mitzvah program at Temple Beth Shalom. He announces: "Mom was Jewish. I'm Jewish. I want to be bar-mitzvahed." When his father, Max, reminds Lester, "You don't have to be bar mitzvahed to be Jewish," Lester responds that he is Jewish because his mom was (that is, became) Jewish, and that "she'd want me to." He declares that he wants to "learn about God." When Max insists, "I can talk to you about God," Lester protests, "No you can't. You don't believe in Him."

Clearly, Lester had done his research and mapped out his strategy. Writers Prestwich and Yorkin bring fine psychological insight to the family dynamic in having Lester open up the dialogue with questions about why he never sees his mother's relatives. "When your mother married me and decided to become Jewish," his dad answers, "her parents had a hard time with that. They refused to come to visit and after a while they stopped talking to us altogether." When Lester expresses anger and hatred for grandparents who never saw him, Max tells him not to hate them. "Mom didn't. She wouldn't want you to, either." At first, Dad says, Mom was hurt and angry, but then "felt bad for" her parents because their small-mindedness caused them to miss out on "the most wonderful thing in her life"—her children.

All this is fair and well-taken, as is the writers' suggestion that Bickford himself needs to overcome "small-mindedness." After all, he tells a friend, "My son is a religious fanatic." Indeed, Max's "struggle" comes across as rather cold and vicarious. He suggests that in order to be able to follow the Alcoholics Anonymous Twelve Steps, he decided to "borrow" the God of a buddy who was a fellow alcoholic. "I believed that he believed and it worked for him. I had faith in him." "Maybe it's time to get a God of your own," Max's colleague tells him. "Everyone needs a little faith now and then."

Reflecting on the theme of faith, Bickford recalls that the last time he was in temple was when he married his wife, Martha. "A lot of good it did her...If faith doesn't keep you out of the path of a drunken driver, what the hell good is it?" Later, when the rabbi (Adam Grupper) asks Max why he resists Lester's search for some kind of faith, Max responds: "I don't know whether God exists or not. But based on what I know, he's not morally fit for the job [Earlier, Max throws in a "she" for good measure.]."

The episode tries to weave together Lester's spiritual quest with Max's experiences in Alcoholics Anonymous and with a subplot involving Max's tensions with his secretary, exacerbated by his shabby treatment of an adoring student. Somehow it does not hang together, especially with Max spending every spare moment trying to make a non-Jewish diner-owner his confidante and girlfriend. The writers are sure to have the rabbi talk about "connection to the community and to God." Somehow the pious language comes across as a formulaic nod to spirituality, just as Max expresses his doubts in a canned, if witty, manner.

Also, Lester's motivations are not explored or clarified in this episode. He wants the bar mitzvah ceremony because he thinks his mother would have wanted it. His father tells him that he doesn't require such a ceremony to be Jewish, thus suggesting that he need not choose certain behaviors out of a posthumous desire to please her. Then Dad turns around and tells Lester that he must not be bitter toward his maternal grandparents, that his mother was not that way. Before we know it, Dad changes his mind, pledging to take Lester to classes, declaring that he wants to be a part of the bar mitzvah experience, and apologizing that "It's not that I don't believe in God. It's that I really don't know, but I'm willing to be surprised." Are the writers aware of these inconsistencies? Or are the contradictions par for the formula?

Backhanded Wedding Nostalgia: "I Love You, Alice B. Toklas"

I Love You, Alice B. Toklas (1968) is an early Paul Mazursky effort. There is a lot that is unworthy in this movie. It was definitely a forerunner in the "Let's mock Jewish mothers" and "Don't love, but leave, Jewish fiancées" genre. Thirtysomething attorney Harold Fine (Peter Sellars) is definitely dominated by his mother (Jo Van Fleet) who keeps his apartment as a satellite of her home, stocked with Manischewitz products. Harold's fiancée (Joyce Miller) has only one desire in life: to marry Harold and to settle down, and she is very much a Jewish mother wannabe. Harold's father is a quiet, passive spectator, with little to offer by way of traditions or values, or even personality.

Then there is Nancy (Leigh Taylor-Young), the nubile Hippie who entices Harold to leave his fiancee at the altar (or, rather, *bimah*), for a guided tour through "drug culture" and an extended period of irresponsibility.

What is amazing about seeing a film decades later, especially a "social commentary" critique-of-middle-class-Jewish-life film, is that (1) the writers' ambivalences seem more pronounced and (2) their original gripes may become softened and sometimes even rendered petty by the passage of time, by both the advance of nostalgia and the advantages of hindsight. Sometimes, as in the case of this film, something else happens: namely, (3) the writers and producers indict themselves for succumbing to trends and formulas.

If *I Love You, Alice B. Toklas* is nothing else, it is ambivalent. The Jewish mother may be domineering, but is she manipulative or just demonstrative? Compared to a lot of Jewish characters in TV and films today, she comes across as rather authentic in being able to use and understand and pronounce correctly a word like *mishpacha* (family), and to actually urge "family values" as a natural and visceral *desideratum*. Ditto for the fiancée, who may want to dress up home life and herself with the latest accessories, but who does genuinely want Harold. So it is, too, with the twin cantors who sing at the wedding(s) that are never completed. They actually sing nicely. Seeing them now, they appear not as a vulgar novelty act, as the writers suggested then, but as a part of a culture that was willing to add flair to the *mitzvah* (sacred deed) of marriage. After all, when it came right down to it, the focus of the seeming excess was not self-gratification or even conspicuous consumption, but the *mitzvah* of marriage.

One does not require hindsight to see bipolar signals here. Sure, the attempted Jewish weddings are a bit schmaltzy. The Hippie life is depicted as downright superficial, self-destructive and self-defeating. No film ever communicated more contempt for Hippie communes and jargon. Sure, Mother is somewhat nouveau riche and out of control, but you can count on her even when you can't count on anything else, including what her son's whims will be a few minutes down the line. Ma, with her slight accent and authentic Jewish vocabulary, does stand for something, as does the synagogue, no matter how gaudy the decorations on either. When Harold's brother returns for a funeral wearing the Hopi Indian mourning outfit, it is not only Ma who decries his obliviousness to his own people's proprieties and customs of mourning. The filmmakers rightly mock Jews who seek spirituality anywhere but in Judaism even more than they spoof the vulgarization of Judaism from within the community.

I Love You, Alice B. Toklas lacks, in retrospect, any moral consistency. It lampooned the drug culture, for example, but provided enough slapstick drug humor to send a signal that nothing's too serious, anyway. It ridiculed the lack of commitment among the Hippies, but had Harold Fine remove his *yarmulke* and run out of the synagogue twice, suggesting that the only way to face the contradictions in life is to bail out, at least for a while. One does get the impression, however, that part of the reason that Harold runs out the second time is that he finds some unworthiness, some persistent foolish-ness, in himself.

Yet, watching this film many years later, one gets the impression that it ends the way it ends because the audience would have expected to have been shocked, would have, in a way more faddish than perverse, delighted in an ethnic version of *The Graduate* (1967) which did, after all, appear the year before and did end with a wedding gone amok. It was not until several years later, with Barry Levinson's film, *Diner* (1982), that the Sixties trend of trashing weddings, especially Jewish weddings, was nullified by the affirmation of Jewish marriage as the redemptive response to human foibles and aimlessness. Indeed, *Diner*'s affirmation is so bold and radical, even in a rather cerebral and low-key film, that one suspects that the reason that the audience of the 1980s could tolerate it was that it was set in a movie about the Fifties, the only decade on which filmmakers could focus in order to break away from the viselike formulas that persisted since the late Sixties.

Chuppah as Object Lesson: "Dharma And Greg"

Dharma and Greg was the story of a straight-laced young lawyer, from true blue blood stock, who met and instantly married a free-spirited and good-hearted young beauty who was raised on New Age doctrine by Hippie parents. The 2001 cliffhanger demonstrated how desperate the once engaging series had become. (It would be cancelled in the following season.) It seems that Greg (Thomas Gibson) cannot trust his wife with a good-looking professor (Kevin Sorbo) whose attentions have left Dharma (Jenna Elfman) somewhat confused. Dharma and Greg try a marriage counselor and make efforts at "communication," but when the professor gives Dharma a ride home on a rainy day, Greg has a fit.

Dharma is indignant. After all, she did not allow anything to happen with the professor. She did keep one of his flattering letters, which Greg happened to find, but finds Greg's superior attitude annoying and unforgiving. While they bicker about their concerns, they get caught up in the tumultuous wedding rehearsal of a young Asian friend, Susan Wong (Susan Chaung) and her Jewish fiancé, Russell Gottlieb (Andy Milder).

The Gottlieb story was a strange side tale on *Dharma and Greg*. It began a couple of episodes before the finale. As soon as Dharma and Greg got involved in a community gardening project, the participants began to bicker. Greg's mother, the wealthy and self-indulgent Kitty (Susan Sullivan, always fun in her role) actually calls in her lawyer when the closest gardener's plants "strangle" some of her own. That neighboring gardener turns out to be the young Asian woman. Instead of coming himself to iron out the mess, Kitty's attorney sends his son, Russell. By the end of the episode, the couple are cuddling on the garden floor. When young Gottlieb's father (Stuart Pankin) finally comes upon the scene and finds them together, Susan prods Russell to tell Dad that they are in love and want to marry. Dad blurts out: "Before I say what I'm about to say, is there any possible chance you're Jewish?"

The Gottlieb saga is taken up again, quite matter-of-factly, in the second of two 2001 final episodes that follow the garden installment. Greg and Dharma are bickering about her having kept her admirer's letter, and Dharma is indignant about Greg's harping on how it is up to him to "forgive" her for an indiscretion that never happened. Their argument spills over into the wedding rehearsal of young lawyer, Russell Gottlieb, and his Asian fiancée, Susan Wong.

At the rehearsal Russell blurts out, "Thankfully, most of Susan's family doesn't speak English, so my parents were only able to offend a select few." We see Russell's dad again, complaining, "Ten thousand Chinese restaurants in San Francisco, [and] we have to shlep up to Mill Valley?" Susan's father responds, "Nothing is good enough for you"—a standard response to Jewish parents in TV series.

Gottlieb Senior can't remember whether his future daughter-in-law is from Thailand or Taiwan. (Actually, it is the latter.) In the wake of such remarks and verbal sparring, Russell tells Susan that she should recognize that it was a big thing for his dad to agree to have the wedding in a Chinese restaurant. Susan is not impressed, countering, "Your family likes Chinese food more than mine does." Here, we find the familiar standard sitcom joke about the Jewish proclivity for Chinese restaurants.

Ever the peacemaker, Dharma asks Susan if there is anything in common between these Jewish and Chinese families. "They're all opposed to the marriage," the young bride responds. Yet the wedding does take place, with rabbi and *chuppah* and guests wearing yarmulkes, in a Chinese restaurant. It is not clear whether Susan has converted to Judaism. That issue is left open, almost as if the silence were a bone thrown by producer Chuck Lorre at any possible religious concerns on the part of viewers. Or, more likely, Lorre does not care. He and Bill Prady, Don Foster and Sid Yeungers, who collaborated on the story and teleplay here, already got across their point: If a Jewish man and a Chinese woman can go through with their marriage despite opposition from both sets of parents, then surely Greg and Dharma can patch up their differences, now that both sets of warring parents (the Hippies versus the Blue Bloods) and good friends are rooting for the success of their marriage, not to mention their own accumulated love and respect for each other.

Strange that the writers made such a big deal out of the Jewish-Chinese concerns. After all, they made it clear all along that Dharma's aging Hippie parents set the precedent for "universal" marriage (or common law marriage) in their own coupling, for Dharma's dad, Finkelstein, is Jewish and self-conscious about it, but proudly partnered with Dharma's non-Jewish mother (Mimi Kennedy).

Dharma and Greg could occasionally be touching in its depiction of Dharma's search for her own identity and bearing, given her confusing upbringing. The 2001 finale revealed that Lorre and Company probably did not intend this pathos. For them, the topic was not interfaith marriage or family conflict following conversion. Rather, the Jewish-Chinese subplot was dragged in to reinforce the moral of the series: Every relationship is hard, so follow your heart, and worry about patching things up later. This is their prescription, not so much for happiness, or wisdom, or for anything, really, at all, except for the longest possible run. But significantly, the series floundered once the writers chose the most familiar and trite of staple TV formulas.

Jewish Weddings and Jewish Gangs: "Diagnosis Murder"

The long-popular *Diagnosis Murder*, which starred Dick Van Dyke as a sweetly meddling physician-sleuth, presented in the fall of 2000 a full-blown Jewish theme that revolves around, of all things, the breaking of the glass at a traditional Jewish wedding ceremony.

It seems that the good doctor has been invited to the wedding of a friend, a dress designer, and her associate, garment entrepreneur Stanley Baumgarten (Don Stark). At the beginning of the episode, we get to meet a pleasant woman rabbi (Joanne Baron), who expresses her joy at being able to fit her *tallit* (prayer shawl) over a designer dress provided by the bride and groom. In response to the groom's fear of cutting his foot with shards of the glass goblet to be broken, the rabbi responds that she uses a mild light bulb and that the groom need not worry.

Writer Terry Curtis Fox has the wedding guests, including the good doctor sleuth and his detective son (played by Dick Van Dyke's real-life son, Barry), witness the bomb explosion that fatally injures the groom the moment he steps on the glass. The next moment we see the bride (Leila

Kenzle) fretting over her groom as doctors battle to save his foot and then his fading life.

In the scene that follows, we join with the erstwhile wedding guests as the same woman rabbi officiates at Stanley's funeral (unfortunately, not pronouncing the words of the Kaddish Prayer too well).

During the course of the investigation, we learn that Stanley had been distributing the drug "Ecstasy" to his models—during his bachelor days, of course—in order to score points with them. As one model explains, the beauties would have hung out with Stanley anyway because he was "short, cute and funny" (and Jewish?), but "like most guys he thought he had to give something extra"—namely, the "Ecstasy." We also learn that Stanley had "rolled over" (that is, turned States' evidence) on the supplier so that Federal drug police could close their case.

Far be it from me to violate the sanctity of the murder mystery genre by giving away plot and resolution. I will not reveal the actual killer, but I can protest that the Jewish wedding scene is used here as yet another media excuse, on big screen and small, to impugn Russian immigrants (and by implication, Jewish immigrants) with gratuitous profiling of the "Russian mafia." I, for one, was saddened that, in this particular episode, Steve Lawrence played one such Russian mobster with joy and aplomb. Also, it should be noted that whatever positive image of Jewish women is offered here in the depiction of the rabbi and the bride is effaced by the implications of the depiction of one of the Russian women.

Sure, there is a Russian mafia and some Jews are involved in it, but where is media treatment of the lives and achievements of the hundreds and thousands of Russian immigrants who escaped Soviet tyranny and post-Soviet chaos and made something of their lives and sacrificed much to remain loyal to their Jewish faith and heritage?

2

FRACTURED FESTIVALS

ℰↄℭℛ

Shabbat And Marriage Taboos:
"Archie Bunker's Place"

In 1979, *Archie Bunker's Place*, the reincarnation of *All In The Family*, began to deal with the theme of interfaith marriage, perhaps the only topic not covered on *All In The Family*.

It seems that Archie's partner, Murray Klein (played by Martin Balsam) introduced his Gentile girlfriend to his mother and aunt. Naturally, both old ladies had protracted melodramatic fits.

What was unusual about this particular encounter is that Edith Bunker (Jean Stapleton) decided to "make *Shabbes*," prepare a Sabbath meal, for everyone. She kindled the Sabbath candles in transliteration and even prodded Archie (Carroll O'Connor) into doing a transliterated *Kiddush* (Sanctification of the Day over wine). The men wore *yarmulkes*, and Edith served chicken soup, chicken and all the trimmings. Dessert was Edith's own special home-spun wisdom: She explained to Murray's mother that it doesn't matter what religion you adhere to, as long as everyone loves each other when they gather under one roof.

Edith and even arch-bigot Archie have become "qualified" to moralize on the higher virtues of interfaith blending of families because they discovered that Edith's niece, whom they have taken into their home, is really Jewish, since her mother was Jewish. The Bunkers have therefore undertaken to safeguard the child's Jewish identity by enrolling her in the local temple Sunday school, and are even dues-paying members of the temple because Sunday school comes as part of a "package deal."

This strange scenario of Archie Bunker raising a Jewish child led to some touching scenes. Especially moving was an episode in which Archie, regretting that he had thrown a fit over his niece's Jewish origin, bought her a star of David necklace as a token of his loving acceptance of her. In another episode, Archie learned first hand the evils of anti-Semitism after the girl's synagogue was vandalized.

The intermarriage issue came to the front burners in the early 1980s. It seems that Murray's own daughter ran off and married a Puerto Rican man, and has two children, Miguel and Rebecca. Murray, who only weeks before introduced his mother to the Gentile woman in his life, wants nothing to do with the children, or with their mother, his own daughter. Not even Archie, now the expert at conducting an interfaith household, can get Murray to forgive his daughter. Only the blind man who frequents Archie's bar can see what producer Norman Lear wants the others to see. If religion is true, he points out, there will be a Final Judgment, so why judge now? If religion is not true, if all religions are equally invalid, then why be concerned about interfaith marriage, anyway?

Writers Bob Weiskopf and Bob Schiller were inconsistent. Why should Archie's niece go to a Jewish school and learn about that heritage if all religious traditions must bow to true love, anyway? Why should Archie preserve his niece's identity if all religious conviction devolves around a Judgment Day that may never come? "Love Conquers All" is old Hollywood's most appealing concept, and it is all the more attractive when religion is reduced to an irrational fear of a judgment day that may never come. What about the joy, the awe, the sense of holiness that makes religious experience meaningful, because, and not in spite of, its restrictions?

The writers of *Archie Bunker's Place* were also insulting. It would seem that Murray regards Gentile women as ripe for sex but not for marriage. *He* can date a Gentile, but his daughter cannot marry a non-Jewish man. Also, there are shades of racism in his obvious hurt at her choosing a Puerto Rican man. No one sets Murray straight on his prejudices and double standards, however. Everyone is too busy pontificating about "true love." No one pauses to consider that if Judaism is worth preserving, then interfaith marriage is not worth glorifying.

The *Seder* in The Absence of The Jewish Mother: "Anything But Love"

Anything But Love (1989-1992) was a pleasant and witty sitcom about Marty Gold (Richard Lewis), a writer from New York who is self-conscious about his Jewish background and everything else; and Hannah Miller (Jamie Lee Curtis), his colleague at a Chicago magazine, a former schoolteacher of undisclosed religious and ethnic background. The premise of the series was that the two decide that they cherish their friendship too much to fall in love, at least right away.

Anything But Love also featured frequent Yiddish expressions and occasional references to Jewish holidays. Marty talks about his Jewishness often and has his own hand mannerisms and cynical, sometimes even morbid, view of things. One character speaks of his "usual bummer-downer attitude." Yet the general implication of the series was that Marty is the way he is not because he is Jewish but because he is Marty.

A clue to the "Jewish" angle of this program was offered in a March 1990 episode about a Passover *seder*. (The word, *seder*, is used several times.) Marty mentions that he'll be visiting his sister for the *seder*. Hannah declares that she's always wanted to know about Passover, and asks why there aren't TV specials about the holiday. (To which Marty responds "You mean you've never seen the perennial holiday special, *Let My People Go, Charlie Brown*?) Hannah persists. She says she wants to attend a *seder*, especially since she's been to a Roman Catholic midnight mass and a Shinto service and has a similar desire to see what Passover is all about.

Finally, Marty gives in to Hannah's "hinting," but only after warning her that his family's *seder* is not orthodox but is "a little looser" than that. He and Hannah arrive at the *seder* after struggling through an unusual spring snowstorm. If it had snowed on Passover in ancient Egypt, Marty quips, Moses would have said, "Dig my people out."

Once at the *seder*, Hannah commits the minor *faux pas* of sitting in Elijah's chair. (Actually, the *seder* features Elijah's cup. Elijah's chair is reserved for circumcisions.) Not even an orientation in the order of the service could prepare her for the big surprise: Marty's sister, unaware that he was bringing Hannah, invited his ex-fiancée, now divorced! Rebecca, the ex-fiancée, is certainly a beautiful and alluring Jewish woman, and mischievous, too, in that she directs Hannah to throw a *matzah* across the room as fast as she can, thus conjuring up rituals to embarrass Hannah.

Most viewers will realize that Rebecca is making such things up. But not a serious word of explanation is offered about the *seder*, not even a translation of the word. The *matzah* is shown but not explained; the drops of wine are taken from the cup (in commemoration of the Ten Plagues) without elaboration. Marty does make a crack about focusing on the Ten Plagues: "This is historically where our cheerful disposition comes from." The implication here, though not in the series as a whole, is that Marty's morbidity is the net result of Jewish tradition.

One understands the lack of inspiration in this *seder*. Clearly, the writer, Janis Hirsch, wanted to lampoon a *seder* without spirituality. There's a cute touch about a brother-in-law and the four cups of wine. The whole purpose of the *seder*, anyway, is to introduce Marty's ex-fiancée, to show that she and Marty share not-so-latent passions, and to offer the rather outrageous scenario of their getting carried away enough to run off to Las Vegas to get married—without even inviting Hannah! With such a scenario, it would be futile, I suppose, to expect the writers to have considered that Jewish marriages do not occur on Passover or for several weeks afterwards, that a nice Jewish boy and a nice Jewish girl who haven't seen each other for years would be able to control their passions during the *seder*. It becomes rather clear that the *seder* is intended simply as an "ethnic" backdrop for slapstick and farce.

At the beginning of another episode, Marty tells Hannah the story of one of his forebears in Russia who was run over by a borscht wagon and had to spend the rest of his life rolling cigarettes for the circus with his tongue. When Hannah comments on how tragic this was, Marty responds: "No, the tragedy is that he intermarried." In the *seder* episode a relative says, "Come on, kids, you can say hello to your Uncle Jack and Aunt *Shiksa*."[1]

Someone obviously has intermarriage on the mind. Time was, by the way, when Jewish men and women were stereotyped as not passionate enough. By emphasizing Marty's and Rebecca's lust for one another, and then having them conclude that it is an unhealthy attraction, this episode deliberately undermined one of the few TV relationships between a Jewish man and a Jewish woman.

What about Marty's mother? It has to be significant that the butt of so many jokes each week, with whom Marty had even reconciled, was not

---

1.   A denigrating epithet for non-Jewish women.

featured in this episode. Did the writing staff decide to trot out Jewish rituals for visual mockery and to relegate the Jewish mother to the background in order to dehumanize her so that the "jokes" would not lose their nasty edge? Whatever their motivation, the writers knew that extracting the Jewish mother would give them—and their character—the latitude to propel Marty into unrestrained revelry and tomfoolery.

Chanukah as Self-absorption:
"E. R."

In its first season (1994-1995), NBC's *E. R.* had been ambiguous regarding Jewish doctors, and the few references to Jews among the patients were also rather second-hand and off-beat. Five months into the series, the only reference to the possible Jewishness of one of the main characters, Dr. Mark Greene (memorably and touchingly portrayed by Anthony Edwards) had been in the pilot TV movie, and that was a response to an anti-Semitic remark that any thoughtful Gentile might have made, also.

From the point of view of Jewishness and religious faith, things got interesting in December 1995 with the second annual Christmas—and, this time, Chanukah, too—episode offered by the series. The episode, written by Carol Flint, is worth analyzing in some detail. Not to be overlooked is a weird segment at the beginning in which some doctors are scrubbing for surgery. One is flippantly discussing investment tips for Christmas gifts and being rather imperious to the gifted African American intern, and is obsessed with beating speed records for that particular operation while using "ethnic" expressions about "chopped liver." Is there a suggestion here that such a "go-getter" physician has become generic for the negative aspects of "Jewish doctors"? Meanwhile, in the same opening segments, Dr. Mark Greene must meet with his lawyer regarding depositions in a lawsuit brought against him by the husband of a woman who died in childbirth. In a sequence obviously intended to fetch sympathy for Greene, he unwittingly picks up the child whom he saved from that mother and returns him to the father, who is visiting lawyers, as well. Had Greene become generic for the nice aspects of "Jewish doctors"?

In the episode's main storyline, an elderly woman is brought into the emergency room after being pulled from her vehicle during a carjacking. The ambulance driver says that she reminds him of a sweet old lady at

Christmas mass, but Dr. Greene is the first to notice her concentration camp tattoos, and declares, "I don't think this little old lady goes to mass." He recognizes that she is a Holocaust survivor.

From police reports of abandoned cars, they learn that her name is Chana Steiner. The patient tells them that she was driving with a baby, her granddaughter, Tirza, who is missing. In Hebrew, the name *Tirza* means "to want" (to survive), an appropriate reference to the descendants of Holocaust survivors, who were understandably seen as miracle-babies, resurrected from the ashes. A nurse observes that Chana refuses to be sedated or to submit to a CAT Scan because she is "hoping to hear some good news." Chana, who is portrayed with grace and charm and thoughtfulness by Joan Copeland, bonds immediately with Dr. Mark Green, because he understands the one Yiddish expression that she uses. She assumes, as several of us viewers did during the pilot episode, that he is Jewish.

Mark Greene tells Chana not to give up. "I guess I don't have to tell you that," he adds, remembering that she is, after all, a survivor. Chana responds that it's easier not to give up when one is young, and has been called a "dirty Jew" in school. Having seen the very worst in people, she understands all too well that the carjackers may hurt her baby granddaughter. After seeing the evil of the Holocaust, she says (and any informed viewer will know that the Nazis had no qualms about killing babies) she learned that the "best revenge" is not to let such evil own you, though "something like this" *can* take away even the accumulated joys of family and meaningful work.

Chana tells Greene that she has just done something that she had not done in fifty years: She has prayed to God. As if testing to see how Jewish Mark is (and probably in the name of many curious Jewish viewers), she asks if he is religious. Greene responds that he learned a little Yiddish from his grandmother, that he is the son of "an agnostic Jew and a lapsed Catholic." Chana quips "You're no good at all. I can't ask you to pray for my family." Greene promises that he will try. (Mark Greene is, I believe, the first portrayal on TV of a child of mixed marriage not raised in any faith.)

With all the cheerful Christmas caroling in the background, and with a Santa Claus-like figure making a mysterious exit from the hospital, this episode almost *had* to offer a happy ending to Chana's saga. The baby is found and brought into the hospital, and reunited with the grandmother in a very natural yet touching way that almost conveys a miraculous aspect to happenstance on many levels. At the end of the episode, Chana's family "brings Chanukah" to her, lighting the *menorah* together in her hospital room, with the prayers recited, much to the pride of all, by grandchildren who obviously know their heritage. "Dr. Greene and I said our prayers," Chana observes, "and that's a miracle, too. I thought that God and I had forsaken each other. And then I found out that He was always with me, in each of you. Bless you." Dr. Greene observes the joyous family reunion, and is obviously pained that his daughter will not be with him after Christmas because she prefers skating with cousins to the designated time with him given by joint custody agreements.

There is no question that this is a moving episode from the "Jewish" point of view. There is some meaningful dialogue here about evil, faith, and the unique struggles and perspective of Holocaust survivors. Granted on all counts. Yet there is also something about this episode that is manipulative, that pushes the right emotional buttons without offering any kind of spiritual coherence or authenticity, Judaically speaking. (Hence, only one of the two Chanukah blessings is recited.) The subliminal messages here are disturbing.

If, indeed, Chana's ordeal were the "main story," how explain that the writer has her silently witnessing the death of a young priest due to gang violence, and not joining in efforts to prevent gang revenge? If Chana's God is only in each of her family, what guidance can she give to other victims of violence who might "take revenge" in ways less constructive than hers? Somehow, Chana's finding her faith betrays a narrowness and self-satisfaction in that faith.

Also, far from restoring Greene to the warm glories of a lost ancestral heritage, the Chanukah experience with Chana actually inspires and liberates him to create a *new* holiday for him and his daughter, the "First Rachel and Dad Post-Christmas Post-Chanukah Pre-New Year's Day Celebration." Since Chana's Judaism is *her* family's thing (again, limiting her Jewish faith), Mark feels free to invent *his* own rituals.

The Chanukah Menorah as Assimilation: "An American Tail," "The Five Mrs. Buchanans"

Chanukah is supposed to celebrate the 165 B. C. E. victory of the Hasmoneans, a small branch of the Jewish priestly family, against Jews who tried to dilute their ancestral faith and its sacred commandments with Hellenistic practices and values promoted by an occupying Syrian regime.

The *menorah* (candelabrum) augmented Temple vessels with a Greek torch of triumph in order to emphasize that the ancient victory was really a Divine response to human efforts to preserve the Covenant with God. Yet there have been recent American treatments of Chanukah, in both television and film, which have exploited the *menorah* for other purposes.

Even as well-intentioned a film as Steven Spielberg's *An American Tail* (1986) uses the *menorah* only as a point of departure. The animated film begins with a Chanukah celebration in which young Fievel the Mouse is presented with an heirloom cap (a kind of *yarmulke?*), which will actually help to identify him when he is later lost.

From Chanukah the scene switches to a pogrom in which the "Jewish mice" scatter when attacked by Cossacks. Like the pogrom scene in *Fiddler On The Roof*, the real length and viciousness of a pogrom is not shown, but, after all, this is a "children's picture." Or is it? Throughout the film the mice are pursued by frightening, salivating, ferocious cats. The deepest fears of children are constantly paraded: getting lost and separated from parents, being exploited by bad people (or cats, as the case may be), ducking malevolent and pouncing human beings. A child psychiatrist told me that the film is a good way for a child to act out his or her fears. It still strikes this reviewer as rather frightening! What therapy does it offer the viewer? Only an "all's well that ends well" message that somehow is not reassuring after all the dark alleys and scary characters.

The film makes a valiant effort to be "Jewish." After Fievel is lost at sea, his parents, thinking he is dead, inscribe a *yahrzeit* lamp with his name in Hebrew characters, but of course, most of the audience can't read it or understand its significance. The *yahrzeit* lamp that no one can read is, in fact, symbolic of the missed opportunities in this film. Instead of letters that no one can read, why not an effort to communicate Jewish values and terms such as *mentschlikhkeit* or *zedakah*? Why not depict the Jewish soul? I'm not saying that the film should have been a documentary or a Hebrew school lesson. The artistry of such a film, if indeed it makes serious claim to a "Jewish" theme, should have consisted in the ability to provide, albeit with a light touch, subtle insights into Jewish values and culture.

The film also makes a valiant effort to depict the immigrant experience, the hopes and sometimes illusions of those who braved the difficult journey to new beginnings. Hence the song about there being "No Cats in America." The all-too-clear message of this film is that being Jewish, at least in a lot of immigrant experiences, is to be frightened and persecuted—mouse-like, if you will. The Italians get the worst (and most uncalled-for) stereotype of them all: They immigrate to escape from their own mafia-types! It's too bad that the writers had to dredge up old stereotypes in the midst of what appears to be a sincere effort to teach mutual understanding and ethnic diversity. (Cats get very bad press, too, for what is, after all, only natural instinct on their part!)

In all fairness to *An American Tail*, it should be said that the Jews are not depicted as being completely passive. They do fight back. They join together with other immigrants to strike back at the cats. All the mice, not just the Jewish mice, are scared: fear of cats binds the different immigrant groups together. Fievel even leads a revolt in America against the cats. Here we may have a subtle message that it is not the older generation, but a new generation that finds courage in the new American environment and takes the initiative to attack old problems. Interestingly, however, Fievel draws from his father's Chanukah stories about a "Giant Mouse of Minsk" (a combination Trojan Horse and *Golem*) to build a secret weapon to frighten the cats away. Here we may also have a subtle message: that one can transfer one's traditions (or at least folklore) for the collective welfare in the new American experience. Does this imply that traditions are to be handed over to the American experience in general, and not preserved as a vital spiritual heritage?

A happily short-lived 1994-1995 sitcom, *The Five Mrs. Buchanans*, offered a similar take on *Chanukah* symbols and stories in the name of "Jewish pride," but ended up sending the most vulgar assimilationist message ever in the television medium. This series, set in "Mercy, Indiana," focused on a virtual sorority of sisters-in-law and their feisty, 70-ish mother-in-law (Eileen Heckart, who delivers her lines with typical aplomb). As for the daughters-in-law, there is a New York Jewish Baby Boomer, Alex Isaacson Buchanan (Judith Ivey); a Midwesterner with social pretensions, Vivian (Harriet Harris); a reformed stripper married to the minister son, with the only biblical name, Delilah (Beth Broderick); and the innocent young Orange County bride with Disneyland work experience, Bree (Charlotte Ross).

In the very first episode, Mother Buchanan, who has nasty one-liners for all, and takes them as well as she receives them, says of her Jewish daughter-in-law, "Oh, there is that delightful Semitic sense of humor." Alex's sister-in-law Vivian tells her, "I've always considered it a minor miracle that the three of us get along so well. Let's face it. We would never have been friends if we hadn't married brothers....You're my best friend and you're a Jew from New York. I never thought I'd be friends with an honest-to-God Jew. Yet here you are and I couldn't love you more if you were my own sister." Alex responds: "So you'll finally introduce me to your other friends?" Quips Vivian, "Boy, you people are so pushy."

Interestingly, such banter did not come up again. The "Jewish" angle of the episodes depended on the writers. We learn that virtually every line—or one-liner—is tongue-in-cheek, anyway, for Alex hosts church meetings and Christmas celebrations at her home. (The depiction of "church women" is rather nasty, by the way.) She is duly thanked by the church women's group for lending her home to their meeting: "In Alex's honor we'll be reading from the Old Testament." Alex, for her part, falls back on her Jewish heritage when she wants the appropriate one-liner. Thus, when her sister-in-law drops off her destructive twin sons, Alex exclaims, "Vivian, as a member of the Jewish community, haven't my people suffered enough?" (Echoes of *An American Tail*?) Yet Alex has a wreath on her door during the winter season and named her only child, a son, "Chris."

As a series, *The Five Mrs. Buchanans* had its moments, but it was generally little more than a five-way volley of one-liners. One does not get to know the characters too well here. In *The Golden Girls*, at least, one felt that one understood something of the background of the main characters as people and not only as types. This rarely happens in *The Five Mrs. Buchanans*. The only episode that was truly moving and artistic was that in which Delilah went to see a psychiatrist to discuss her infertility. The laugh track and one-liners stopped, and a tour-de-force performance by Broderick was possible. Even that scene began with a one-liner, "I've never been to a psychiatrist before, but my sister-in-law is a Jew and she swears by you people."

The Five Mrs. Buchanans was, in the main, little more than a tinny version of *The Golden Girls*. It was chintzy in its production. One got the impression that most scenes took place at Alex's home because the producers were too cheap to build another living room. One of most humorous episodes was that in which Mother Buchanan's youngest, newly-wed son, Jesse, was featured. None of the other sons had been depicted. The producers, it seems, were too cheap—or dogmatic—to hire some male actors.

Ironically, it is precisely this chintziness in production, resulting in the one home set, Alex's living room, which led to the series' most vulgar episode, written by Michael Patrick King. The episode was probably well intentioned, though also marred by gratuitous laughs at the expense of holiday alcoholism. The premise was amusing enough: Alex accidentally breaks Mother Buchanan's Baby Jesus. After offering the requisite "Oy vay," Alex tells her sisters-in-law that maybe she could say that "the Romans did it."

Mother Buchanan cannot forgive Alex for breaking the Baby Jesus that the elder woman hand-painted years before, and is offended when Alex observes that the statue is "just a symbol." Mother Buchanan responds, "I should think that anyone who would marry a Buchanan could at least learn to respect this family's religious traditions." It is at this point that Alex "stands up" for herself: "I *am* part of this family. After twenty years of decorating 'this family's' Christmas tree and making 'this family's' Easter baskets....I don't remember your ever coming here for the big Chanukah celebration. How do you think that makes me feel?"

Here was a scenario never before seen on a TV sitcom: namely, the Jewish member of an interfaith family demanding that Chanukah be given the same attention she gives to Christmas! The episode concludes with the "moral": "The spirit of the season is not in our symbols but in our hearts." Yet to anyone who takes his or her religion seriously, the symbols are the way to bring spirit to the heart.

Indeed, at the end of the episode, when a burnt fuse threatens to disqualify the decorations put up by the family on Alex's house for a local contest, the family decides to use the Chanukah *menorah* to shine on the Christmas lights. As Mother Buchanan says, "Doesn't the nativity look beautiful in the glow of candles?"

Until I saw this final scene. I never fully appreciated the Hebrew words recited after lighting the Chanukah *menorah*: "These lights are sacred through all the eight days of Chanukah. We are not allowed to use them for any of our utilitarian purposes." This episode was the ultimate misuse of the Chanukah lights for a misguided series' message of religious syncretism, a scenario, I fear, that will appear more and more on TV in the name of "Jewish pride," and that began, in a more "secular" vein, with *An American Tail.*

Chanukah as Slander of Jewish Children: "Hiller And Diller"

Sometimes, it's the low-rated and annoying and short-lived sitcoms that make TV history. The 1997 series, *Hiller and Diller*, is a sad case in point.

Produced and often written by Lowell Ganz and Babaloo Mandel, it represented a TV "first": depicting Jewish children as nasty and rude and without any saving graces.

Ever since the first episode, I was troubled by the series, starring Kevin Nealon (of *Saturday Night Live* fame) and Richard Lewis as best buddy sitcom writers. Nealon is sympathetic and likeable in his role as a dedicated family man, and ditto for the rest of the cast members playing his wife and children. The husband-wife dynamic is nicely drawn, but it's another story with Lewis' side. It's hard to figure out why Nealon's character, Hiller, is so devoted to Lewis' character, Diller, who is whining and erratic and never acts from principle or values.

Enter Diller's children. We are told immediately that he is sole guardian because their mother has run off. His twelvish son is introduced as a pyromaniacal, foul-mouthed shifty operator. His fourteenish daughter dresses in a manner that would be deemed inappropriately suggestive for a twenty-year-old, and has no worthy interests or social graces. Diller himself has no integrity. After exploiting his friendship with the Hillers to get his children an interview at a private school (after they have wreaked havoc at their other school), Diller wants his friends to go along with him in a bogus promise to endow a gymnasium at the school in order that the faculty and board will not expel his destructive children. Even as he tries to hatch his plot, his son is summoned by the school authorities and charged with involving the school dietician in a cafeteria scam.

Unfortunately, the moribund series (which had the most insipid and annoying theme song ever) lingered long enough to spawn a "Chanukah-Christmas" episode. It begins with Diller's Jewish children, joyful, pleasant and having good, clean fun, none of which has characterized them before, while singing Christmas carols at Hiller's house. Hiller asks Diller whether he wants his kids to have some sense of their roots and heritage. Diller responds with some flip reference to an aunt's "enormous breasts." Undeterred by that response, Hiller asks Diller why Jews eat *latkes* (potato pancakes) on Chanukah. Diller's "witty" answer is that Jews are supposed to eat food cooked in oil in order to "celebrate the bad complexions of the ancient Hebrews."

Interestingly, the audience roared as soon as it heard the word *latkes*. Why? Could this be the net result of legions of TV sitcom "humor" that suggest that Jewish rituals and customs and beliefs are a joke? Have audiences been so conditioned by the relentless prattle of self-mocking Jews? This episode had no qualms about making a mockery of the lighting of the *menorah* without even bothering to try to explain the meaning of the Festival.

True to form, Diller's children are incapable of sustaining even the "Christmas spirit." Son Zane bullies the other children into forming a makeshift cheese business, destroying their fun on the festival. The reason? "Christmas isn't about fun," he says. "It's about the story of cheeses." "That's Jesus, you moron," a young Hiller tells him. The message is clear: Diller's kids are dense to spiritual nuances and always looking for an opening to make a quick buck. Not even Christmas can save them, and Judaism, which is nothing but a joke, cannot redeem the silly one-liners, even in its TV role as object of mockery.

Toward the end of the episode, writer Alex Herschlag tries to account for the Diller behavior by having the children's dad offer bitter reminiscences of his childhood Chanukah experiences. Seeing one's parents argue over brisket, however, is no excuse for one's children's bad conduct or for the distrust and suspicion that Diller stirs up at the office. The latter comes across as particularly unpleasant behavior in the season of "peace on earth and goodwill." Baby Boomer angst becomes justification for denigrating the next generation of Jewish children.

Thanksgiving as Jewish Holiday: "Avalon," "Family of Cops"

In his film, *Avalon* (1995), Barry Levinson intends to offer us autobiographical tribute to the first generations of a Jewish family in Baltimore. He especially cherishes the grandfather, Sam Krichinsky (a touching performance by Armin Mueller-Stahl), the grandmother (Joan Plowright, in an equally affecting performance), and the grandfather's brothers. Through the adorable eyes of young actor Elijah Wood, who, we assume, portrays Levinson as a child (young Michael), we experience vignettes of a family history, both amusing, moving and suspenseful: unfair school-teachers; violent crime striking close to home; the subtle traumas of moving to a more spacious home and yard in the suburbs from the warm extended family network of the city; the arrival of Great-grandpa from the Old Country; even the mesmerizing screen patterns of early TV. The film, which features excellent performances all around, offers insight into the risks and pitfalls and worries that went into the founding of family businesses. Particularly memorable is the performance of Aidan Quinn as Michael's dad, Jules.

The great strength of *Avalon* is that it hits close to home in its depiction of family struggles, of the relationship between generations and their parents and in-laws, of sibling relationships and family quarrels. It offers a respectful, but not overly romanticized, glimpse into the immigrant generation, centering, in this case, around Sam who, as he never tires of repeating, arrived in this country on the Fourth of July of 1914. By keeping the immigrant generation sharply within focus, it offers insight into the toll that sociological migrations took on family ties. Yet the main focus of the film is on the first generation Americans, especially as seen through the eyes of Michael or through his impressions of family stories.

The image presented here is of parents who were caught up totally in the trend to move to the suburbs and in the economic pressures to pay for the changes. Prominently conspicuous by its absence is any semblance of Jewish involvement or of Jewish life either in the immigrant generation or the first generation. Sometimes, we hear a Hebrew expression or a Yiddish word as background, identifiable only to one in the know. Once there is a reference to a woman as a "woman of valor" at a funeral, but this is a family without *shivas*, without any bar mitzvahs, without reference to Hebrew School or the State of Israel or to the synagogue. In one scene, we learn that Michael's parents (and cousins) were married by a justice of the peace, even when the couples were Jewish. (One recalls that a previous Levinson film, *Diner*, offered one of the most beautiful depictions of a Jewish wedding in a film, and made that event the climax and even the redemptive point in the movie.)

The Baltimore Jewish community was, and remains, one of the most active and distinguished in the country. I submit that during the years presented in this film, only the most assimilated family that made a career of shunning Jewish life could not have been touched in at least one branch or household by synagogue or Jewish organizational life, and that this was just as true of the suburbs as of the city neighborhoods. The only Jewish organization depicted in the film is a family club, which comes across as symbolic of all family networks, and not specifically of Jewish ones. Even the great-grandfather is depicted here as admired for his ability to hold liquor—a "distinction" found in the lore of many ethnic groups.

There are not even any vignettes of Jewish holiday observances in this film. Did the family never have a *seder*, never share a Rosh Hashanah dinner? Time is marked in this movie by the celebration of family

Thanksgiving dinners. Yet the immigrant generation is depicted as being inept at getting the holiday right. Grandma asks: "To whom do we give thanks?" Was a Jewish woman from the Old Country so religiously unaware and unacquainted with the Festival of Sukkot, the first Thanksgiving? We find references here only to a "holiday gift." The song, "O, how we danced...." seems to have become the substitute for Jewish music. Even the Holocaust is virtually stripped of its Jewish significance. Grandmother's refugee brother arrives from Europe after World War II, and even in the touching reunion scenes there is no reference to the plight of the Jews. Instead of Yiddish, a Slavic language is spoken. The Holocaust survivor represents the persecuted relatives of people of any background.

I don't understand what Levinson means to convey in this film. Does he intend to have the family come across as so assimilated and uninvolved Jewishly? If so, does he mean it as a critique? Does he just want to show "the way it was" with his family? If so, is he prepared to stand by the impression he gave of a life completely devoid of Jewish causes and concerns? If not, how honest is the film? And what good is a film about families-in-general who happen to be Jewish, if it offers no insights into Jewish life? My own suspicion is that Levinson wanted to create a family-saga-in-general. Is that not the vacuousness of nostalgia for the sake of nostalgia?

As a result of the glorification, and even, sanctification, of nostalgia for its own sake, *Avalon* is a manipulative film. It knows what buttons to push, but it offers no perspective, no judgment, no searching. It set back the Jewish family film saga by fifty years. It is more of the 1940s than of the 1990s, of the era which would present the Jewish family only to the extent that it is like any other. The Thanksgiving motif only serves to make the kind of statement that a film of the 1940s or 1950s would make: "We're as American as you are! We now fight over the turkey instead of over *matzo* balls!"

Thanksgiving received similar status as the Jewish holiday of choice in a well-meaning and promising CBS TV movie, *Family Of Cops* (1996), the first of a series of three about the same household. The film did succeed at breaking stereotypes, but it fell into *Avalon's* paradigm.

Unique in its premise and casting, *Family Of Cops* featured Charles Bronson as Inspector Paul Fein, a widowed Jewish father who is a policeman and has two policemen sons, a public defender daughter, and a wayward daughter accused of murdering a wealthy businessman. The movie is well-cast, although the crime part never rises above formula melodrama and action scenes. This film, however, is significant in other ways.

While Jewish policemen and public defenders have long been part of the human landscape and law-and-order lore of big screen and small screen alike, this TV movie goes out of its way to depict the Jewish cops as virtually interchangeable with two-fisted and danger-loving types of any other religious and ethnic background. That is fine. The notion—or stereotype—of all Jews bringing uniquely cerebral qualities to their professions ignores the basic human truth that there are all different kinds of personalities in any religious or ethnic group, the Jews included. The old Yiddish writers understood this well in their depiction of the *ba'al guf*, the hefty and ruddy Jewish types who used their hands for physical labor and sometimes fighting, and not only for talking or studying Torah.

Family Of Cops goes out of its way to make the point that *this* family is not going to put up with any anti-Semitic slurs, especially from criminals and gangsters. We just know that eldest cop son Ben (Daniel Baldwin) will throw a punch at the hoodlums who regale him and his father with comments like, "Did you get some Hebe judge to write out this warrant?" Nor are comments like, "Why don't you be a smart Jew boy?" allowed to pass. Yet after a while writer Joe Blasberg may be doing his characters a disservice by suggesting that their two-fisted approach to things is a reaction to slurs or to assaults on the family honor. It seems truer to human nature and to many drawn to the law enforcement profession to say that we have here people who thrive on crisis and on confronting criminals.

As far as the "Jewish" angle is concerned, *Family Of Cops* may be indicative of a new trend in television portrayal of "Jewish" themes. This trend may be described as the "subliminal" approach. There is a reference to Avrum Weiss being the best in daughter Katie's public defender office. Later, an Orthodox rabbi with full beard is shown walking down the hospital corridor—not addressed nor given any lines, just shown walking by. Also, a physician wearing a *kippah* (*yarmulke* or head covering) is shown talking to the family. Could it be that at the climax of Twentieth Century TV, a "Jewish" program is one that acknowledges that there are religious Jews in the world with split-second shots, and that relates by suggestion that you can have an O. K. public defender with such an old, Jewish-sounding name as Avrum? Indeed, this film actually does something rather brave in a subliminal way, at least for TV dramas present and past. It blurts out the maiden name of Fein's deceased wife, Lasky, thus suggesting a marriage of two Jews to each other! Yet it remains ambiguous about the religious background of Ben's wife, and nonchalant about the probable Catholic background of the youngest son's girlfriend.

Apart from the suggestions and subliminal stuff listed above, there isn't too much that is really Jewish about *Family Of Cops* in any meaningful or noticeable way. No one in the family offers even so much as *"Baruch Hashem"* ("Praised be God") when key evidence is found to clear the youngest daughter. At the end, one of Ben's small daughters tells him, "Daddy, you have to kiss the *mezuzah*," but the line seems so disjointed, almost gratuitous, that it hardly makes a difference. Not that it isn't good to hear such a bit of dialogue. Yet it is unsatisfying and disappointing when disconnected from the rest of the drama. No one even finds a way to explain what a *mezuzah* is, and why should they?

Thanksgiving is, after all, when Jews do what all other Americans do to celebrate the blessings of their country. That holiday belongs to all Americans, and all Americans belong to it. This is a great blessing of American democracy and values and ideals; but one would hope that producers and writers would get beyond *Avalon's* "We celebrate Thanksgiving, too" posture. This film only exacerbated that all-too familiar stance by declaring "We can be cops, too," "We can throw punches, too," or "We have wayward daughters, also."

3

CORRUPTED JEWISH USAGES
AND BELIEFS

ಬಂಡ

Matzah as Communion With Hollywood:
"State And Main"

David Mamet's 2000 "film," *State and Main*, is really a photographed stage play, in which dialogue and scenery are almost at cross purposes, perhaps by intention. The tack may be to show that idyllic country scenes do not necessarily showcase idealistic natives. The Vermont town that a vain, calculating and desperately overbudget movie company would exploit out of urbane arrogance and bottom-line necessity is more than up to countering by maneuvering for its own ego needs, financial opportunities, and power plays.

So chivalry and virtue are dead or at least in hibernation, in small town America as in Hollywood. Selfish actors and pretentious writers can be despoiled and humbled at the intersections of small town byways. Hollywood movie companies are constantly locked in bargaining and manipulations that may infect the local courthouse (and, we are explicitly told, the Electoral College) as well. What else is new, or, rather, why was all this stuff being rolled out in a play-thinly-disguised-as-movie?

Oddly, or perhaps not so oddly, the strands that unite all these disparate elements, which Mamet does not even try to resolve, are the Jewishness of producer Marty Rossen (David Paymer) and the suggested Jewishness of writer Joseph White (Philip Seymour Hoffman)—these, and an old city newspaper whose bannerhead includes one of the Ten Commandments, "Thou shall [sic!] not bear false witness."

Before addressing the Jewish/Ten Commandments angle, it might be helpful to regard *State and Main* as a second draft of a recent genre of play, created by the Coen brothers and by Mamet himself. First came the Coen's film-imitating-a-play, *Barton Fink* (1991), about a young Jewish writer who goes to Hollywood in the 1940s and is surrounded by madmen and, even worse, by vulgar Jewish producers who exploit playwrights and pervert their art in order to hoard grist for the mills of movie production. The Jewish playwright there is a lone bystander, whose idealism is a tense mix of naivete and arrogance, and whose perspective and nobility and only chance of sanity rest in his remaining a solitary observer of the *meshugass* (craziness) that is all around. The dramatic tension abides in the question of whether he can do that with greed and insanity and even cruelty lurking and lying in wait, either to pounce or to seduce.

The other first draft of this scenario is *The Winslow Boy* (1999) by Mamet himself. The theme here, too, is integrity versus lurking sensationalism and vulgarity in a highly stratified and snobbish late nineteenth-century British society. Here, a refined and religiously grounded family choose to defend their son at any cost when the latter is falsely accused of cheating. In *State and Main*, neither the lead actor who pursues under- aged girls, nor the producers who cover up for him at every turn, care anything for the honor and virtue of children, but neither, for that matter, do children have respect for adults who are not wealthy matinee idols.

So what is *State and Main* really about?

The film declares that standards have been totally surrendered by our society to the "values" of celebrity and money-making. Here it is not only the entertainment industry, or the super rich, or adults, or Jews, who are compromising and perhaps suffocating morality. Everyone has a share in that. When characters are adjured to close ranks and circle the wagons to defend and protect the making of the movie above all else, the mandate to be faithful to "our community" refers specifically to the society of filmmakers of every ethnic background. This is the "new covenant" that Mamet portrays with mixed romanticization and ridicule.

It would seem, however, that the role of Jews in that new covenant is to bring certain colorful ethnic trappings to it. The townspeople eat *matzah* (unleavened bread) as they watch the film finally being made, symbolic, perhaps, of their buying in, or at least eating in, to the "communion" between show biz and small town mercenaries. The day that a briefcase with $800,000 in cash is redirected from manipulations within the film colony to payola to protect the star (Alec Baldwin) from local government—this is dubbed the *yomtov* (festival or holiday). Once the Jewish producer calls the opportunistic local prosecutor a provincial "*shegetz*" (a vulgar expression for a male non-Jew), Yiddish epithets are exalted to the "liturgical" status of being the most expressive putdowns that can be invoked in the verbal war against the disingenuous "normal community," whom the film community regard as backdrops rather than as counterparts.

Jews still have an important role in Mamet's "new covenant." In addition to expediting the "creative process" and bringing a colorful vocabulary to the negotiations, they are the ultimate stand-outs in every community, the relentless spindoctors among the filmmakers and the lightning rods of adoration or resentment in both the movie team and the small town. The local bookshop owner wants the writer because he represents accomplishment among the minority of book-people; to the leading lady he represents the mystery of sex with the circumcised. To the local prosecutor a tough Jewish negotiator is a "cheap Hebe," but *the* opponent to beat in order to prove one's courtroom prowess.

At times Mamet seems to tell us that the Jews assume these roles because they ask for them, provoke them, even beg for them. Certainly, his Jews have no moral edge or perspective here, though his writer character, Joseph White, spends an inordinate amount of time trying to flee the town and show business in fits of guilt. It is his Gentile girlfriend who cherishes the "Thou shalt not bear false witness" commandment on the local newspaper and who goes to great lengths to concoct a ruse that keeps Mr. White on the honorable path, using set-making skills against the filmmakers. Is it also the role of Jews to win the sympathy and charity of non-Jews who take the Commandments seriously and are the only moral salvation of post-religious Jews?

The "Jewish" elements in this film certainly grow out of a publicized "reawakening" of Jewish identity within our playwright/filmmaker. In his depiction of Jews in *State and Main*, has Mamet come that far from *Homicide* (1991), which equated intensified Jewish identity and commitment with appropriation of, and by, a people of self-preserving exploiters? Does he now project the same "Jewish" characteristics onto the filmmaking community?

Mezuzah, *Mikvah* and Apocalypse:
"Millennium"

The Fox Network's *Millennium* (1999) certainly knew how to produce creepy, eerie and disquieting scenarios. Fairly early on, it offered a rather startling episode with Jewish themes.

The script by Marjorie David is fragmentary in that its shards evoke all kinds of stereotypes and negative images, and one is hard put to find any message in all this except the truism that fanaticism can be bad and scary.

The episode begins with a young husband's leaving the house to buy an outlandish snack to satisfy his pregnant wife's cravings. He is attacked by masked men with a taser who break into the home and kidnap the wife. By the time a team of government investigators arrive, the husband, who turns out to be a Jewish doctor, is awaiting some kind of ransom call and the *mezuzah* has been removed from the door.

What kind of kidnappers would take a *mezuzah*? Right then and there I guessed that this would be *Millennium's* Jewish fanatics showcase, and that it would all have something to do with the messiah and the Temple Mount (what else?). Once the millennium-fanatics busting team referred to the *mezuzah* as "prayers in the Torah to keep everyone from harm" (as opposed to Divine teachings to be reminded of upon entering one's door), one had to expect distortions and bad impressions.

Sure enough, the kidnappers are Hebrew-speaking (albeit in broken fashion) and take the petrified mother-to-be to a *mikvah* (ritual bath), where they intend to deliver the child in order to inaugurate the third Temple. (One fears that this child's parents will never subsidize a trip to Israel, should mother and child survive this horror.) There is even, though just for a moment, a suggestion of the possibility of human sacrifice, but only for suspense. Still, the impression of ruthlessness and barbarism remains.

The writer can't wait to give us a lesson in Jewish genealogy, alerting us with aplomb that the father's name is Cohen and that the mother's family were both *cohanim* (priests) and Levites, as if such combined lineage matters in Jewish law and tradition. Then we are given some ill-digested Dead Sea Scrolls fare to the effect that this group plans to raise the child as a messiah-priest while they blow up the Dome of the Rock Mosque to build a Third Temple.

Our investigators soon discover that the crime is without fingerprints because the kidnappers grafted on artificial skin developed in Israel for burn victims. (This was probably the first time in TV history that one of Israel's marvelous scientific and medical achievements had been given a sinister twist in order to spice up a dramatic plot.) The writer is also intent on telling us that the robe discovered on the young mother, who is mysteriously released, was made at a vestment company in Williamsburg, Brooklyn. This is, of course, where ultra-Orthodox Hasidim live. Yet it is slanderous to feature them in this "exposé" of fanaticism, since they would never support an effort to reclaim the Temple because of their belief that the messiah must arrive and change the world *before* one can even think of rebuilding the Temple.

Most appalling of all is a scene in which a woman, a spiritual seeker who has joined this cult and who once had a connection with the Cohens, is stoned by the group for releasing the mother. This well-meaning Jewish person is denounced as a "woman, betrayer from the time of Eve." Her execution, not to mention the politically incorrect rhetoric, is reminiscent of proverbial depictions of Jews as zealots and stoners, stereotypes found initially in New Testament literature, and then taken out of context by anti-Semites down through the ages. As if to add defamation to insult, the villain behind the cult is none other than a hero of the Six Day War.

I suppose that the message in all this is that fanaticism can rear its ugly head in all religions, and that all religions may feed off one another with fanaticism. The arch-villains in this series, a (non-sectarian?) "millennium syndicate," hope to use these Israeli fanatics to hasten the end-time. As long as a Middle Eastern war brings Armageddon it doesn't matter to the millennium folk whether the Jews have found a real messiah or simply raise an anti-Christ to provoke the Christians. The end-time is the terrible, chaotic and exciting goal, either way. Our writer does manage to convey the images of Jewish fanatics so bumbling and inept that they let key witnesses get away, can't land escape helicopters, and are klutzy enough not only to slip and fall at climactic moments, but to get impaled to death in the process. Is saving grace for the Jews therefore to be understood as a lack of coordination in hatching vicious plots, the mind being crafty but the body clumsy? Is that why these Jewish zealots allow their victims to live? One hoped for more religiously authentic reasons, like compassion and reverence for life.

The episode has some strong moments. The fear of the kidnapped mother-to-be is well-depicted in her shaking (to highlight the threat of human sacrifice?). The two principals among the investigators are engagingly and thoughtfully portrayed. The African American woman agent obsesses a bit on the apocalyptical literature, wondering how "that kind of knowledge in the world" can be taken in stride. Her partner responds, "Nobody owns the End or the truth." Does that mean that no scripture contains the truth and that there will be no End? If everybody believed that, then no one would be interested in Jews or Christians or in any other TV fanatics of the week.

The Talmud Ignored:
"Reasonable Doubts"

Reasonable Doubts (1992) featured Mark Harmon as a police investigator who works with a hearing-impaired assistant district attorney played by Marlee Matlin, who is deaf and who won an Oscar for her role in *Children Of A Lesser God* (1986).

One episode featured Uncle Murray Shaffner (Pierre Epstein), who is the uncle of the district attorney, Arthur Gold (William Converse-Roberts). Shaffner is defending a child murderer, a psychotic serial killer. Gold is seeking the death penalty, but his uncle sincerely believes that the death penalty is wrong. So Uncle Murray tells Arthur: "If you have an ounce of your heritage left in you, you will give him life instead of the death penalty."

While one appreciates the sincere opposition to the death penalty by the character (and writers?), we ought to be troubled by their suggestion that to be loyal to one's Jewish heritage is to oppose the death penalty. I can understand a writer and his character invoking loyalty to the Jewish heritage to oppose some unethical act that would bring shame on God and the Jewish People (dialogue rarely, if ever, heard on TV). But this is a gross misrepresentation of the complexity of Jewish teachings and traditions regarding the death penalty.

The Mishnah, the foundation code of Talmudic law, compiled in the second century, records a telling discussion:

> The Sanhedrin (Rabbinic court) that puts to death one person in seven years is termed tyrannical. Rabbi Eleazar ben Azariah says, "One person in seventy years." Rabbi Tarfon and Rabbi Akiva say, "If we had been in the Sanhedrin, no one would ever have been put to death." Rabban Simeon ben Gamaliel says, "They would have [thereby] increased the shedders of blood in Israel." (Makkot 1:10)

In this and in subsequent deliberations, the ancient Hebrew Sages debated the issue of capital punishment from several vantage points. They made it very difficult to actually put someone to death, but they did not want to erase the biblical laws of capital punishment which lent absolute authority to the sacredness of human life for the first time in the ancient world.[1]

The oversimplification of classical Jewish teachings on capital punishment is not the most troublesome and even offensive aspect of this episode of *Reasonable Doubts*. However, of far more concern, I believe, are good old Uncle Murray's words to the assistant D.A. that capital punishment is wrong because no society has the right to kill as Uncle Murray's parents were killed at Auschwitz because they were deemed unworthy by the state. Here we have a blatant and gratuitous comparison between laws applied to hardened killers and a racist war against an entire people that made a mockery of all laws. Now it is true that Matlin's character is allowed by the writers to respond to Uncle Murray that the situations are different. Uncle Murray is given the last word: "That killer didn't will himself into a monster any more than my parents are responsible for the fact that they were Jews."

One appreciates Uncle Murray's sincere crusade for justice as he understands it, and his affirmation that his experiences as a Jew and as a child of Holocaust victims inspire and animate that crusade. One can respect his words to Arthur, "Your mother would be proud of you if you defended the underdogs instead of persecuting them." One cannot help being offended by the gratuitous use of the Holocaust, and by the suggestion that being a prosecutor of crimes (here called the "persecutor") is not as worthy an aspect of the process of justice as being a defender. If the Jewish heritage is invoked for the latter, it should be invoked for the former, as well.

Forfeited Jewish Customs:
"Chicago Hope"

When, in 1995, actor Mandy Patinkin announced his intentions to leave the CBS series, *Chicago Hope*, in order to spend more time with his family, viewers like me, who appreciated Patinkin's sense of values, sighed with

---

1. On the biblical roots, see Nahum N. Sarna, *Exploring Exodus* (N.Y. Schocken Books, 1986), pp. 185 ff.

relief that his character, Dr. Jeffrey Geiger, would no longer be TV's preeminent Jewish doctor. I had hoped that the way Patinkin was written out would offer less offensive images of Jewish physicians than Geiger and Adam Arkin's character, Dr. Aaron Shutt (who remained).

Who really cared about a doctor's being haunted by a nasty Jewish mother or conflicted in his relationship with a mad wife who drowned their son? In an early episode, Geiger was dating an African American physician while still deeply attached to his institutionalized wife. He gave her some song and dance about only expecting to marry a Jewish girl. That was before the writers made it clear that his mad and infanticidal wife was not Jewish—and, therefore, that his speech to the black physician was, in retrospect, a bit dishonest, if not racist.

As I see it, Dr. Geiger, as painted by the scripts, could always have been easily replaced, anyway. Brashness and cockiness come in varieties other than Jewish stereotypes. Gentile doctors can use the word *megillah* in wrong contexts, too. A number of the younger doctors depicted here had those qualities in less whiny ways than in the behavior patterns assigned to Geiger and Shutt. Other doctors could have been brought in to say sexist and insulting things to the unabashedly ambitious and calculating woman physician well-played by Christine Lahti. Another obnoxious Geiger trait, a delight in second-guessing other doctors, might also have been reassigned.

The best writing in *Chicago Hope*'s depiction of its two Jewish doctors was the often touching brotherly bond that distinguished their relationship. Unfortunately, but not surprisingly, there was never an effort to explore the nature of bonds among Jews in any meaningful way. Why suggest that there is a different quality of bonding among Jews? How interesting will such bonds remain without some unique link of commonality? In a first season script by producer/writer David E. Kelley, with John Tinker and Dennis Cooper, Geiger and Shutt did two procedures simultaneously in order to try to buy time for an older man with both brain and heart problems. Even here, the friendship bond is explained as little more than shop talk and common brooding and self-recrimination.

The apogee of the social skills and spiritual depth of our two Jewish doctors was reached in the second season (1995-1996) when the hospital lawyer (memorably played by Peter MacNicol) turned to Shutt and Geiger, in that order, to be his adopted baby daughter's godfather, and was turned down by the former who was busy whining to his wife that he didn't like her any more (and after one of TV's strongest glorifications of interfaith marriage!). Geiger almost declines this request because he does not feel comfortable with the "you being Catholic and me being Jewish" thing. Geiger does agree on the condition that there be no speaking in strange tongues or flames dancing on anyone's head. So much for Geiger's concept of religion in an episode penned by John Tinker that is far more respectful of Catholic ritual than of the capacity of certain Jews to graciously and sensitively respond to the heartfelt requests of friends.

I remarked above that certain unpleasant qualities of Dr. Geiger are universal enough to be interchangeable with any other characters that might come along to replace him. Ironically, I find that the writers have given him a role that he, as a Jew, ought not to have been assigned, and have given to the Gentiles some specifically Jewish customs that are not identified as such. All this came out in the farewell episode for Patinkin, written by Tinker, as well.

The Jewish custom that is not acknowledged as such is the ethical will, a statement of values and hopes that one intends to be a guide to loved ones, especially children, after one's death. There are at least two references to an ethical will in this episode. Not that Jews have a monopoly on ethical wills, but there is a unique Jewish tradition of them, as classic volumes by Israel Abrahams and Jack Riemer have shown.[2]

One would have hoped that TV's preeminent "Jewish doctor" might have been allowed to cite this tradition, especially because doctors work with patients and should have some knowledge of these things, if only for counseling purposes.

Here, it is a Catholic hospital lawyer, played by MacNicol, who sets the moral tone with his ethical will. This is the character, by the way, whom the writers had made a clown and butt of humor before restoring his dignity and then killing him off. It should be noted, too, that this character is killed off as the victim of machine gun shots by marauding black youth in a prominent stop in the Chicago city train system. Chicagoans had been flattered that the two major medical series of the 1990s, *E.R.* and *Chicago Hope*, were set in their city. I'm sure it did no good for public relations, or depiction of blacks, or even day-to-day morale, when these programs

---

2.   See Israel Abrahams, ed., *Hebrew Ethical Wills* (Philadelphia: The Jewish Publication Society of America, 1926), and Jack Riemer and Nathaniel Stampfer, eds., *Ethical Wills: A Modern Jewish Treasury* (N.Y.: Schocken Books, 1983).

stepped up their depiction of graphic violence (as they did, almost as if in competition with one another), both to provide fodder for their increasingly lurid emergency room scenes, and for plot devices.

Be that as it may, it is the friend's ethical will that restores to Dr. Geiger his equilibrium, perspective and purpose in life. Not Judaism. Not Jewish family. Not Jewish community. Not Judaic ethical traditions, including the spiritual legacy of ethical wills, one of the most famous and beautiful, by the way, being that of Liebman Adler, the first rabbi in Chicago (!) and the father of architectural genius Dankmar Adler.[3]

What is the mission that Geiger gets from his murdered friend's ethical will that he is really not equipped to do? He takes an indefinite leave of absence from his medical practice to raise his friend's adopted baby daughter as a good Catholic!

Unable to get over the drowning of his own son, and missing the role of parent, Geiger breaks with everything in his life and background to take on this new mission in fulfillment of the request made in a Christian ethical will. Abraham Heschel once wrote that Jews are "messengers who forgot the message." I doubt, however, that this episode was intended as social commentary on Jews' failure to recognize their own time-honored traditions. It may simply come from the inability or refusal of writers and producers to see Jews as any kind of messenger whatsoever, but only as colorful, highly verbal and neurotic ethnic types.

Yiddish as Euthanasia: "Chicago Hope"

During the 1999-2000 season, its last of first-run episodes, *Chicago Hope* threw the Jewish community a curve ball with a vexing episode about Dr. Jeffrey Geiger (Mandy Patinkin), an elderly, dying Jew, and baseball.

The hour began with Geiger taking a class of medical students along on morning rounds, instructing them that it is the physician's job to instill in patients a "sense of hope." If miracles don't come, he adds, the doctor must see that the patient is comfortable and able to enjoy whatever time he has left.

3.　　Cited in Morris A. Gutstein, *A Priceless Heritage: The Epic Growth of Nineteenth Century Chicago Jewry* (New York: Bloch, 1953), pp. 103-104.

When Geiger comes to the room of Mortimer Gould (Sid Conrad), who is up in his eighties, the doctor serenades him with "Take Me Out to The Ball Game" in Yiddish, and jokes with him that men with his condition are reputed to have been "accomplished" in the "sexual department." Both aspects of Geiger's bedside manner are, when one thinks of it, a bit inappropriate. Combined together, they make for a strange association of Yiddish culture with off-color humor. Indeed, in most TV drama, Yiddish is utilized only as a language of expressive off-color words. The episode has much worse associations for the Yiddish language in its store.

The Mortimer Gould saga is badly alternated by writer Gardner Stern with stories about a doctor banished by an indignant Geiger for cloning experiments, and about a fundamentalist Christian woman who denies medical procedures to her physician son on the grounds that he has "healed" the mother and members of her circle while he has been in his comatose state. The mother tells the young female physician on the case that no procedures must be done to bring her son out of the coma, for the healing is the will of the same God who won't allow anyone into heaven without belief in Jesus.

So, in addition to the gratuitous juxtaposition of Yiddish song with off-color "therapy," the writer provides a gratuitous jab at Evangelical Christianity and at cloning experiments. The hour is, in many ways, moralistic and judgmental, but what are the values that guide its preachments?

It would seem that the writer and company are advocating compassion. Would-be cloners are by definition without feeling, as are fanatical Christians. Jeffrey Geiger, though impulsive, is the paragon of compassion. He bonds with his elderly Jewish patient and sings in Yiddish to him. He learns that baseball has been important to this man since childhood and that he courted his wife, now deceased, through baseball. Gould laments lying in the hospital, with tubes coming out of him, without children or family or enough living acquaintances even to get a gin game together. He asks Geiger to end his misery, to spare him from having to return to a depressing, smelly old folks' home.

We next see Geiger emerging from Gould's hospital room to tell colleagues that his friend and patient quietly passed away, ostensibly to the choruses of "Take Me Out To The Ball Game" in Yiddish. The implication is that Geiger did not have to euthanize, that just his presence and the Yiddish syllables helped to free the soul so that his friend could depart gently into the beyond. Yiddish therefore becomes associated with putting a sick, elderly gentleman out of his misery. It is a language of the so-called "sage-ing" movement, the growing push to regard old age as one long preparation for a "smooth" and "seamless" passing.

The problem with the episode, however, is that it offers skewed perspectives on Yiddish song and culture and on the way that life, whether of youth or of the aged, is regarded in Judaism. Cantor Charles Bloch, a distinguished recording artist of Yiddish song, points out that the most beloved Yiddish songs offered a moral lesson, a warning against becoming obsessed with profit and superficial pleasures, a mandate to be a *mentsch* (decent human being) and to embrace *Yiddishkeit* (Jewish culture). By that standard, writer Stern and singer/actor Patinkin give a very limited understanding of Yiddish song. True, baseball is an important part of American culture and of the Jewish experience of it. Solomon Schechter once said that to be a rabbi in America, one has to know baseball. In a drama purporting to deal with spiritual matters of life and death, the reduction of Yiddish culture to assimilation of a baseball song, however sacred in the ballpark, is a disservice to Jewish life.

It is a profound disservice to Jewish religious teachings to imply that active euthanasia, or even a nod to euthanasia by autosuggestion, is in order for any elderly person who feels lonely, frustrated and who is in pain, or who believes that he has outlived his era. To validate such a program with Yiddish song adds insult to Judaism and to possible injury or self-injury of a human being. This is not an approach to illness and pain that is true to the teachings of Judaism, as expressed eloquently by Abraham Heschel: "If society should decide to reject my services and even put me into solitary confinement...would I then feel compelled to end my life? Human existence cannot derive its ultimate meaning from society, because society itself is in need of meaning. It is as legitimate to ask: Is mankind needed? as it is to ask: Am I needed?...Every moment is a new arrival, a new bestowal. Just to be is a blessing, just to live is holy...All it takes to sanctify time is God, a soul and a moment. And the three are always there."[4]

---

4.   Abraham J. Heschel, *The Insecurity of Freedom* (Philadelphia: Jewish Publication Society, 1966), pp. 76, 82. See, also, Leon R. Kass, "Death With Dignity and the Sanctity of Life," *Commentary*, March 1990.

4

MISGUIDED MOURNING
AND AFTERLIFE

℘℃ℜ

Shiva as Kung Fu:
"Babylon 5"

I n 1994, the syndicated television science fiction series, *Babylon 5*, offered a telling episode about a *shiva* (week of mourning) in outer space. It seems that the "Babylon Project" is a space station where aliens and earthlings have common ground to try to deal with their interpersonal and intergalactic problems.

Into this arena comes a rabbi, nicely played by Theodore Bikel, who tries to get his niece, Susan Ivanova (Claudia Christian), a commander on the space station, to say *Kaddish* for her deceased father. The niece steadfastly refuses. Finally, the rabbi goes over her head and appeals to the commander to make her sit *shiva* so that, as he explains it to the commander, she might find comfort and be able to fulfill the obligation of praying for the departed.

As it happens, the commander believes that she should sit *shiva*; he says that she must express her grief. Yet she protests that her feelings are her own and that whether or not to display those feelings is her choice. Needless to say, she is angry at her uncle for going over her head. She does tell her uncle, the rabbi, that she is dispensing with *shiva* not because she has ceased being a Jew, but because her dad was "not a loving man, though in his own way, I felt he loved me." She says that she blames her father for denying her his love after her mother committed suicide and her brother died in a tragic accident. The rabbi understands that she can't forgive her father for leaving her with unfinished business, but warns, in well-written lines of dialogue, "Without forgiveness you cannot mourn, and without mourning you cannot let go of the pain." "You cannot run away from your heart, not even in space."

Ultimately, she decides that she wants her uncle to stay and to help her sit *shiva*. The custom of *shiva* is depicted respectfully and meaningfully. There are moving reminiscences, which help the rabbi's niece to cherish her father's memory. There is an effective reading of the Memorial Prayer which gives a sense of the Jewish belief in life after death. If anything, the expectations for the healing powers of a *shiva* period may be raised too high by this hour. Such healing and comfort from so many terrible tragedies can only come through years of spiritual preparedness, achieved by growing faith and cumulative acts of love and reverence for God. The Kaddish prayer, after all, is not a prayer for the dead, does not speak of death, but of God as Source of strength and comfort.

The episode, written by Lawrence G. DiTillio, does foster an appreciation for Jewish traditions and acts of piety. It also demonstrates that religions, even those as all-encompassing as the skies are expansive, must work their wisdom on human beings who carry much complicated emotional baggage; for God has only people (and maybe space aliens) to work with. I liked the way that the rabbi was depicted as having his human foibles. He could show childlike awe upon first seeing the space station, saying that Babylon 5 is a *"nes gadol*, a great miracle." He joins his niece in eating a new food, "treel," obviously some artificial or extraterrestrial concoction, and one of the few foods readily available, for, though not sure if it is kosher, he can say, "I don't recall it being mentioned in the *Torah*." Though most rabbis I know would err on the side of caution, there is a very Jewish concern expressed here about making the commandments adaptable to novel circumstances.

My only qualm about the episode is its equation of the "Jewish" story and a parallel plot about an African American kung fu fighter challenging a heretofore invincible veteran alien fighter. At times in the hour, it seemed as though the kung fu sequences were being presented as rather silly and barbaric when contrasted with the wrenching emotional issues being dealt with in the *shiva* sequences. By the end of the episode, however, it appeared that the writer was glorifying the kung fu match as "a tradition" on a par with *shiva*.

Convoluted *Shiva*:
"Saying Kaddish"

Under the auspices of the "Interfaith Broadcasting Commission," the Jewish Theological Seminary of America produced, in 1989, a sixty-minute drama, *Saying Kaddish*, written by Nessa Rapoport and Debbie Goodstein. Dr. Rachel Roth, a distinguished researcher, has died before her sixtieth year, a victim of cancer, leaving her husband and two daughters. The elder daughter, Talia, played by Tovah Feldshuh, returns home for the funeral and *shiva* with her young son. Talia, a physician, has been away in California for quite some time, and left the role of nursing their mother to her younger sister, Annie, played by Star Jasper. Talia is uncomfortable with the *shiva* traditions; she feels at once confined and at home in the family house; she both leans on and provokes her father. Is she beset by grief, or guilt, or problems finding a spiritual home in the traditions of Judaism? The answer seems to be all these and more.

Feldshuh and Jasper are just fine and likeable in their roles. Some of the best scenes are those with the two sisters trying to understand one another and to forgive each others' shortcomings before these become a barrier between them. One only wishes that the writing allowed the sisters—and their father, and the rabbi, and other characters, for that matter—to come across with more humor, more wit, more grace and a bit more warmth in their outlooks, dialogue, and interaction with one another. True, the characters are in mourning, and true, not every character—not even *any* character—in a drama has to be a Cary Grant or a Carole Lombard. To be sure, the characters are in an unrelenting search for their personal and spiritual identities; the sense of pain and searching and the atmosphere of a *shiva* house are well-depicted here. Yet the writers have so emphasized the angst, guilt and spiritual search that they have left the impression that this family (and perhaps families in general, or Jewish families in particular) are interesting to the extent that they are hurt and angry.

Indeed, I would go so far as to say that the characters in *Saying Kaddish* are not very interesting apart from their suffering. We learn nothing about Talia the physician or Annie the teacher. We don't even know their fields or specialties. The only scenes in which the characters bare their souls are when Talia listens to a Danny Kaye record from her childhood, or when the sisters play ping-pong with their father. This *shiva* period, which does, after all, represent Judaism, comes across as totally isolated from every other aspect of life, as the crucible in which they must work out all the familial and "Jewish" struggles in their lives. To a large extent, by the way, things are worked out between the sisters and between the daughters and their father. So we are presented a *shiva* with a happy ending, as *shivas* go.

The writers deliberately chose to isolate the *shiva* for a family's emotional marathon. The drama does get across the point very well that the *shiva* period must be as little invaded by the workaday world as possible. The father has to make it clear a couple of times to business colleagues that he cannot look over even important papers during his week of mourning for his wife. In a nice scene with her little boy, Talia addresses the child's confusion over the covered mirrors and other *shiva* procedures (including the tearing of the garments) by explaining to him that these practices show that their world has changed and that the mourners can no longer be the same. There is also some fine use of the camera in getting across the spirit of the *shiva* candle in shots to highlight a photo of the deceased or the family saying Kaddish. Talia's becoming more open to the traditions is underscored with a nice shot of her in front of a *mezuzah*.

Indeed, for sheer atmospheric and educational communication of the meaning of *shiva*, this film effectively balances explanation and dramatic effect. It is, thus far, the best example of such balance in films produced under Jewish religious auspices. There are, however, a lot of missed opportunities and crossed signals here also. The scene with the rabbi is problematic. The rabbi is sympathetically depicted. His eulogy is appropriate and he is helpful to the family and seeks out Talia for discussion. Talia tells him that she does not rebel against God as much as against tradition. She states that she considers herself "spiritual" but finds no meaning in the rituals, that she must make her own path. Instead of telling her outright that the traditions are the cornerstones of Jewish spirituality, the rabbi waxes historical and therapeutic: What about 2,000 years of tradition, common history? Don't you find comfort in all these people who knew your mother, here each day, keeping traditions, saying the words and the tunes that you've known since childhood? The rabbi's words offer no real response but do encourage people who are resistant to variations of synagogue melodies.

The dichotomy between "spirituality" and "tradition" remains unaddressed. The writers merely assume that Talia's moves in the direction of participation are indication enough that the issue of such dichotomy has been treated. This, I think, was a mistake. Talia expresses a most respectable emotion when she responds to the rabbi, "How can I believe in a loving and righteous God in a crazy world?" It is good that Talia brings up the subject of God, because the rabbi never does! During a pivotal scene in a Jewish religious drama that will reach more people than all the sermons in every synagogue combined, the rabbi mouths these words: "You say you feel too little. Maybe you feel too much."

While not an inappropriate response to her concerns that she is numb to her mother's death and to the traditions, this is, by itself, a trite and incomplete response, since no respect is given to her larger questions—namely, what traditions have to do with spirituality and with facing personal loss. No explanation is given by the rabbi at the very beginning when the garment is torn—not a word about how Judaism finds every opportunity to experience God's presence through blessings recited on every possible occasion, including times of sorrow and anger unresolved. Nowhere does the film get across the point that *shiva* is more a continuity than a discontinuity with Jewish spirituality in that the prayers recited are almost identical to those recited every day in the synagogue or at home. Even the Kaddish prayer does not mention death. It is a prayer in praise of God, read originally to thank God for the gift of Torah, repeated in between important sections of each service, and recited by mourners to affirm God's kingdom even in times of grief and mourning in order to accept God's comforting and supporting Presence no matter what we must face in life. Through the Kaddish prayer, Jews declare loyalty to God and affirm their faith that God is faithful to us despite the unfairness that we inevitably encounter. One would have hoped that a drama about *Saying Kaddish*, presented under the auspices of a theological seminary and placed in the hands of talented writers and actors, would have gotten some of these points across.

The writers actually promote conflict between "tradition" and "spirituality" in their depiction of the hour's most interesting character, Uncle Manny (engagingly played by Dan Frazer), who is Orthodox. They portray him as both lovingly impish and annoyingly inflexible. Uncle Manny takes it upon himself to teach Talia's son *Shema Yisrael* (unfortunately, in a flat key), and his actions later elicit a surprisingly cordial response from Talia. Yet during the *shiva* service, this same uncle tells Talia, "Where I come from, men and women pray separately," eliciting from her the hostile retort, "I don't understand, Uncle Manny. You're here to pray for a woman. You can't pray with women?" Interestingly, this film under Seminary auspices, which has gratuitously injected the controversy over the role of women, chooses to debunk the tradition of separating the sexes during prayer, which is not common practice, anyway, at the vast majority of *shiva* services under Conservative auspices. The film also suggests that the *shiva minyan* (prayer quorum) is intended to "pray for a woman." *Shiva* is really an attempt to affirm God despite the loss of a beloved family member. Strange, by the way, that in a drama which purports to convey Judaism's approach to death, not a word is said about the afterlife. When Talia's little boy tells his grandmother's best friend (Phyllis Newman) that he is looking for his grandma Rachel, she immediately replies, "I don't think she can hear you, sweetie." That's as much as we're "told" about the afterlife.

There is much with which this family must deal in this *shiva* period, and in this hour-long drama. Yet everything is, if not completely, then all too neatly, resolved by the end of the *shiva*, and of the drama. Even the case of Annie's non-Jewish boyfriend, who returns into her life for the *shiva*, is dispatched by a difficult decision that she makes. While my instincts and emotions and religious beliefs support her choice, and while the soul-searching and feelings of the *shiva* period (especially this one) could well result in such a decision, the general patness of the plot leaves this and other resolutions of this family's difficulties rather unconvincing. Also, the film is ambiguous, not only in its depiction of tradition, but of the daughters' feelings for their mother. At one point Talia, after asking her father what he is going to do, and while embracing him and her sister together (in one of the best scenes), whispers something to the effect of "Loved her." Does she say that she loved her mother, or that her father loved her, or that "we" loved her? Whether by poor elocution or writers' design, it remains unclear.

Despite these concerns, both theological and dramatic, *Saying Kaddish* does convey some authentic and sincere spiritual searching on the part of all its characters. In writing, direction and acting it was a welcome step in the right direction for drama in Jewish religious broadcasting.

Ignored Afterlife:
"Max Glick," "Murphy Brown"

Everybody, including Jews, wonders what it is that Jews believe about the afterlife. So the question is fair game for television series. Have the television treatments been fair?

The *Max Glick* series from Canada was rerun in syndication on the VISN Interfaith Cable Network (later swallowed up by Hallmark). The program was produced in the 1990s to present a 14-year-old Jewish boy growing up in a small Canadian town in the mid-Sixties. Unlike the counterpart U.S. series, *Brooklyn Bridge*, this series showed signs of a thoughtful attempt to explore issues of Jewish identity and interfaith relations.

The *Max Glick* series succeeded at depicting a warm relationship between Max (engagingly played by young star Josh Garbe) and his rabbi (Jason Blicker), who, although a bit off-beat, is presented as an authentic, warm and thoughtful religious person with side interests in guitar playing and stand-up comedy.

Before the series gets to the afterlife, it solidifies Max's relationship with the rabbi. Max first declares his admiration for the rabbi when he hears his horrified grandparents describe how the young bearded rabbi was picked up by the local constable (the father of Max's Polish-Catholic girlfriend, Celia), for refusing to acknowledge the constable while *davening* (praying) with his *tallit* and *tefillin* (objects worn during prayer). The angry constable therefore put the rabbi in jail. Not long after Max's grandfather, Augustus, an elder of the synagogue, bails the rabbi out, the rabbi has taught Max that bar mitzvah (which Max has undergone before the time-frame depicted in the series) merely "opens the door to being a man."

In an amusing episode, written, as most, by Phil Savath, the guiding force in the production of the series, Max and Celia have kissed, and both are feeling guilty, waiting for lightning bolts to fly. Max not only feels guilty about having kissed a Gentile girl, but resents that at least *she* has confession in which to deal with her guilt. He asks the rabbi how Jews deal with guilt. "Usually by writing an autobiography," the rabbi responds with a typically cutesy answer. "That's why they call us the People of the Book."

Sensing Max's genuine concern, however, the rabbi tells him that we *do* have Yom Kippur which reminds us that we have to try to lead a better life in the coming year. But Max doesn't want to wait until Yom Kippur. He asks, "Why don't religions just standardize procedures?" He says it is unfair that the rabbi can forgive him only for sins committed against the rabbi, but not for what he does to someone else or to God. After all, the priest seems to be able to forgive Celia for everything.[1]

So Max decides to try out confession, and has so much pent up guilt that he takes up most of the priest's time listing every peccadillo since age three. Yet, in the end, Max decides to wait until Yom Kippur instead of going back to the priest, and kisses Celia again in the meantime.

While cute, this episode is indicative of the problem with the relationship between Max, the rabbi, and Judaism. It was honest and well-intentioned, I believe, and raised issues that Jews do wonder about. It never does get around to pointing out that in Judaism there is opportunity to confess sins in the *Amidah* prayer three times a day; that one does not have to wait until Yom Kippur and is indeed not supposed to.

The most pleasing and the most disappointing episode (both!) from the point of view of Jewish religious themes is that in which Max's grandfather Augustus (Jan Rubes) is involved in the purchase of a cemetery for the synagogue. The episode, written by Charles Lazer, leads to discussion of life after death in Jewish belief.

The opening scene with board members gathered at the proposed cemetery site is very good at depicting opinions at synagogue board meetings—pro, con and in-between. It also initiates a humorous rivalry between Augustus and another board member over a prime location plot. There will be attempted bribes of the rabbi and board members and a cute resolution to the dispute.

The opening scene also shows that Max's father, Henry (Alec Willows), is uncomfortable with any discussion of death, and seeks refuge in another preoccupation especially appropriate to one who was a teenager in the early 50s. There is a fine sub-plot, well-written and well-played,

---

1. The writers made the priest friendly to Jews and to the rabbi, and sincerely concerned about Max. But in order not to miss the opportunity to include one old joke they have him tell Celia that while he knows the penance for kissing (outside of marriage), he has to look up the penance for kissing a Jewish boy. The gratuitous one-liner, very much out of place given the tone of the episode, suggests anti-Semitism and anti-Judaism when these are clearly not issues.

about Dad's undergoing the various stages of facing mortality from denial and bargaining to acceptance.

Later, Max and his school friend discuss the recent death of Ian Fleming, the creator of the *James Bond* series and describe life after death from the points of view of their respective faiths. The Christians speak of Heaven and of their concern that people who don't believe in Jesus may not end up there. The Buddhists don't worry about Heaven, but look forward to an incarnation to a better life in another body. Max has nothing to contribute to the discussion: "In my house, they don't really talk about Heaven."

One of Max's Catholic friends says that he thinks about Heaven every day and even says a prayer every night in case God takes him in his sleep. Max jokes, "And you say *I* worry too much." Obviously the writer chose to make a joke about Catholic versus Jewish guilt at the expense of a very important doctrine of Judaism. No one tells Max to check out the popular *Adon Olam* hymn (traditionally recited upon rising and going to sleep as well as on Shabbat morning) which expresses the same sentiment of not fearing even if God takes one's soul at night, or the many other prayers where life after death is affirmed—even physical resurrection of the dead.

Here is the problem with this episode, symptomatic of Judaism on *Max Glick* and in so many other TV series. The series are good at depicting the questions of Jews and their lack of knowledge about Judaism, but not at responding.

Max's Dad says, "We're Jewish. We don't have Heaven. If I get run over I'm just another grease spot on the pavement." Here is the perfect opening for Max to find out about Judaism. Max tries, but all the rabbi can say is that "Heaven and Hell aren't mentioned in the Torah at all. Life after death wasn't all that important to the ancient Jews." Yet judging by Rabbinic literature and by the fact that the Bible does have, albeit sketchy, references to an afterlife, we can certainly make a case that life after death was at least as important to the ancients as to Max, who is so frustrated by the rabbi's responses that he observes of the Sages, "Those guys were too busy making up a million rules about eating and drinking and washing their hands." Actually, "those guys" held that belief in life after death and the resurrection of the dead were *cardinal* teachings of Judaism, and were responsible for similar beliefs in Christianity and in Islam.

Max does try again to ask the rabbi about life after death while the rabbi is playing chess with the priest, who is fascinated by the discussion and also a bit shocked by the rabbi's stubborn open-endedness. When Max

tells the rabbi that he thinks his dad is scared because he has nowhere to go when he dies, the rabbi turns around the discussion by asking Max what Max could do to help his father with these concerns. (Indeed, the most touching subplot in all this is the well-made point that Max's desire to give his dad comfort is his father's best comfort.) Soon the rabbi has Max joking, too, about how Jews "don't agree on anything." The rabbi adds: "We don't neglect the afterlife out of spite, Max. But the seeking is as important as the discovery."

After a while, I felt like shouting at the TV set: Why doesn't the rabbi just say that Judaism does believe in the afterlife, but provides no map or compass because the emphasis is on performing the commandments and doing God's will in this life? The Hebrew Bible demanded that Jews separate themselves from the death-centered pagan religions and exercise their power to make this life holy. The tradition elaborated that Jews must believe in God's faithfulness to take care of the rest, in this life and beyond.

Max Glick picks up on this a bit at the end when he quotes an "old Jewish proverb" (actually, a Biblical mandate!), "Choose life." (Deut. 30:19) Unfortunately, the episode itself offers a "resolution" in Grandpa Augustus's remarks that it doesn't pay to worry about life after death, anyway, so one should find comfort in being remembered by children left behind—not a comforting thought to those who are childless or to those whose children have predeceased them. What was pleasing about this episode was the sense of family warmth and spiritual hope that it exuded. What was disturbing is that it achieved this despite what it said, or didn't say, about Judaism!

Even less satisfying, as far as Judaism is concerned, was a meaningful and clever episode of *Murphy Brown*, aired in November 1993, and written by Rob Bragin. Murphy (Candice Bergen) has become obsessed with death, and concerned about how she will explain it to her child. She corners producer Miles Silverberg (Grant Shaud) and tells him that since her son, Avery, is "half-Jewish," she wants to know, "Well, what do you believe happens when we die?" The "you" here is directed to Miles as a Jew who should be able to represent Judaism. The "we" refers to humanity in general. Miles responds: "Oh, sure. You can't start with the easy stuff, like why we play hide the *matzah* on Passover.... Ah, we don't really talk that much about heaven and hell and all that stuff. We're supposed to focus on the here and now. We're sort of like the Unitarians that way, only they don't have to eat *gefilte* fish." Murphy reacts: "So let me understand this.

You've got one of the world's major religions. You've been around over 5,000 years, but the subject of the hereafter never came up."

That's where the matter rests: Judaism, which gave the concept of the hereafter to Western religions, is depicted as having nothing to say on the subject, and, in general, to be virtually indistinct from Unitarianism except in what its people eat. Now it is true that Judaism emphasizes the deeds done in the here-and-now to make life holy. It is also true that many Jews would answer as Miles did, out of ignorance and secularism. It is, however, possible to communicate with humor and yet respect the Jewish view that ultimately we have faith (*emunah*) that God will be faithful to us to guide us in the Afterlife as in earthly life if we have tried to be faithful to God's teachings.

If the reader thinks that a concept such as "faith" is too heavy to be handled with both humor and respect, consider another segment of the same episode in which Murphy asks colleague Corky Sherwood (Faith Ford) her opinion of the Afterlife. Murphy is amazed that Corky has no fears or worries about death. "When my time comes, I'm going to Heaven," Corky says with such surety that she gets one of the biggest laughs on the show. Then she elaborates: "It's right there in the Bible," quoting the verses effectively but getting a few more laughs by confessing uncertainty as to the exact source.

Corky even shares her vision of Heaven—a place where all streets are paved in gold, where there are lots of famous people, and where the buildings shine with the brilliance of one thousand lights. This allows Murphy to quip: "So you're saying Heaven is like spending eternity in Las Vegas?" Murphy goes on in this vein, but cannot shake Corky of her vision of Heaven. Finally, Murphy says—and in admiration rather than exasperation, "A part of me would like to believe the way you do. You have no doubts. You're perfectly happy and content." Corky's response is immediate: "Well, it's not that hard. You have to have a little faith." Corky even invites Murphy to her church, where the Sunday service is followed by a pot luck lunch for singles. It sounds a lot better, and comes across as far more spiritual and caring a scenario, than Miles's *gefilte* fish *a la* Unitarianism.

Indeed, if faith can be explored with good humor with respect to Corky—and with real respect for Corky's faith—why couldn't the same thing have happened to Miles? Corky's quirks endear her in the dialogue; Miles' mannerisms elicit cheap laughs. Maybe the quality of depiction of the character and the character's faith depends on the level of respect.

Murphy's dialogue on death with Miles ends with his confession that he was "obsessed" with death as a child: "Some kids would play 'Doctor.' I would play 'Funeral.'" He describes how he would put his arms on his chest, pretend that he was dead, and "wait for all the kids in the neighborhood" to "bring sponge cake." Yet he overcame his fear of death when, as a child, he began choking over a Cracker Jack peanut when his parents' car hit a pothole. He says he remembers a "near death experience"—seeing a tunnel of light, his Aunt Shirley (though she was alive and living in New Jersey), and a Voice telling him it was not his time yet, but also telling him, "I told you not to eat in the car." Murphy's response, "You're basing your whole faith in the Afterlife on a pothole and a peanut," sets Miles to fretting and sighing on the prospect of becoming topsoil. So much for his "faith." So much for the Jewish view of the Afterlife, as depicted on these programs.

Choosing Hell:
"Deconstructing Harry"

In his 1999 film, *Deconstructing Harry*, Woody Allen plays a novelist who has written a book about family and friends and bared everything about his affair with his third wife's sister. Harry abducts his nine-year-old son from school to take him on a ride with the prostitute-du-jour to his alma mater, which is honoring him. Allen mocks wryly the adulation of academics as well as the murderous scorn of those who have been betrayed. His point is that the feelings of sycophants and friends and even family do not matter much in the scheme of things, anyway. What matters is whether the literary characters created are varied and real and interesting enough to comprise a worthy audience to the foibles and frustrations of the writer.

Deconstructing Harry is the most imaginative and in many ways the most pathetic (that is, affecting) of Allen's films. Though it drags at points, it generally flows quite artfully from the real life sins of Harry to their glorification or rationalization in some of his short stories. The short stories are Allen's most clever flourishes ever, and are truly works of art. They contain within them all the stereotypes of Jews and wholesale mockery of Judaism that have been the stock in trade of Allen's previous work. You get the same easy laughs at the expense of Jewish names (and even the name of the rescuer of Holocaust victims, Raoul Wallenberg). The stories show a brother- and sister-in-law engaging in quick sexual intercourse in front of a blind grandmother (in the tradition of *Hannah And Her Sisters*). Yet, until the penultimate sequence, the one in, of all places, Hell, Allen manages to parody his own established formats with good humor.

What does not ring true here is Allen's suggestion that his rantings about Jewish life have provocation. Thus, in a sequence in which Harry has been accused by a religious relative of denying the Holocaust, he responds: "Not only do I not deny the Holocaust [but] I think records are made to be broken." Needless to say (except perhaps to Woody Allen), no provocation could ever make such a line appropriate, and Allen himself seems to acknowledge that Harry's religious relatives don't deserve that kind of affrontery. In one of the short story sequences, Allen depicts a female Jewish psychoanalyst who overnight becomes "Jewish with a vengeance"—namely, religiously observant, much to the consternation of her husband. Out of fear of her "wrathful and vengeful God," she praises Him for everything, even reciting a prayer in bed over oral sex with her skeptical husband. In the "real life" segment that parallels this story, Harry feels estranged from his sister, Doris, because she has become observant together with her husband, whom Harry resents. He tells them that religions are all private clubs that formulate concepts of "The Other" in order to determine whom to hate. Doris, for her part, decries Harry's religion of "nihilism, sarcasm and orgasm."

Yet there is something quite touching about the way that Allen communicates that Harry still regards his sister as a "wonderful kid" who has been as devoted to Harry as to her religious convictions. Allen definitely does not condemn Doris's religious observance here, unlike his character, Harry. In fact, his critique of excessive observance for its own sake in the short story is rendered all the more authentic and effective by the tenderness he shows for Doris in clear criticism of Harry. Although clever, the other short story sequences, particularly a nasty "exposé" of Harry's parents, lack this knowing quality. The only other sequence that carries moral weight as a short story is an impressive allegory about an actor, nicely played by Robin Williams, who discovers that he is intrinsically "out of focus." As for the acting, Kirstie Ally is most effective as the mother of Harry's son. Most of the other stars in the film, especially Billy Crystal, are used as exaggerations of persona for which they are well-known, and which are already overdone, whether in Allen's previous work or in their own.

By the end of the film, Allen convinces himself, and tries to snow us into believing, that the movie is about knowing one's limitations, and getting on with one's life. True, *Deconstructing Harry* demonstrates, in many ways, the most self-awareness of any of Allen's films. But it is not a meditation on self-awareness. It is, rather, a deliberate choice and action on Allen's part. In one segment, half story and half daydream, Harry takes an elevator into Hell (the commentary in the elevator is delicious), and meets his father in Gehenna. Not surprisingly (for easy laughs in an Allen film), Dad is wearing a *yarmulke*. He has been consigned to Hell for being too critical of Harry (of course). For a precious moment it seems that Harry will find closure and renewal and even achieve a kind of *teshuvah* (repentance). Instead, like an annoying old habit impeding and even discouraging growth and maturity and decency and awareness of responsibility, the Hell scene degenerates into Dad qua "religious" Jew rejecting the Heaven option (speaking for Allen?): "I am a Jew. We don't believe in Heaven." When Harry asks his Dad where he wants to go, the *yarmulke*-wearer says, "To a Chinese restaurant." (Allen and the writers of the contemporaneous television series, *The Nanny*, seem to relish the same, tired, American Jewish jokes.)

In one fell swoop, then, Jewish beliefs in Heaven and in the sanctifying power of dietary disciplines are traded away—and for what? For the "ultimate one-liner" that follows—an off-color joke about Hadassah women. Again, a cheap Woody Allen remark about Jewish women and their largest and most accomplished philanthropic organization. In this movie, that crack is the definitive statement on Heaven and Hell—unlike the earlier pictures, where such references were little more than asides and stage whispers.

Right before our eyes, Allen chooses Hell—for Harry, for Harry's dad (who represents previous generations) and for himself. *Deconstructing Harry* is not a commentary on bad decisions; it is a bad decision. It is a choice for Hell, and rejection of Heaven for the sake of two-or-three one-liners about Jews, Jewish women, and Hadassah. One can't help thinking of a saying from the Talmud: "In the Hereafter the Holy Blessed One will slay the evil impulse in the presence of the righteous and the wicked. To the righteous it will appear like a high mountain, to the wicked like a single hair. Both will weep. The righteous will weep and exclaim: 'How were we able to subdue such a high mountain as this?' The wicked will weep and exclaim: 'How were we unable to subdue a single hair like this?'" (Sukkah 52a)

5

CONSTRAINED CONVERSION

ജ൙ര

Cowardly Conversion and Baby-Naming:
"A Year in The Life"

Praised by some critics and by the self-congratulatory network blurbs as superior television and vintage heart-warming drama, NBC's three-part 1986 miniseries, *A Year In The Life* was heralded in as the golden age of television reincarnate. It was the story of an upper middle class Seattle family who try to emulate the Kennedys with annual family touch football games. The family under scrutiny experiences tragedy and disconcerting change, and each of the four children has adjustments to make—one son must focus his life on more than just charm and past glory, one daughter must face up to an unhappy second marriage, another son feels he must break his engagement to his college sweetheart when he falls in love with another, and a fourth daughter is married to a Jew who wants her to convert to Judaism.

For the first time in TV history, network promos made a big point of indicating that conversion to Judaism would be explored.

The drama, by the way, was a little better than the average miniseries, but rather humorless and slow-moving. The acting was uniformly nice. The cast was good, children and teenagers as well as adults. I especially enjoyed Jennifer Cooke as the jilted fiancée, a spoiled but sensitive Home Coming Queen type thrown over for a Bohemian spirit. David Oliver as the

youngest son, who did the jilting, and Sarah Jessica Parker as the free spirit
he decides to marry, were quite fine, as were Richard Kiley as the patriarch
and Trey Ames as the grandson who trains him for a bike race. No one
could fault the casting.

As for the conversion to Judaism issue, I think I can honestly say that
this was, to date, the biggest tease in TV history.

When I heard that conversion would be discussed, the natural questions
were: Will she convert? Will they show it? How will they broach the
subject? Will they talk about the differences between Judaism and
Christianity in a miniseries so close to Christmas? It was rather shocking
that they'd even deal with the theme in a series that literally measures itself
from Christmas to Christmas!

One finds in the opening episode a few of the staple jokes, as old as
Abie's Irish Rose or *Bridget Loves Bernie*. Shall the baby be named
Emerson Greenberg, an old family name on the Christian side, or Moishe
(Moses), the Jewish family name? At a family songfest the Jewish son-in-
law requests and gets *Hava Nagila*.

A little farther along in the opening sequence, a bombshell is dropped.
When, in a very charming scene, the husband and wife are playing a
pleasant "Would you rather" game on the subject of their unborn child and
his/her future, the husband nonchalantly asks: "Would you rather be a wife
who *offered* to convert to Judaism or was asked by her husband because it
was important to him?"

"Why was it important to him?" she replies.

"Because of the way he was brought up."

"Well, what if she, the wife, never really felt strongly about organized
religion ... that the world would be a whole lot better place without any
of that stuff?"

"I think he would respect that."

"But he would still want her to convert."

"Ahum."

"Why?"

"Because although he agrees with her in principle," replies our Jewish
husband, "emotionally he's just not as evolved as she is."

"Well, she'd like to think about it," the wife concludes.

Now this is a moving and most pleasant scene from start to finish. In
fact, Jayne Atkinson and Adam Arkin as Lindley and Jim Eisenberg are the
nicest and most appealing couple you'll ever see on television, sensitive
and lovable. The Jewish husband is depicted as being the kindest, most

devoted, most responsible person in the bunch, and it is to him and his wife that the eldest son comes when he needs money and understanding. (There may be some touches of the medieval image of the Jew as money-maker and money-lender, but the Gentile family is quite well off and Jim and Lindley help out at her father's business.)

What is significant about the scene just cited is that (1) the entire issue of conversion is discussed in the third person, as if the parties were not involved, and not in an "I-Thou" fashion (to use Buber's phrase); (2) it is emphasized that Lindley never had any strong religious feelings, anyway, as if to say that it's all right to discuss conversion with a Gentile who never made a religious commitment, but not with a Christian with a crisis of faith; and (3) Jim regards Judaism as a nostalgic way station on the road of evolution, anyway, so any conversion to Judaism as a more meaningful worldview and way of life is *ipso facto* negated by this attitude. Also, there are no Jewish parents and relatives shown in this show (which may be a blessing considering the way they have been depicted in other series and films). It is clear that Jim is extolled for his individual qualities and not as a representative of an alternative religious culture.

If these three points seem to indicate oversensitivity on my part, consider that this is the one and only time that conversion is seriously discussed in this miniseries, within the first two hours and not during the remaining four! Right after this discussion Jim joins the family in carol singing at their church, doing his share of candle-holding, and we're not talking about Chanukah candles. True, he does give his brother-in-law a *yarmulke* as a Christmas gift "to cover the bald spot" but the significance of the skull cap is not discussed, nor is the subject of conversion seriously broached again.

Did she or didn't she? The depiction of the marriage of Jim and Lindley Eisenberg degenerates into slapstick on the tensions between the cravings (for bagel and lox and everything else) of a bedridden pregnant wife and her worn-out husband who satisfies her every whim, and of their temporary sexual setbacks after the baby is born and he must adjust to seeing his wife as a mother.

Did she or didn't she? In one scene the bedridden, pregnant Lindley asks her husband to bring the rabbi some ice-cream and some for her. Is this a joke? Is she referring to Jim or to the foetus as "the rabbi," or is there actually a rabbi with her? Of course we have here deliberate ambiguity, rendered further ambiguous by the spoof of a husband catering to his pregnant wife, best left to the classics like *I Love Lucy*.

In the last segments of the miniseries, Lindley teaches Yiddish words to her nephew, such as *Zaideh* (grandfather), *Kinder* (children), *Shayneh* (pretty), and one is not sure whether her own father is disinterested, amused, immersed in his own problems, or simply putting her off in his response. The ultimate tease comes at her brother's engagement party, when she tells an older woman, a family friend: "I'm thinking of converting." "Converting what?" her friend asks, whether for clarification or out of amusement. "Converting to Judaism," Lindley answers.

Not only are Lindley's choices ambiguous, but so, in this film, are the reactions of her family and others to what might or might not have been a decision to convert to Judaism.

Did she or didn't she?

Whereas in the miniseries the "conversion" issue was just a big tease, treated with such timidity as to leave us wondering whether daughter Lindley ever went through with it, we find that several months later, in the series, the issue of conversion is handled rather bluntly and even dismissively.

In one of the earliest episodes of the season, Lindley and her husband Jim are being interviewed by an official of a rather exclusive nursery school. When asked about race, Jim responds: "We're white. We're Jewish white." Lindley interjects before she even realizes what she is saying: "Jim is, I'm not. I mean, I'm a converted Jew."

This one exchange of dialogue is more provocative than anything said about conversion in the three long segments of the previous year's miniseries version. But the dialogue continues. Lindley apologizes to Jim for saying she isn't Jewish. "It kind of came out of me," she says.

In addition to her (momentary?) denial of Jewishness, Lindley's refusal to attend the naming of her baby daughter in the synagogue (because she's not "into rituals") is also highlighted here. She apologizes again, this time for not attending the ceremony. Her husband Jim says that it's not like the ceremony can be repeated; it's a once-in-a-lifetime thing. Lindley protests that she would not have been comfortable at the ceremony. "Is this what it's all about?" Jim asks. "Your being comfortable? If you had an idea about how important this was to me, you would have been there." He adds: "I expect you to keep your word. What if you don't feel like being married? What if you don't feel like taking care of the kid? We're not talking about feelings. We're talking about commitment."

Lindley protests that it's not that simple, that it's not an issue of "commitment," but that she "can't pretend to be someone I'm not and I can't lie to myself."

Jim wonders if she has lied to him. When she responds that she never said that she would go to the ceremony, he insists: "This isn't about the ceremony. This is about the whole deal and about the fact that you are backing out of something that you have put no effort into. No effort!"

I have reproduced much of the dialogue verbatim because we find here a common tendency in television series—namely, an attempt to deal with religious issues and concerns, usually where Judaism is concerned, in brief and quickly paced dialogue (typical of the way television approaches all issues) and to come to some immediate resolution or compromise intended to satisfy the audience and, at the same time, to "develop" the characters.

The only problem with such a machine-gun approach to relationships and spiritual and psychological issues is that it raises more questions about the characters and their relationships and about the issues being "explored."

Consider the dialogue I have just reproduced. Does Lindley regard herself as Jewish or not? Her slip of the tongue may be a Freudian slip and betray an inability to deal with Jewishness, or it might simply be the result of adjustment to the newness of the Jewish identity. The writers are not content to explore this one issue in a short conversation. They add to the problem by depicting Lindley as "uncomfortable" with the baby-naming ceremony. Is she uncomfortable with Judaism or simply with rituals or maybe with that one ritual? Does she not realize that rituals are a part of Judaism? Is she "lying" when she says she wants to be Jewish, or is she just avoiding a ceremony that means nothing to her when another ceremony might mean more?

At one point Lindley does indeed say that the baby-naming ceremony isn't as important as a communion or a baptism or a bar mitzvah. Is she making a distinction between rituals? Are the writers making a point about the possible ambivalences of those who convert to another faith? Is there a suggestion that Lindley is only now asserting herself after converting under the emotional duress of her husband's feelings ("Do you have any idea how important this was to me? If you did, you would have been there.")

I am not sure whether the writers considered these questions at all, or whether they believe that these questions are eclipsed by "dramatic" concerns or by artistic "freedom." Yet I suspect that the writers were not very thoughtful precisely because of the mixed messages implied in questions raised by the drama, and because of an unfortunate tendency in this series to depict women as being somewhat unstable, and unsure of themselves.

With regard to the image of women, *A Year In The Life* has no female characters who match the strength and conviction of the male head of the household. (The matriarch seems to have had character and wisdom, but she was killed off right away in the miniseries.) It seems to me that Lindley's "conversion problem" makes more of a statement about the way women are depicted than about conversion itself, which is only superficially and rather gratuitously treated here.

Interestingly, despite the less than impressive characterizations of women, this is the first TV program which featured a rabbi who happens to be a woman, and the service she performs for the baby-naming is touching and appropriate indeed. But even here, the implication of the ceremony, at least to the most discerning viewers, would cast aspersions on the competence and sensitivity of the rabbi. The episode makes it clear that the rabbi has arranged the ceremony just for the couple and the baby—a secretive baby-naming as opposed to the traditional Jewish concept of a baby-naming of a girl being done before the congregation. More important still, what rabbi would do a baby-naming without the mother present, especially if the mother is a convert to Judaism? The impression given is of Jews sneaking around to do a ceremony without the presence of the mother, who as mother and especially as a Jew-by-choice should be present at this ceremony which could easily be postponed until she is ready to attend.

At the end of the episode, Lindley tells her husband Jim that she volunteered to do something once before and found it hard to go through with it. She tells him that she promised to go hiking with her father, and froze in her path when she had to climb down from a high place. All his reasoning, reassurance and bribery could not budge her. "The more he tried to make it better, the worse it got," she says. Finally, Dad just sat in silence "for what seemed to take forever," and Lindley said that if they took one step at a time she could do it. It's not that she didn't want to hike down the mountain. She did. It's just that it was too overwhelming to do all at once.

Jim looks on with an understanding nod, and the program literally ends with Jim overhearing Lindley read the *Simchat Bat* (Babynaming for a Daughter) ceremony to the baby, with conviction and heartfelt expression. But that one touching scene—an example of TV's least inspired tendency to "fix" problems with quick and happy "solutions"—does little to resolve the mixed signals in this episode about conversion, the image of women, and the image of Jews, who come off here as insensitive to converts.

Exploitation of "Conversion" and of Jewish Periodicals: "Picket Fences"

One of *Picket Fences'* most memorable flirtations with Judaism (of many, too many) was a 1994 episode in which the sheriff's youngest son, Zack (Adam Wylie), expressed the desire to become Jewish. The elementary school principal complained that seven other pupils in the class of a Jewish teacher, Jason Steinberg, have declared the same desire. According to the principal, it's an "epidemic."

We soon learn that Mr. Steinberg began telling the class about Judaism because one of the Jewish students was called a "kike," and instead of sending the perpetrator to the principal, the teacher wanted to use the opportunity for "educating," but not, he said, for proselytizing, simply to discuss the "history of the faith." At a meeting with the teacher and some other concerned town leaders, the principal declares that if a Protestant teacher were converting Jewish children to Christianity, Steinberg would be leading the lynch mob.

It seems that the teacher has done his "indoctrinating" well. Zack keeps reciting the "*Shema*" (Deut. 6:4) at every opportunity, almost like a mantra or charm. When his mother, a physician, is arrested for ignoring a court injunction against treating a pregnant Christian Scientist, Zack "sits *shiva*" (the traditional week of mourning) until his mother is released, and also recites the *Shema* at the bedside of a sick woman. Zack tells the woman's husband that he is trying out a Jewish prayer because he already tried "Our Father" and it did not work.

The sharp and unprincipled Jewish attorney, Douglas Wambaugh (Fyvush Finkel), has taken the case of the Christian Scientists against the (Catholic) hospital's physicians, who want to continue to treat the woman. Wambaugh, who more and more assumes the role of the Sophist who will take any side of an argument that will prove lucrative or at least stimulating to him, tells the woman's husband to decide whether he, Wambaugh, should go into court full force, or come up "a little short," enough to keep the husband a Christian Scientist in good standing, and to represent his faith with "integrity," while managing to let his wife keep her doctor. The husband tells Wambaugh that he believes that getting his wife out of the hospital will save her life, at least her spiritual life, and Wambaugh seems to understand, which, of course, makes his offer all the more offensive, as the writers appear to intend. Yet the writers also seem to want the Catholic priest to look more pragmatic than understanding and caring. Reflecting on all the litigation in which the hospital might be involved, the priest tells Zack's mother, the physician: "You should have left her in the restaurant," adding later: "I make this comment as a member of the board, not as a priest."

There are a few cute scenes in which Zack explains his interest in Judaism. In one such segment, he defends Judaism when his older brother, who says that it is his duty to protect him, warns him that "Jews get picked on." First, his brother tries to discourage Zack by telling him that he will "lose Christmas." But Zack says that he will gain Rosh Hashanah, Yom Kippur, Passover, eight presents on Chanukah, and extra vacation days.

Later, Zack's brother tries to "deprogram" him by tying him to a chair, forcing him to eat *gefilte* fish and to listen to songs from *Fiddler On The Roof.* To dissuade him even more, and this is most significant, the brother displays a tremendous photo of Wambaugh the Lawyer wearing a yarmulke, as if to say: "You'll become like him." Their father, the town sheriff, happens to come in on this scene, and tells his older son, who says he is only trying to "cure" Zack, that Judaism "isn't a disease."

Now it is Dad's turn to question Zack, who says he likes Judaism because of its three basic rules—"love learning, love God, do good deeds." Zack adds: "But the best thing of all is to be kind to animals....They say that's a pure good, because being kind to animals is being kind but not for a reward." (While kindness to animals is a part of Jewish Law and reverence for animal life basic to the dietary laws, Jewish tradition regards as the greatest kindness the dignified burial of the dead human being, who can no longer do us any favors, but who is considered as worthy of respect in death as in life.) When Zack's dad tells him that Christians believe these things, too, Zack responds: "Yea, but they still got that hell." Zack had said that Jews "don't have hell," and "that's a load off my mind." Of course, Judaism does have its concept of hell. In Jewish lore, hell is both sweltering and freezing. (Jerusalem Talmud, Sanhedrin 29b)

Fortunately, no one has told Zack that the price of admission to the Jewish community is ritual circumcision or we would get a lot of *mohel* jokes. Actually, we already got some "genital humor" from Wambaugh in a statutory rape case, when he referred to his brother-in-law the *mohel* who has good malpractice insurance—"a two-inch deductible."

In a nice scene, Zack appears before the school board to explain his new-found interest in Judaism. He says again that he thinks Jews have "nice rules," adding that he enjoys their "hats without propellers" and their bread which is "better than saltines." He says that he is not so sure about Jesus being the son of God, not because his teacher caused doubt, but because his father opened up that can of worms by saying that Santa Claus is not real. He is able to ease the board's concerns about indoctrination on the part of Mr. Steinberg by testifying that his teacher taught him that besides religious rules, there is no difference between Jews and Christians.

Particularly noteworthy in this particular episode, however, is not so much the account of a youthful interest in Judaism (though this is unusual enough), but the use of a public school Jewish teacher's writings in an inquisition to indict him for proselytism. Before the school board, the principal cites an article that Steinberg wrote in a periodical called "Judaism Today" in which he decried intermarriage and assimilation and declared that Jews "must aggressively encourage conversion." As far as I know, this is the first and only reference to Jewish periodicals ever made on TV, and David E. Kelley and Company invoked it in a negative context.

Lest the reader think that I am being overly sensitive, consider that in the very next episode of *Picket Fences* we witnessed what is probably the one and only reference to a Jew spending all night in his synagogue praying. Who is that Jew? Wambaugh. What are the circumstances? Wambaugh has taken the case of a fellow student who has shot Zack's thirteen-year-old brother, Matthew, right in school, with premeditation, in front of everyone. When the boys' older sister, Kimberly, who works for Wambaugh, tells Wambaugh that he doesn't have to take every case, that her brother may never walk again, Wambaugh replies: "Ninety-eight per cent of all criminal defendants are guilty. If you'll always want to be on the right side of justice, you'll never make a living as a lawyer." It is then that Wambaugh says, "I probably can't know your pain, not completely. I was in the temple all last night praying for Matthew. God will take care of him."

Kimberly responds, "I don't want to hear any talk about God. I don't think there is a God. No God would let a thirteen-year-old get shot.....And I don't want to hear about your going to temple and how religious you are. I don't give a damn how much you pray. That doesn't make you a moral person. You take any case, whatever will bring you a fee. You can spend all day in your stupid synagogue. That doesn't make you moral. Right now I don't believe in God. And I don't believe in you."

Wambaugh responds with something about how there are two victims in this case, Kimberly's brother and the boy who shot him. He says he can't help her brother right now, but he will do what he can for the other boy. Kimberly answers that his response is "not good enough, not even close"—and we have to agree. We have to concur because Wambaugh has vacillated throughout the series, and even throughout this episode, between being an ambulance chaser and a defender of all victims, and he comes across as insincere.

So the writers give us our first TV mention of Jewish periodicals only to make the first TV suggestion that employers of Jews in the public sphere should keep an eye on what they write. They make the first TV mention of prayer vigil in a synagogue only to offer the definitive TV representation of a hypocritical and conflicted Jew. They have Kimberly echoing references in Christian scriptures to "Pharisees and hypocrites" and to corrupt synagogues, and viewers can't help agreeing that in Wambaugh's case, at least, she is right! The writers do see that the accused teacher is exonerated though there is not much they can or will do with Wambaugh. When Zack, during his Jewish phase, said he "prays to Hashem," and a family member translated, "the Jewish God," the statement was allowed to stand, implying a tribal deity.

The sad truth is that while *Picket Fences* did bring clever twists to social issues, David Kelley and Company had little to offer when it came to issues of religion and morality. Their attitude toward religion, any religion, is best described by the words of a friend of the young boys which the writers with insincerity, I think, have the parents rebuke: "Religion is like a fart. Your own smells good, but everybody else's stinks."

Compartmentalized Heaven: "Party of Five"

The Fox Network series, *Party of Five*, offered a premise that was both the dream fantasy and ultimate nightmare of every child—namely, being left behind by parents (killed in an accident) to go it alone with siblings, working out an ethos of sharing household chores and making moral choices, and being able to rely on selective memories of one's parents for guidance, thus avoiding any adult authority. This series had no other theme but ambivalence—ambivalence over the absence of parents, over the power of older siblings, over religious identity, even over the truth of one's memories of deceased parents.

In a 1994-1995 episode, three of those ambivalences were juggled around. The girlfriend of an older brother is regarded as a usurper by an adolescent sister as soon as the girlfriend moves in with her boyfriend in the dead parents' bedroom. The other siblings come to resent her as well, though she was beloved by them before moving in. Likewise, Julia (Neve Campbell), the sister most antagonistic to the live-in girlfriend, begins to resent even the memory of her mother, wondering after seeing an old, incomplete journal entry whether her mother has had an affair with a fellow musician. A younger, 13-year-old sister, Claudia (Lacey Chabert), acts up by contemplating conversion to Judaism, after she sees her Jewish boyfriend Artie (Michael Shulman) preparing for his bar mitzvah and begins to ponder her own religious needs and the issue of whom she might marry some day. Julia, the older sister, who fears anyone or anything displacing the memory and beliefs of their deceased parents, reacts with vehement opposition to Claudia's so much as considering abandonment of the parents' faith.

As far as I know, this episode by Amy Lippman and Christopher Keyser is the first on television to depict wavering about conversion to Judaism rather than conversion itself. There is even some implied ambivalence toward young Artie's strong ties to his Judaism and his willingness to share his feelings: "Being Jewish is important for me. It's hard enough for me to be kind of…seeing someone who isn't Jewish. If we get married it would just kill my grandmother." She asks him what they would do about religion if they marry. He responds that "statistics on the failure of mixed marriages are staggering," and suggests that it would be nice if they believed in the same thing. When she responds, "I guess one of us could switch, like…convert," he replies, "I couldn't do that. I couldn't." All the while that the writers have Artie mouth standard synagogue and youth group rhetoric about mixed marriage, they suggest that Artie may be too controlling in all this.

Claudia says: "Religion is a very personal thing. Just because their parents believe in something, it doesn't necessarily mean that their kids have to." Upon seeing Claudia experiment with lighting Shabbat candles, older sister Julia protests: "You don't just change your religion like you would change a stupid sweater. It's a part of who you are."

Artie continues to offer "sage" advice about Judaism: "You don't have to be kosher. We're not kosher. If you're really becoming Jewish, you should never apologize for complaining." (Actually, had the ancient Israelites apologized to Moses for complaining, they might have reached the Promised Land a lot sooner.) Artie tells Claudia that the Mourner's Kaddish is a prayer to remember the dead. (Actually, it is a prayer recited by the congregation at various intervals of the service to affirm God's sovereignty in life and in the world, one such recital being by mourners who affirm this despite the grief and loss that have shattered their world.)

The episode comes to two conclusions. First, Claudia decides that she has to learn more about Judaism, and that this may or may not help her to understand what religion means: "I just can't figure it out. About religion. If it's something you believe in, or if it's just...something you are. And if it's something you are then how can you convert? But if it's something you believe in, then how can I convert until I believe in it?...Maybe becoming Jewish could really be important to me some day, like it is to you. I just have to learn more about it."

Later, Claudia decides that although Judaism is a "beautiful religion" and she "could believe in it" (note the politically correct deference that is given, in passing, of course), and although she likes the idea of eight presents on Chanukah (that line's been overdone), she ought to stick to her own Christian denomination because that's what her parents believed in. After all, she adds, she wants to believe in the same heaven as her parents did and not make any radical changes because "I kind of need to know that we'll all be together." So Claudia understandably opts not to upset the religious apple cart in a family already shaken by terrible events. That's understandable, even admirable.

Why, however, bring Judaism into all this, especially when the final "decision" suggests that Jews, like doggies, may have their own heaven? Any topic brought into this program was bound to reflect its general ambivalences, which were built into the plot and chiseled into the writing. It is shocking that the writers made no effort to feature concerned adults as resources for guidance (not even clergy). But that was par for the course among the upscale waifs in *Party of Five*.

TV's Unconversion:
"Living in Captivity"

American television sank to an all time low in its depiction of "religious" themes in a Shukovsky/English sitcom, *Living in Captivity*, which premiered in the fall of 1999 and, happily, did not last until the winter. Yet this short-lived exercise in vulgarity and stupidity wasted no time in offering an episode on the theme of "conversion" to Judaism.

Could this episode be the ultimate revelation of the kind of "spiritual sensibilities" that have shaped one of America's most successful team manufacturers of TV fare? Do we have here the resonance of the undertone and the imprint of the soul of other Shukovsky/English sitcoms, like *Murphy Brown* and *Love and War*, stripped to the core, without artifice? Writers Dan Cohen and S. J. Pratt did, of course, bear a lot of responsibility for this episode, but were they simply providing grist for the company mill?

This nasty piece of work begins with a vicious swipe at a Jewish mother who calls to "remind" her daughter that Yom Kippur is coming, to insult her Gentile son-in-law and to raise questions about how future children will be raised—all in one condescending sentence that is left to the imagination. (Why is it that these series, which usually leave so little to the imagination, are so polished at unheard stage whispers, as well? Maybe because they have thus learned how to save money by not adding additional characters.) The daughter's response is a put-down of Jewish parenting: "Mom, I don't know how we are going to raise our kids. That will be the nanny's problem."

In the next scene, the husband is "reading up" on Judaism and discovering such "facts" as strange ways that Orthodox Jews have sex. As soon as he tells his wife that he is considering conversion, he is obliged by the tired Shukovsky/English formula to make nasty remarks about his WASP Presbyterian heritage. (No wonder the mainline churches are a threatened species. The media are killing them.) The wife is equally obliged to joke about her marrying a Gentile man because he was so "exotic" as to "smell like wheat, have no allergies, and never talk about food." Later, she'll even warn him to put his hammer away after putting up a *mezuzah* because "Jews don't use tools." (This makes us wonder how Jews did put up *mezuzot* for all those thousands of years.)

Most disconcerting of all was the depiction of the rabbi/*mohel* (circumciser) played by Shelley Berman. The character seemed quite at ease reducing all of Jewish teachings and history to: "They tried to kill us. They didn't. Let's eat." Berman seemed to go along with the real theme of this episode: that circumcision is a barbaric test of either the courage of the convert or his blind love for his wife, and that "Judaism" is no more than an ethnic bonding which entails the use of earthy Yiddish expressions in jokes that can be mastered by apprenticeship to a good comedy coach. The half-hour is unrelenting in making the circumcision frightening and cruel in order to justify the view of the self-hating Jewish partner that it is "barbaric." Circumcision (actually, only the token tiny cut for ritual purposes on the already circumcised) is even portrayed here as a deterrent to juvenile delinquents.

Interestingly, a few years before doing this episode, Shelley Berman appeared on a Jewish talk show in his home town of Chicago and advised: "Do not give the audience what they want. Give them what you want to give them....what you think is good....There really is no special kind of altruism other than you give of yourself with risk, with the danger of failure." Was this "risk" and this "failure" worth the fee? Did Berman think that he gave his audience something "good"?

The conversion does take place (with the vulgar suggestion that tradition demands that a convert's friends hold his legs during circumcision). The episode implied through Shelley Berman as the rabbi that conversion to Judaism entails a wink and a change of menu. Readers should be aware that in Jewish law and belief, a convert is as eternally bound to the Holy Covenant (Genesis 17) as a born Jew. In this sitcom, the only struggle in conversion is the struggle against circumcision. When the husband hears about circumcision, he says, "O my God." The rabbi pipes in: "He's not your God yet." It is the belief of Judaism that Gentiles can be close to God by virtue of the Covenant with Noah (Gen. 9) without having to become Jews to be saved or to be regarded as good people. Jews are called upon to preserve in a more intensive way the perspective and teachings about God that they are to hold in trust for all humanity.

The episode becomes television's first instance of an "unconversion." At the end, the "convert," who is drunk, has a vision of Jesus telling him not to convert, and right at his "You're a Jew" coming out party. (In this series, Gentiles are drunks, Italians are part of the mafia, and only blacks get to burst stereotypes, to the point of being reduced to little more than anti-stereotypes.) It is not made clear whether the "vision" is the result of drinking, but there is an (unintentionally?) moving scene in a church where the convert confesses his "straying" from Jesus in front of many crucifixes. The writers squeeze in some mockery of Christianity (and the suggestion that the church scene may be an hallucination, also) by having Jesus do line-dancing at the party—intimating, perhaps, that it was a guest who struck the "convert" as Jesus. That is left open, but the serious and impressive scene in the church lingers in the mind of the viewer.

The episode was entitled by the writers and the producers, "The Unkindest Cut." Does that refer to the Jewish mother's barbs about her son-in-law or to circumcision? Again, it is left open. To me, it describes the episode's wholesale mockery of Judaism.

PART TWO

OUTLANDISH JUDAISMS FOR BIZARRE JEWS: TV'S DECONSTRUCTION OF JUDAISM

ക്രൗ

6

MISPLACED JUDAISM

℘◑℘

The Absence of Judaism:
"Duddy Kravitz"

B ased on Mordecai Richler's novel, the movie, *The Apprenticeship of Duddy Kravitz* (1974) may have been the first major Canadian treatment, on film, of contemporary Jewish life.

Critics generally observed that Duddy, a poor Jewish boy who is willing to do anything to make a buck, comes off as a likeable, if ruthlessly ambitious fellow. The film had this effect by zeroing in on the way young Kravitz was snubbed by wealthier Jews and Gentiles alike. Kravitz uses the affections of a Gentile woman to acquire property from an anti-Semitic land-owner. He also exploits the friendship of a good-natured, epileptic, Gentile, young man, squeezing work out of him for no pay, and endangering him so that he becomes paralyzed.

Yet we're not supposed to get too upset with Duddy. True, his old *zaideh* (Yiddish for "grandfather") has a few qualms about his behavior. But Duddy really can't help being such a rat; he feels sorry about it, and even the Gentile woman and man whom he used cannot be *that* angry with him. After all, Duddy is a kind of hero. He gets a nice piece of land from anti-Semites, and has big plans. He shows up his rich uncle, makes his dad proud of him, and spits in the eye of an arrogant Jewish gangster. (Richard Dreyfuss has such an innocent face!)

The film's comedy highlight (there is much clever humor) is a bar mitzvah movie that Duddy makes with an alcoholic, has-been producer. (Duddy plans to make a business of such films.) It provides a good glimpse of a handsome synagogue, and then cuts back and forth from the bar mitzvah boy and his *fressing* (gluttonous) family to the adolescent rites of young African natives and their partying tribes.

Visually, then, *Duddy Kravitz* is a film where Jewish rituals appear primitive and quaint (and therefore inefficacious), where the Jews are either ruthless or old-fashioned, and where the Gentiles are naïve and too trusting.

Now Jewish producers and writers have the right to say these things about some Jews and the way they practice Judaism. *The Apprenticeship Of Duddy Kravitz* is a milestone in that it depicted an amoral Jew, who is never taken to task, morally speaking, by the Jewish community. While, admittedly, Jewish communities can do more to hold their adherents to moral standards, it is not clear whether this film wants to convey even that legitimate critique. Otherwise, it would have found a creative way to allude to fundamental Jewish teachings:

1. Jews are enjoined not to be misleading in business. Jewish Law even warns against "wronging with words," against getting up the hopes of a storekeeper when one has no intention of buying in the first place. (*Mishnah Baba Metzia* 4:10)

2   Jews are taught not to cheat in business. One cannot, for example, put better wheat on top of poorer-quality grain in order to deceive a buyer. (*Ibid.*, 4:12)

3. Jews are prohibited from exploiting laborers. Rabban Gamliel used to buy wheat back at lower market prices from sharing-tenants to whom he lent it for sowing. (*Ibid.*, 5:8) One cannot even increase the measure to be carried by a rented animal once the amount has been agreed upon. (*Ibid.*, 6:5) Laborers are not to be asked to work earlier or later than the customary work-hours of a given locale. (*Ibid.*, 7:1) They should be allowed to eat a certain amount of the produce while farming.

These norms and values originate in the Torah. "Thou shalt not oppress a hired servant that is poor and needy, whether he be of they brethren, or of thy strangers that are in thy land within thy gates. In the same day shalt thou give him his hire...for he is poor, and setteth his heart upon it, lest he cry against thee unto the Lord, and it be sin in thee." (Deut. 24:14-15) "When thou comest into thy neighbor's vineyard [whether as a passer-by or as a harvester], then thou mayest eat grapes until thou have enough at thine own pleasure; but thou shalt not put any in thy vessel. When thou comest into thy neighbor's standing corn, then thou mayest pluck ears with thy hand; but thou shalt not move a sickle unto thy neighbor's standing corn." (Deut. 23:25-26)

Is it appropriate for a major film about Jews to completely ignore these teachings, or to fail to censure its antihero for violating them?

Faith Redefined: "Keeping The Faith"

Keeping The Faith, a 2000 rabbi-priest buddy picture, boasts the stellar cast of Edward Norton, Ben Stiller and Jenna Elfman, and Norton's directorial debut. Writer Stuart Blumberg respects his clergy most when they are involved in a love triangle after a girl they both admired most in the eighth grade returns as a beautiful, high-powered corporate executive.

In an interview with Charlie Rose, Norton described the film as a takeoff on the screwball comedies of the Thirties and Forties, such as *The Philadelphia Story*, but actually Blumberg's script is a *fin-de-siecle* nod at *The Jazz Singer*, moving from the cantor to the rabbi, but with the same premise: Love conquers all. If one wants to follow the heart, one cannot be bound by the attitudes and faith of one's fathers or mothers. But another angle is added here: If one's love is deep enough, then one's faith will be reaffirmed.

I couldn't help thinking of the well-known passage in the *Shema* (a major morning and evening prayer), that the heart leads people to stray from the commandments (Num. 15:39) and of Jeremiah's knowing caveat that "the heart is deceitful above all things." (Jer. 17:9) *Keeping The Faith* is not commentary on these themes as much as confirmation of the old biblical concerns. It is symptomatic rather than insightful.

The screenplay is crafty enough. The film, while not a work of fine artifice, has a certain effectiveness. While sitcomish in the writing, it offers a bit more finesse than the usual TV fare in the cutaway shots and editing (though at least one such transition uses Hebrew lettering for the Divine Name to accent some toilet humor). The craftiness here consists in the impression that the film is advancing New Age "enlightenment." Visually, the suggestion is that the synagogue is at its best when the sanctuary is emptied of chairs and when Jews gather to practice their own version of Eastern meditation. But the real message is far more orthodox in the annals of American film: True heaven is romance.

In order to understand what this film represents, we need to take a look at what it actually says about religion. Whether consciously or subconsciously, Blumberg respects the priest more than the rabbi. Norton reported in the same interview that Blumberg wrote the screenplay with him and Stiller in mind. One hopes that the respective depictions of clergy were based on the quirks of the proposed actors, but the consistent, unrelenting undertones of the screenplay suggest deeper ambivalences. Rabbi Jacob Schram is vain, selfish, and compulsively self-advancing. Since his youth, he has collected rabbi-hero cards (an Orthodox version of baseball cards), not so much out of respect for their teachings as to succeed at acquiring every possible card and thus to beat the "competition," namely, the other, rather limited group of collectors. The suggestion is made that this same aggressive spirit leads the rabbi to seduce his old schoolfriend who has blossomed into a beautiful woman, in violation of his friendship with the priest.

Blumberg depicts a rabbi who wants sex and companionship with a Gentile woman but is unwilling to give up his congregation. Schram is able to make the synagogue grow, but the implication at every turn is that the crowd is attracted and misled by superficiality and emptiness. The New Age innovations are praised here but come across as hollow, as does the relationship between the rabbi and his girlfriend. The film keeps insisting, even protesting, that Schram is doing a lot of good things, but it says nothing good about him and about his constituency. The synagogue members are either throwing their daughters at the rabbi or involved in trendy spirituality or in self-promotion. The senior rabbi, played by Eli Wallach, is a seasoned lackey with no real advice to offer.

The only touching and meaningful relationship in the film is that between Norton as the priest and Milos Foreman as the older and wiser priest. The only virtue in the film is attributed to Norton's Father Brian Finn. True, at one point, he is ready to throw away his vows for his childhood friend. But he goes to the woman's apartment only after she begs him to come, unlike the rabbi who heads there in hot pursuit. The priest remains loyal to his faith much longer. True, the film opens with the priest in a fall-down drunk state, but it offers disclaimers along the way that he is usually not a drinker, but has been driven to it by his "friends." No disclaimers are made in behalf of the rabbi, except his mother's statement that he is a "good person."

Blumberg has his characters observe that it is easier for the woman to seduce the rabbi than the priest because there are no "vows" involved. The suggestion throughout the movie is that Jews have no code, no authority, no discipline, that their only way of exercising religious community is to learn how to manipulate one another as pleasantly and efficiently as possible. In another movie that would be an interesting critique of American Judaism. This movie seems to expect that we adore the rabbi and his innovations *lamrot hakol*, "in spite of everything," as the Hebrew saying goes. That is especially disappointing in view of the fact that this is the first and only film in memory to speak of a rabbinic calling, if only for a moment. The movie quickly gets bogged down in requisite circumcision jokes (and now incense jokes for Catholics). Had it even asked the question whether a rabbi can betray a calling, or whether a rabbi has the same calling as other Jews, it might have achieved a certain depth.

The real religion advocated by this film is, I repeat, the Hollywood glorification of romantic love. As rabbi is told by priest (who comes around to the romance-religion, of course): "Do you think God is going to drop a gift like that in your lap a second time?" Voyeurism and phone sex are as effective rituals of this religion of love as are those of synagogue and church.

As I mentioned above, not even the New Age methods preached here—meditation, breathing, etc., which are depicted as worthy innovations, especially in the synagogue—are given reverence and homage in the film. Though we think we are being given a Deepak Chopra-type spiritual adviser in the form of a bartender, we end up with a living infomercial for interfaith marriage—a Sikh-Catholic-Muslim with Jewish in-laws! Ann Bancroft as the rabbi's Jewish mother is trotted out solely to offer a *mea culpa* for all Jewish parents who ever opposed the intermarriage of their children in the name of tribal, as opposed to romantic, religion. It would seem that Love Conquers All has lived to mock both monotheism and New Age trends in the new millennium.

Even the term "faith" takes on new meanings here. It is not faithfulness, as in the Hebrew Bible, to a Covenant through loyalty to God, Torah and the Jewish People. Nor is it the risk taken for Divine grace in the theology of Paul of Tarsus. It isn't even the faith in one's own potential of the New Agers. Rather, as Elfman's Annie puts it, the rabbi must have faith that "other people will understand." It is a faith that other people will accept the "ethic" of indulging in selective peccancies: "Give all the people in your life credit to deal with this. It's the twenty-first century!" Sin now, confess later, and put your faith in the public's capacity to forgive.

So Rabbi Schram confesses on Yom Kippur eve: "I'm not sorry for loving a Gentile woman, but I'm sorry I didn't put more faith in you to let me do what I want." Of course, he gets the job as senior rabbi, and he gets the woman, and the writer even throws in the strong probability that she will convert. The film thereby purports to take up the cause of conversion, as well. Annie tells Jake: "Your faith is a huge part of what I love about you." She chides him for not being tolerant of others to whom faith comes less easily, but this is cynical because he is not cited for his faith in God but chided for his lack of faith in his public's adoration. What could have been a nice insight into agnostics who struggle to convert to Judaism becomes, in reality, the canonization of romantic comedy to sanction and define faith, conversion and confession. One wonders whether the New York "megasynagogue" that lent its beautiful sanctuary to the filmmaker is pleased with the message and with the use of that distinguished and historic pulpit as an arena for what has become a stock scene, first on the small screen (with David E. Kelley) and then on the big: the "punching out" of rabbis by Jews or Gentiles.

In addition to the film's text of romantic religion, there is a subtext here that should not go unmentioned. This is another in a long line of films about the "*Shiksa* Goddess" (played in the Sixties by Cybill Shepard and Lee Remick) who are superior to Jewish women at everything, including controlling Jewish men and their mothers. That quasi-racist subplot is insulting both to Jewish women, Gentile women, converts to Judaism and—especially in this film—to Jewish men, particularly male rabbis.

Mitzvah Redefined:
"Law And Order (Special Victims Unit),"
"Son of The Beach"

In the 1999-2000 season, the popular crime series, *Law and Order* spawned *Law and Order—Special Victims Unit* (sex crimes, of course) which continued a long tradition of arrogant and self-righteous Jewish characters. Whereas previously these were all minor characters, the spinoff immediately "promoted" such Jews to leading and recurring roles.

Writers Robert Palm and Wendy West gave us a compelling account of a suspected child-killer who had served time for committing that same crime some years before. The evidence and an iron-clad alibi seem to point away from this man. Also, his psychological history suggests that his convicted crime had been the result of hallucinating on drugs when the victim happened to come to his door while soliciting for a cause.

Yet, as Morris Klein (Terry L. Beaver) from the State Attorney General's office points out, "Outraged citizens could care less about civil liberties when kids are at risk." He tries to convince Captain Donald Cragen (Dann Florek) to hold the past offender even though his alibi has been corroborated. A new mechanism for "civil commitment" (to mental institutions) is being tested, pending a mental health bill that would allow ex-offenders to be held indefinitely. "As a *mitzvah*," Klein begs, "can you buy me some time?" Cragen responds, "This goes against everything I believe, Morris. You've got twenty-four hours, not a minute more." Later, Cragen tells a colleague that he cannot abide such "situational ethics." The past offender becomes a Christ-like martyr to internet pedophile sites, to an enraged public, and to well-meaning Jews.

This episode is significant for a number of reasons. It is, to my knowledge, the first time that the word "*mitzvah*"(commandment)was used in prime time, at least without translation and explanation. The implication, then, is that both men are Jewish, for the term has no widespread usage in American English outside of the Jewish community. In this context, it is used to mean "favor" even more than "good deed" (as it is popularly, but wrongly, translated). It is *not* a good deed, however, either in American law or in Judaism, to deprive a citizen of his rights by keeping him imprisoned when there is no justification for incarcerating him. Indeed, in Jewish Law it is a heinous sin, the opposite of *mitzvah*, to bear false witness, to pretend even for a moment that confirmed testimony demands penal action when there is no such testimony. The writers also tell us that the proposed "civil commitment" law will allow the authorities (in this case, Jews) to choose their own psychiatrists (in this case, a Dr. Greenblatt). Even if we are being handed a "good Jew," "bad Jew" scenario, or good Jews doing bad or overzealous things, who ends up being synonymous with arrogance and abuse of power?

Another troubling but noteworthy definition of *mitzvah* was provided in a 2002 episode of Howard Stern's deliberately vulgar series, *Son of the Beach*. Writers David Morgasen, Timothy Stack (who plays the central character) and James R. Stein have Tex Finkelstein (Southern accent and many gallon hat), mogul of the United Broadcasting Monopoly, describe "doing a thirty-two rating" as a "*mitzvah*." Here, *mitzvah* obviously no longer means Divine commandment, but a self-serving (and lucrative) goal. Gone is the Talmudic principle that one must serve God by performing the *mitzvot* (commandments) for their own sake, without thought of a worldly reward.

This episode is a spoof of "reality TV." The head lifeguard, middle-aged, out-of-shape Notch Johnson (Stack) and his loyal crew are invited by Mogul Finkelstein to win a million dollars (after garnering much media attention) when their favorite charity, a home for the retarded, burns down. (Needless to say, the opportunity to mock the disabled is not lost here.) Their challenge is to weather it out on "Penetration Island."

Finkelstein puts them through lurid, gory, and gruelling, not to mention sexually exploitative, paces. When one of his particularly cruel machinations is exposed, lifeguard Kimberly speaks for her comrades: "Mr. Finkelstein, you make me sick. Playing with people's lives in front of the whole world? When are you TV executives going to see that you've taken the whole reality thing too far?"

The writers want to make Finkelstein lovable in a Wizard of Oz sort of way, but totally vulgar. He is depicted as sexually exploiting would-be starlets even while in a business conference. He interjects Yiddish into his Goldwynisms: "I want to shoot the *kibbitz* with you." He draws analogies between his televised garbage and Jewish sacred literature: "You see, my *goy*," he tells another indignant female lifeguard (actually, the "proper" gender form for such offensive language is *goya*), "*Penetration Island* was never just a television show. No thanks to you, I reckon, this is the biggest damn *megillah* in the history of the mass media."

So the word *megillah* (a sacred scroll of the Holy Writings) is used alongside *mitzvah* to depict television's goal of big viewer ratings. And Jason Alexander, beloved to current audiences after *Seinfeld*, is cast in the role to make the character more likeable. One wonders, however, how Alexander, *mitzvah* and *megillah* will look to audiences thirty years hence.

The Holy Ark as Negation of Ritual:
"Touched by an Angel"

Touched By An Angel began the 2000-2001 season with an effective, but puzzling piece about the Ark of the Covenant and Middle East politics.

It seems that a Professor North (William Russ), an instructor at a small college, is obsessed with finding the Ark, and is about to succeed. A newly-created angel-in-training, nicely played by Valerie Bertinelli, is assigned to keep the good professor in tow. She is the egghead among the angels, a veritable computer without much in the way of interpersonal skills, but is well-suited to pose as a student in the professor's class. The other angels guide her on her first assignment. It soon becomes apparent, however, that this is a job for all the angels plus reinforcements.

The young angel-in-training makes it difficult for her colleagues who are trying to prevent the professor from finding the Ark. After reading the entire Bible for the first time in one sitting (can angels do that?), she interprets the Prophet Ezekiel to reinforce his theory that the Ark is buried under Mount Nebo. Professor North has concluded that the Ark was hidden in caves just outside of Jerusalem. He cites a passage in Second Maccabees that suggests that Jeremiah hid the Ark on Mount Nebo.[1]

Professor North is determined to find the Holy Ark by hook or by crook. He even lies to an adoring and enthusiastic student whose grandmother has sent him an ancient scroll, a family heirloom, just before her death. North has the document carbon-dated, and tells the student that it is not authentic, though it is so important that it corroborates North's theory about the whereabouts of the Ark. We learn from his sister-in-law, the president of the college, that he has squandered money from grants and otherwise connived to find the Ark. She warns him, "You know what it's like over there right now. You could get killed." He is so encouraged by the student's scroll that he pretended was "worthless" that he quickly plans an expedition to Israel and steals his sister-in-law's valuable mantelpiece to finance the trip.

The entire staff of angels conspire to prevent North from discovering the Ark, but he is implacable. Angel Monica (Roma Downey) admonishes him, "You're a desperate man and you'll use desperate measures to get what you want." When North discovers the cave that houses the Ark, he is ready to kill its guardian, Micah (Roy Dotrice), who turns out to be another

---

1. The passage is in II Maccabees 2:1-8. It describes the Ark as buried by Jeremiah near the "mountain where Moses went up and beheld God's inheritance." While it does seem to refer to Mt. Nebo, where Moses was permitted to look at the Promised Land before his death, some scholars associated "inheritance" with the commandments given at Mt. Sinai.

angel. But all the angels line up before the splendor of the sacred object and block his way.

The writers, Martha Williamson (the chief producer), Burt Pearl and Luke Schelmaas, do a pretty good job of conveying a sense of the holiness of objects and places, as understood in the Bible. North finally understands the sacredness of the Ark, and, in the presence of the angels, forgoes the opportunity to seize it. While doing the requisite soul-searching before the heavenly bunch, he owns up to his "real" motivation for his dogged pursuit of the Ark: His beloved pregnant wife, the sister of the college president, was killed in a taxicab while rushing to surprise him on one of his earlier expeditions in search of the Ark of the Covenant. It seems that when, as kids together, they saw *Raiders of the Lost Ark* four times, he determined to find the real ark, and was encouraged by his wife every step of the way, both before and during their marriage. He tells the angels that his deceased wife had always said that she didn't care if they lived in the past or in the future as long as they lived together.

Angel Monica tells Professor North, "You have broken many commandments to find the Ark. You have to find peace. You won't find it by violating a holy place."

Somehow, however, neither the psychological nor the theological explanations ring true to the plot and the characters. Is Professor North searching for the Ark as a tribute to his departed wife? Isn't the drive to find it basic to his character and personality as an individual and as an archeologist? What's wrong with that? And would it be a desecration of everything holy for the Ark to be found? Or would it be an amazing testimony to the historical claims of Scripture?

The script belies the true concerns of the writers. At the beginning of the hour, Professor North comments for a while about the situation in Jerusalem, with Jews and Muslims arguing over control of the Temple Mount. He says that the enmity has been unchanging. Thus, we find the "same names, same places, even the same bloodshed going on in the same Palestine, the same Jerusalem, the same River Jordan, the same Temple Mount where Solomon built his Temple." The same point is more subtly made when Angel Tess (Della Reese), in the guise of the carbon-dating expert, questions North's declaration that finding the Ark would be the greatest archeological discovery in the history of the world. "What would be the greatest?" she asks. "The fame it would bring the finder or the war that would be fought over it? You see, Professor, they keep calling it 'the lost Ark.' It's not lost. It's hidden. And there's a good reason for it to stay hidden. It's not a movie. It's real. And it's holy."

Yes, the script makes a plea for preserving the integrity of holy things. But its chief point is that the Ark must remain protected and set apart because of political and social conflicts. It can only make matters worse. Therefore, it is hidden.

There is definitely a suggestion here that the sacred is explosive, provocative, and therefore should be withheld from battling men. One is reminded of a legend of the Midrash that when Moses was about to receive the Torah on Mount Sinai, the angels protested that human beings were not worthy of such a holy Scripture. But then God scolded them, "Do you steal or kill or commit adultery that you need to keep the Torah in the supernal regions? The human being needs the Torah; hence, it is being given to humanity." This episode of *Touched By An Angel* makes the opposite point.

It is true that Scripture ordained that the Ark not be touched except by its designated carriers. But since Scripture prescribed the building of the Ark, one could argue that there is an obligation to promulgate such a discovery. Scripture does not prohibit searching for the Ark. Could it be that the writers of *Touched By An Angel* regard the Ark as the film, *Raiders of the Lost Ark* (1981) depicted it, namely, as a secret weapon that can be exploited by its possessors, including, potentially, by Nazis?

Rabbinic legend does relate that sparks from between the cherubim cleaned the roads of scorpions and thorns as the Ark passed, and that these sparks became a sweet incense that impressed the nations. However, the Ark is not depicted in biblical literature as a weapon. It falls into the hands of enemies, but does not serve them. Both the pagans and the Israelites incur Divine wrath and Divine plague when they mishandle the Ark, but the Ark does not itself bring plague.

At the end of the episode, the angel Monica tells Professor North, "Remember, your heart is an Ark." He becomes a changed man, making amends and apologizing before the college directors. He explains to them that he has found something better than the Ark, namely, that he has "found God…peace," and now feels responsibility for that discovery, to be expressed by integrity in everyday life.

The suggestion that internal transformation is more precious than adoration of external ritual objects is perfectly in keeping with the teachings of the Torah and Prophets. But Scripture does go to great lengths to inculcate its readers with a reverence for holy objects as a vehicle to living God's commandments. For all the reverence for the Ark tendered in this episode, it conveys the message that ritual objects only increase divisiveness and violence in the world. Had the series, *Touched By An Angel*, been saying all along that sacred religious objects are toxic to the religious and to the irreligious alike?

7

Misapplied Nostalgia

ℰℭ

Covenant as Ethnic Chain:
"Thirtysomething"

ABC's *thirtysomething* focused its first episode of the 1990-1991 season on the birth of a son to (Jewish) Michael Steadman (Ken Olin) and to his (Gentile) wife, Hope (Mel Harris), their second child. Michael's mother (Barbara Barrie) visits with her boyfriend, Dr. Ben Teitleman (Alan King), and the latter insists on a *b'rit milah* (ritual circumcision) for the baby. Michael and Hope have to decide where they stand on the matter of the *bris*. Obviously, the birth of their first child, a daughter, did not raise so many questions about religious identity. Or did it? Did those concerns then fade away? Or is there just something more mystical or primal about a boy and his circumcision? Or is the program merely affirming some popular conception—or the writers' conception—in the latter assumption? Hope reflects that the fuss over circumcision is "a little bit sexist." But the program gets across the message that if the birth of a son raises more issues for Michael, it is because of Michael's unresolved relationship with his deceased father (who abandoned the family) and because of Michael's reluctance, for many reasons, to accept his mother's meddlesome companion.

The episode was extremely well-acted (not unusual for the show), filled with meaningful dialogue (not always the case on a program known for talking many issues to death), and profoundly moving. Above all, this episode was sincere, genuine. It may not have been knowing or even informative, but it was honest.

The message was an honest one because Michael learned, quite painfully, that he must come to terms with how he views other Jews, and therefore how he views himself; how he regards his wife, whom he facetiously describes to his cousin Melissa as Hope "who lives upstairs. She's not Jewish"; and with what Judaism means to him. Also, the writing and directing were most effective in that, whether intentionally or not, the slow-pacing of the episode gave a sense of the pain of making big decisions amidst day-to-day tasks (work, guests, etc.).

The jokes about a *bris* are par for the course, but are offset in the end by a rather moving if eclectic ceremony, in which Teitleman—I think unintentionally on the part of the writers—emerges as an Elijah figure as understood in Jewish lore—as a rather forceful guardian angel who sees to it that ritual matters receive proper attention. Most troubling in this episode are Michael's remarks. Michael says that the *brit milah* "just feels like something I'm supposed to do." But it gives him all kinds of fears that he'll become "too Jewish." Yet being "too Jewish" to him does not mean being ultra-pious. He relates something of what it means to him when he tells his Gentile friend Gary: "Next thing I know, I'm five-feet-two, in a '68 Lincoln, driving four miles an hour, shouting 'Goyim!' out the window." Yet Michael does not have to worry about being "too Jewish" (even in such a stereotyped way) because he is not even sure what it means to be basically Jewish. "Am I a Jew?" he asks. "I can tell a great Jewish joke, but do I really feel like a Jew? What is a Jew supposed to feel like?" He does not know what to answer when Hope asks him to explain why he wants a *brit milah* for his son: "You're the Jew in the house," she says. "Just explain it to me."

All Michael really knows is that he is contemptuous of his mother's companion because he seems "too Jewish," too pushy about the ritual. Alan King portrays this Dr. Ben Teitleman with just the right blend of "loud" and "obnoxious" (according to Michael) and "O.K. guy" (in Hope's words). That Ben is depicted as constantly appraising people's homes and possessions as a hobby is troubling, but I won't pause to decry this unfortunate stereotype of the representative of Judaism. The other Jews are not so stereotyped, at least not the women. Michael's mother is restrained and understanding (though more concerned about her "relationship" than about Judaism) and Melissa is quite likeable for a troubled free spirit. The show gets across in the end that whatever problems Michael has are because he is Michael, a particular individual from a particular family, and not because he is a Jew. It also quite emphatically enables best friend Gary to tell Michael (regarding the latter's comments about fellow Jews): "How come you Jews can say stuff like that? If I said something like that you'd kill me!"

The episode does manage to editorialize that the way Michael regards other Jews is problematic, and severely warps his own self-image as a Jew. Yet the writers are unable to make a pointed and even unequivocal statement that Michael's joke-stereotypes are warped and self-destructive. Even so, Michael's lines come across not as the natural questioning of one in search of identity, but as rather pathetic monologues of one whose method of questioning is itself troubled.

Writer/director Richard Kramer is never able to make Michael's concerns touching because he obviously believes that Michael is "interesting" as a character to the extent that he constantly indulges in mockery. Yet Hope's questioning—nay, her anguish—is profoundly moving. Hope is upset that Michael shows signs of Jewish anti-Semitism and has not done anything about their daughter's identity. At one point she tells Michael, "Don't use that dumb *shiksa* tone with me." When Michael responds that he never called her such a thing or "even thought it or even remotely implied it," the viewer understands that the issue is not what Michael has done or said, but that Hope feels isolated and excluded by his very indecisiveness. One is deeply touched by her cries, effectively punctuated by a confrontation with Michael in the rain: "If our son's going to be a Jew, if our children are going to be Jews, then I want to know why and what it means, for them and for me and for you." One feels her anguish as an outsider when she asks her mother-in-law: "Is this baby a Jew? And what does *that* mean? Where am I in all this?....Whatever we do, it just comes back again, whatever we do." These lines are truly poignant.

As for the final point raised, and suggested in Hope's dialogue even more than in Michael's—namely, what does it mean to be Jewish—the episode poses the question all right, but in a way that makes light of both the question and of any possible answer. Cousin Melissa is given the line that sets a rather flippant tone at the beginning of the show, "Everyone has a *bris*. Roots are in." The characterization of the "Reform *mohel*" sends out contradictory signals when he describes interfaith marriage as a "glass...half full" and urges them to send the children to religious school, telling them that marriage is "hard enough without all this." He adds, "You two are in uncharted waters. I think a religious life would help. But, then again, that's why I get the big bucks."

Do the writers intend to invoke the stereotype of the money-grubbing Jew—or, in this case, *mohel*? Perhaps they want to paint the *mohel* as somewhat flippant (even to the point of insensitivity, including making fun of the baby's name), either to make him Michael's kind of Jew or, perhaps, to suggest that any *mohel* would have to be flawed or opportunistic to in any way sanctify the failure of the Jewish parent to make a decision. (The point of information is never given that a child can be converted at birth if there is a decision to raise it as Jewish and if ritual immersion follows later on.) As it turns out, Michael barely agrees to the *brit milah* ceremony, and then only because Hope "works it through" for him by helping him to conclude that she really does understand his desire to be part of something (with at least the male child) and his fear of failing the group or being failed by them. That bit of five-minute auto-analysis suggests that Judaism is on a par with Michael's basketball team.

The episode never does get around to explaining the significance of the *brit milah* as affirmation of Covenant with God in Judaism, a Covenant which embraces both men and women. Nor are we helped much by Dr. Teitleman quoting his father who speaks of Judaism as a "golden chain that links us all together....[Nobody] says we got to keep it going. But do you presume to break it?" If there's anything worse than reducing Judaism to a basketball team, it is reducing the Covenant to a chain gang. The classical belief, after all, is that God wants Jews to keep Judaism going. Depiction of Judaism on television might actually be interesting if it tried to grapple creatively with that notion.

Tradition as Pleasant Prison: "Sofie"

Liv Ullman's 1993 directorial feat, *Sofie*, based upon a novel about a Jewish family in Denmark, is a fascinating study, not so much of Jewish family life, as of the attempt of a Swedish filmmaker, in the Ingmar Bergman tradition, to appropriate local Jewish history into a particular genre and style of film. The novel by Danish-Jewish author Henri Nathensen already reflected certain Scandinavian quirks of storytelling, and so Ullman's task was made easier. She does, however, deserve a lot of credit for offering fine attention to detail of plot, characterization and setting (which become tedious or overdrawn far less often than the length of the picture would indicate) and for eliciting excellent performances from a perfect cast. Karen Lise-Mynster is memorable for her portrayal of Sofie from a young woman in her late twenties worried about whether life would present her a husband, to the middle-aged mother of a son who is determined to venture out to new frontiers. The entire cast is equally memorable.

One is certain just from the authentic feel of the picture that Ullman has recreated Danish city and village life in the era of the 1880s through the early twentieth century. The representation of Jewish rituals and observances, such as Shabbat meals and the bar mitzvah ceremony, is also most accurate. Of particular interest is a presentation of synagogue music in a traditional Danish congregation of the period by cantor and choir. Ullman, probably following the novel, is also careful to indicate in the dialogue where her characters depart from traditional observances, especially when it is duly and appropriately noted that enjoying a cigar on Shabbat afternoon is the ritual of certain protagonists which they know to be an infraction of religious observance.

As with many films of the Bergman stamp, however, Ullman's *Sofie* both respects and defies restraint. Sofie resists the temptation to marry a Gentile, but her marriage to a Jewish man is so disastrous that she finds herself flirting with his brother, leading to more disastrous consequences. The implication throughout the film is that every act of restraint (especially for reasons of Jewish tradition) leads to further, more shocking and dangerous temptations. On the one hand, the film would have us admire Sofie for honoring her parents and her family heritage. On the other hand, it would have us applaud the resentment that she builds up, and even expresses, regarding her parents' complicity in her bad marriage; and yet, the film never suggests that marriage of a Jew to a Jew is in and of itself a debilitating and constraining experience. (Beginning with *Northern Exposure* [1990-1995], many television series have made that suggestion.) One of the most touching and loving marriages ever depicted on film is that of Sofie's parents, a Jewish marriage in which siblings and in-laws are also honored and treated affectionately.

There is no question, however, that Ullman has produced this film out of respect and admiration for Jewish traditions and culture, out of regard for Jews as citizens in their respective Scandinavian countries, and out of a desire to show that Jews experience the same feelings and concerns as everyone else. There is, however, a certain ambiguity in *Sofie* that prevents this film from having any real message about Jews and Judaism. At the bar mitzvah celebration for Sofie's son, Aron (a good Jewish name that is definitely becoming popular again in films), Sofie's father gives a traditional family speech expressing the hope that the bar mitzvah boy will be a good Jew, one who loves his neighbor as himself. (The original Hebrew from Leviticus 19:18 is actually quoted.) Then an uncle gives his speech about Judaism being a "blood bond." On his deathbed, the grandfather repeats his charge to Aron, urging him to "love his neighbor" and to "Never forget who you are, your roots." The first part of the charge could come from any number of faiths, and the second is an echo of Alex Haley. The uncle's speech is pure ethnicity. One would look in vain in this film for the suggestion that in Judaism love of God and of Torah not only inspire love for fellow human beings, but are themselves services that Jews perform for humanity by preserving a teaching and vision for the world.

The film makes its point, though, that there is a certain mystery and wonder in being a Jew which transcends one's personal happiness or unhappiness and brings unique meaning and continuity to life. This is suggested by the film despite Sofie's comment, "My life didn't have a meaning until Aron. But Aron's not going to be fenced in." Perhaps more than anything else, the theme of this movie is a tension between continuity and personal fulfillment, between tradition and self-expression. It happens to give tradition a slight edge, but only until the first decade of the 20th century. Then tradition becomes "roots" or identity—something to be proud of, cherished, prized, but not necessarily something to restrain us or even to inspire restraint. Indeed, a *Kol Nidre*-like melody is played as background to shots of a madhouse, the ultimate symbol of self-imprisonment.

It is appropriate that this film appeared during the year that commemorated Danish and Swedish cooperation in the rescue of Jews during the Holocaust. And it is a fascinating coincidence, too, that in the concurrent (October 1993) issue of *Commentary*, David Klinghoffer of the *National Review* told of his conversion to Judaism, the heritage of his adoptive parents, even as he sought out his birth mother, a Swedish woman who explained that she placed him with a Jewish family because "in Sweden the Jews have a good name."

Ullman has, by and large, presented her Danish Jews with a good name, at least until the formulas of recent Swedish film and of an old Danish novel set in.

Jewish Ritual as Mantra:
"Independence Day"

I have to admit that I was impressed with *Independence Day*, the 1996 film tale of alien invasion of the earth produced by Ronald Emmerich and written by Emmerich with Dean Devlin. It is a very clever parody on the old Saturday matinee serials, but a very serious parody, too, which makes the suspense all the more gripping, the humor all the more funny, and the touching moments surprisingly affecting.

Independence Day uses certain ethnic clichés, to be sure, but for no less a reason than to drive home the lesson that the loss of humanity's quirks would be the most tragic aspect of the loss of humanity. It makes its point on the grandest possible scale, that all humanity shares the same fate, whether in environmental recycling or in intergalactic warfare. It may even have a few biblical overtones, such as the danger of looking back too much, *a la* Lot's wife, and the coziness-cum-convulsion of the Noah's ark venue—though I confess I may be reading these references into it.

The film also boasts a superb cast, headed by Jeff Goldblum, Eddie Murphy, Judd Hirsch, *et al*, including two fine child actors and a lovable canine hero, not to mention the appropriate musical score by David Arnold, itself a clever nod to the old serials. So we can well understand that the success of this film is far more than the special effects, though the latter are sensational and memorable.

The "Jewish" aspects to this film are significant. *Independence Day* poses a milieu in which David Levenson (Goldblum), an M.I.T. under-achiever, immediately breaks the aliens' code and dashes, and heads over with his old-fashioned Jewish dad, Julius (Hirsch), to warn the president. Levenson's ex-wife happens to be the White House press secretary, so with clever use of some gizmos, David gains instant entre to the White House and, with his dad, becomes part of the presidential entourage and, ultimately, the engineer of world survival. (Oh, the neat coincidences of comic strips on film!)

David's dad, Julius, sports a *yarmulke*, and even leads the huddled remnant of the Washington elite in a "*Shema Koleinu*" ("Hear Our Voice, O Lord") prayer during the fateful moments of truth. He is a knowledgeable Jew who uses Yiddish expressions as second nature. "I look like a Jewish *schlemiel*," he tells his son, when he realizes that he is about to meet the president and is not wearing a tie. Though dad has had his own struggles with faith ("I haven't spoken to God since your mother died"), he responds with Hebrew prayers when prayers are needed, assuming the grandfatherly role amidst the survivors, dispensing cigars as well as victuals.

The writers offer a paeon of sorts to Jewish old men, who have certainly been the glory of synagogue life, and are a pleasant memory to many of the now middle-aged Baby Boomer generation. (Hirsch does well playing the Jewish dad, but let's not forget that Eddie Murphy could have done a fine job, too, judging from his cameos in *Coming To America* [1988]). There is also an obvious concern for Israel in this film, reminiscent of American Jewish response to the 1967 war. The point is made more than once that it's a shame that Israel and her neighbors, including Iraq, are not working together.

It should be noted, too, that while David is deferential to his father's Jewish knowledge and piety, he turns back the prayer book and *yarmulke* to his father. David does not pray, Jewishly or otherwise. He "respects" religion. He gladly witnesses a black colleague's (Christian) wedding ceremony. The film leaves all religious presence, however overbearing, to David's father. (Interestingly, the religious and ethnic background of David's wife is kept vague.) When someone tells Dad, "I'm not Jewish," the latter responds, "Nobody's perfect." But David relies on human know-how.

Salvation in *Independence Day* comes not from the Jewish God, but from the "*Yiddishe kopf,*" the old notion of "Jewish brains," even on the part of an "underachiever." The Jewish hero also possesses impressive stocks of courage. Yet salvation does not come from "the Jews" as such. Apart from David and his dad, the Jews in this film are depicted as nerdy or as over the top.

Independence Day is a wistful glimpse into Jewish ethnic self-perceptions of the 1950s and 1960s, and a tribute to America reflective of the post-Holocaust Jewish experience: "We're fighting for our very right to live," the President says. The Fourth of July will no longer be "just" an "American holiday," but a testament to "world survival." Now the film is most generous to many racial and ethnic groups. It definitely fosters equal opportunity saviors. The overriding values are recognizable as the middle-class Jewish liberalism mixed with a certain religious nostalgia of a generation ago.

Independence Day extols human know-how in the face of peril. It is fear which instructs and redeems humanity, and not religion, according to this film. Religion, Jewish learning and ritual, happen to be the mantras by which the doctrine of human self-redemption and the case for world unity are made. The film does suggest that any war for one's country rather than for all humanity is not a just cause. It doesn't let us forget the Vietnam War. Could it also be a nostalgic tribute to the American anti-war movement of the Sixties and to illusions of decline in violence and hatred forever shattered by the terrorist attacks on America of September 11, 2001?

Several years hence, when nostalgia for the Sixties, by Jews and others, will have been superseded by other Jewish and general nostalgias, and current fears and challenges (inevitably) displaced by new ones, this film will still be appreciated for its energetic appropriation of old-time movie heroics and histrionics. What a pity that, fear of alien invasion aside, the Jewish gesticulations so conspicuously highlighted here yield no real perspective—and certainly no Jewish take—on human unity and national integrity. Is this film documentation evidence that, in the Nineties, some talented people who wanted to make a "Jewish" statement just didn't know how to do so?

Jewish Tradition as Vestige: "Brooklyn Bridge"

In his long-running 1980s' hit series, *Family Ties*, producer Gary David Goldberg extolled the American-family-in-general. In his 1991-1993 show, *Brooklyn Bridge,* he romanticizes the Jewish Brooklyn and the Jewish family of his own youth. There is no mistaking that the family of *Brooklyn Bridge* is Jewish. Marion Ross, as Grandma Sophie Berger, sports a big Yiddish accent, echoed by Louis Zorich, who plays her husband, Jules. Peter Friedman and Amy Aquino are most engaging and loving as the first generation American parents, and Danny Gerard and Matthew Louis Siegel offer affecting composite portraits of Goldberg and his brother as 14-year-old Alan and 9-year-old Nathaniel. Indeed, Siegel rivals the young Jerry Mathers for cuteness and charm, and Gerard rivals Fred Savage of *The Wonder Years* for early teen poise and perspicacity.

At its dramatic best (which was fairly consistent), *Brooklyn Bridge* provided portraits of family life which are heart-warming and not sappy, touching but not corny. Particularly touching and well-drawn is the relationship between the brothers. The loyalty of the younger brother to the older brother was poignantly painted in an episode in which the latter does not win a televised baseball contest in which he represents the neighborhood on TV. The scenes between father and son are also profoundly touching in this episode. In another moving episode, the loyalty of the younger brother to his aunt, who announces her imminent divorce, is depicted. When Nathaniel asks his elder brother if he thinks that their parents will ever divorce, Alan responds that he doubts it because they need each other too much. These moments of sincere and authentic concern and insight abound on *Brooklyn Bridge*.

On the Jewish level, however, *Brooklyn Bridge* is both revealing and disappointing. There are aspects of the opening song which sound like an old Yiddish melody, yet the authentic Yiddish song is one accented by the concepts and vocabulary of traditional Jewish life—*Torah, Am Yisrael* (The Jewish People), *zedakah* (sharing), *mentschlikhkeit* (decency), *emunah* (faithfulness). There were no Jewish values or concepts explained on this program. Certain Jewish observances and holidays, such as *shiva* and Sukkot, have been mentioned, but mainly to show how they get in the way of the children's activities and how they are observed not so much out of conviction but to please Grandma. Alan gives up a baseball game with his Irish girlfriend to make the quorum for the *shiva minyan* (mourning week service) of an uncle whom no one liked. It is then that Grandma shares her philosophy that family is "people who don't really like each other getting together to do things they don't really want to do." The same philosophy is applied by *Brooklyn Bridge* to Jewish life and observances.

In the episode in which Grandma Sophie is upset by her younger daughter's announcement of an impending divorce, the boys' mother explains to them that Sukkot is the Jewish Thanksgiving. Not a word is said about the *sukkah* or the *lulav* and *etrog*. Alan refers to Sukkot as one of the "rare up Jewish holidays," as if there's nothing "up" about Rosh Hashanah, Yom Kippur, Passover or Shavuot, or even Chanukah. His main concern is not being able to watch the football game because Grandma frowns upon TV-watching during holiday dinners. Alan tells his mother that he's checked Jewish Law and found no prohibition against watching TV. He insists that TV watching on the holidays should be a house-to-house decision. His mother doubts that he will convince Grandma.

Is Grandma observant of Jewish Law, or does she simply frown on distractions during family dinners? When she hears that one of her daughters is getting divorced, her first impulse is to cancel the dinner, to send away her guests—in effect, to cancel the Holiday. Once she returns to the table and the family discussions become too graphic, she instructs her son-in-law to send the two boys to the store to buy Grandpa Jules some cigars. It would appear, then, that Grandma is not consistent in observance of Jewish Law, which she invokes as a kind of table etiquette but not as a religious observance. For she sends the boys to shop on a Festival, and thus to violate the Holiday observance, once the propriety of her table is disturbed by talk of divorce, which is, albeit sadly and reluctantly, permitted by religious law.

The question that must be asked is whether Goldberg and episode writers Peter Schneider and Ben Cardinale are aware of this TV Grandmother's inconsistency, whether or not she represents an actual portrait of a real-life grandmother. Is Goldberg attempting to depict the lives of somewhat traditional Jews who observed Jewish Law only when it fit family needs? There were once many such Jews in Brooklyn, which probably has many more authentically Orthodox Jews today. If that is what Goldberg is depicting, and that is his right, since it certainly corresponds to historical reality and maybe to personal memory, the question is whether he has an obligation to point out to the viewer that this grandmother is inconsistent, that this family did not have a fully observant life, that Sukkot and *shiva* mean more to Jews religiously than simply dinner table etiquette.

Since the program offers a knowing perspective on many of the assumptions and actions of all generations in the family, where is its perspective on Judaism? Once Judaism has been invoked, isn't there an obligation to convey a sense of the values and observances of Judaism in which the family may fall short? Doesn't Judaism deserve to be represented to the audience with at least the same authenticity and respect as the religion of baseball?

Regarding fourteen-year-old Alan's Catholic girlfriend, Grandma Sophie does voice her disapproval, but never explains why she disapproves. If the "Jewish" family is to be portrayed with authentic concerns, and not merely as an ethnic backdrop for the glorification of inter-ethnic romance, don't writers and producers have an obligation to put some meaningful and coherent words in Grandma Sophie's mouth? Without words to cogently explain her feelings, the feelings and values and beliefs she represents, albeit eclectically (at least according to this particular TV series depiction), ring rather hollow and chauvinistic.

Interestingly, the writers of *Brooklyn Bridge* did attempt to depict nostalgia for spirituality in an episode about the "once in a blue moon" Saturday that Dad had off. It is made clear that Grandpa did not observe the Sabbath. He uses the morning to inspect a used car he's been admiring. Dad plans to take the boys to buy underwear at a once-a-year sale, and Mother and Grandma plan to go to the laundromat. Yet the men end up going to Coney Island and the women to a Danny Kaye movie; and Saturday night they all sheepishly confess their caprice, and gather for the weekly ritual of dinner and TV viewing.

Writers Brad Hall and John Masius have every right to depict the Brooklyn Saturday if that is their memory, rather than the classic Shabbat. What is remarkable is that in this episode about a Saturday, the writers did allow for some nostalgia regarding "Old World" Jewish observances. At Saturday evening dinner Grandma reminisces: "Our whole village would stop on *Shabbos*. No one would work. The men would not plough, the women would not sew, from sundown Friday [through] all day Saturday. The whole village—praying, thinking, singing. My mother, my father—they would forget all their troubles. Life was hard for six days, then for one it was beautiful."

This description of Shabbat is as nice as one could find. One can, I think, give the writers credit for a fine and sincere attempt to explain Shabbat to a general audience. But then they go and spoil it all by giving Grandma some extra lines: "Well, the world has changed now. But as long as we're all together, Saturday is still special." The dialogue goes downhill from there. Little Natie responds that Saturday sure is special, with *Jackie Gleason, Gunsmoke* and *Your Hit Parade*. Grandma pipes up, "See, things haven't changed so much." Sabbath holiness has been replaced by diversity in entertainment.

This dialogue about Saturday may well be authentic reconstruction of certain family attitudes. It may even be taken as a critique of the times, though I doubt that this is what the writers intended. We must consider the responsibility of the writers. They have every right to depict a family philosophy that the Sabbath is passé, but as broadcasters they have the obligation to indicate that many Jews still observe the Sabbath, and that all Jewish religious movements advocate Sabbath observance. The impression they leave is that the old world Shabbat is inevitably replaced by the Brooklyn Saturday, and that nostalgia for a Brooklyn childhood in the 1950s is more sacred than Judaism.

Jewish Ritual as Family Neurosis:
"Frank's Place"

Frank's Place, a likeable and engaging series about a Creole restaurant in New Orleans, offered fascinating glimpses into aspects of Black culture. One of the few regular white persona in the cast is a Jewish lawyer, Bubba Weisberger, played by Robert Harper. Does Bubba's helpful and kind personality, his sense of responsibility and friendship, bespeak a rootedness in specifically Jewish values and observances?

After Bubba told another character that Jews like to drink I should have realized that Judaism or at least his Jewish family was bound to be depicted in this series as a cause of alcoholism and neurosis rather than as a source of positive values. I dared to hope that a show which excelled at exploring both the noble and the scoundrels in the African American community, at depicting both the pious and the crooked in one setting, might at least be even-handed in another setting. I was sadly mistaken.

A 1987 episode had Frank express his desire to see the "ancient ritual" of Chanukah. So Bubba invites Frank to the annual "nightmare" experience at his mother's home on Shabbat Chanukah, the Sabbath of Chanukah. That way, I expect, Frank could see two "ancient rituals" at once—the Sabbath and Chanukah.

The only positive thing that one can say about the episode is that it offers a good history lesson. Appropriately, the Jewish mother here is depicted as very much the Southerner and, in fact, her grandchildren, Bubba's niece and nephew, speak with very thick Southern accents. This is as it should be. The myth that all Jews are from New York and have only recently immigrated to other parts of the country is handily shattered here. (Also, Bubba happens to be a very blond individual, and hence the myth that all Jews are dark-haired is appropriately shattered, as well, as Harry Kemelman tried to do, by the way, in his description of Miriam Small in the Rabbi David Small murder mysteries.) Bubba's mother describes how her great-grandparents arrived in Charleston almost two centuries before.

Unfortunately, however, the episode exults in advancing the myth of the domineering, neurotic, Jewish mother. It seems that Mrs. Portnoy has simply relocated to *The Glass Menagerie*. Bubba's mother may present something of the noble history of Southern Jewry, but it is, out of snobbery—and not reverence—that the history lesson is offered. She constantly shoots arrows at Bubba, in the most vicious and annoying ways, about his not being married, his not being attentive enough to her, his all too frequent visits to Frank's bar, etc., etc., *ad nauseam.*

This scene is enough to spoil anyone's Shabbat or Chanukah meal, especially Bubba's. His mother even accuses him of killing his father, and tells him that his deceased father was bitterly disappointed in him—in front of the entire family and a couple of visitors. In order to shock his mother, Bubba tells her that Frank is his lover, and this puts Mother in her place so that she no longer cares whom he dates, "as long as it's a girl." Bubba is quite proud of himself for so having tamed Mother with his playful "shock treatment."

The episode does pay some attention to rituals. Mother lights the Shabbat candles (with English blessings). The grandson says the blessing over the Chanukah candles (also in English), and the niece recites some appropriate Chanukah narrative. It is clear that the point of all these rituals is to show that Mother uses them to dominate her son. Thus, she asks Bubba to recite the *Motzi* (Blessing over bread) in Hebrew, which he does quite well, though it is a "command performance." Mother then explains that Chanukah is "like Thanksgiving" for "us"—a "time for all the family to get together"—"for a change." The latter phrase is obviously intended to make Bubba feel guilty for not visiting more often. With a mother like that, it is little wonder that he prefers Frank's bar. Also, why suggest that Jews use Chanukah as a substitute for the "American" Thanksgiving, as if Jews cannot join in Thanksgiving as full-fledged Americans, especially when the American Thanksgiving is based on the major biblical festival of Sukkot (Tabernacles), and not on the relatively minor Chanukah festival.

I'm not sure which I resent more: the association of Jewish rituals with neurosis and bullying, or the distortion of those rituals. If a television writer is going to show rituals, why light the Chanukah candles after the Shabbat candles and so violate the Sabbath? Why show people with the *dreidel* and giving out Chanukah *gelt* (money gifts) on the Sabbath, when pious Jews refrain from handling money on Shabbat?

In all fairness to *Frank's Place*, it does show neurosis and unhappiness and bullying in some Black families, as well. The funeral director is a mother who dominates her daughter (or at least tries) and the rest of the town mercilessly. At least she has a sense of humor and some redeeming moments.

Frank's long-lost uncle visits him in this episode, and brags about his unusual and exciting jobs and his frequent travels to exotic places, including Israel, of which he says: "You've got to see that place one day.

I don't know what there is about it, but it's someplace different, special." It turns out, however, that the uncle has never been to Israel or to many other places beyond the small Mississippi town where he lives; he is, in fact, a Walter Mitty character, a postman, who has everyone in the New Orleans restaurant believing his fantasies, but always enjoys the warmth of his obviously fine wife and their children as he follows his mail route throughout the year.

In contrast, the Jewish family depicted here is a network of neuroses whose only interesting and pleasant aspects are some antiquated, quaint rituals. Sure, everyone is fascinated by Israel and by Jewish "customs and ceremonies," but there is no warmth, spirituality or kindness in the Jewish family. All they're good for is nasty one-liners about their own rituals. The message is clear. The Jewish holidays merely exacerbate the ever-present tension and rancor. In contrast, the Christmas spirit, in which Bubba finds refuge at the end of the episode (while visiting Frank's Place, of course),—the Christmas spirit brings out song, love and good will. Bubba is clearly happier watching his Christian friends observe their holiday at Frank's Place than spending Chanukah with other Jews. At the end of the episode, everybody joins in the "born is the king of Israel" carol, thus further highlighting the triumph of the Christian spirit above Jewish neurosis. Who would *want* to be the king of Israel, anyway, after seeing all this?

Several episodes before, *Frank's Place* had featured a good segment about a scoundrel who poses as a Black minister. There's a scene in which Bubba joins the minister and their mutual friends for dinner after attending the minister's debut service. When the minister invites Bubba back the next Sunday, Bubba replies: "I'm Jewish, Reverend." "Well, I'll stick to the Old Testament," the Reverend answers. "I've got a sermon on Moses that will knock you naked." Bubba answers: "Well, as enticing as that may sound, I'm already not practicing one religion and I don't want to feel guilty about two." Later, Bubba jokes that he'll observe one of the minister's baptisms if the minister will accompany him to Kol Nidre services. "Kol Nidre," quoth the minister. "It sounds like a bad woman."

At the end of the Chanukah episode, Frank asks Bubba: "When's Passover? I'm sure I don't want to miss it. What are you going to do? Shoot Roman candles at your mother's dress?" Fortunately, the series quietly disappeared a spell thereafter, sparing us its versions of Passover, Yom Kippur or any other Jewish holiday.

Scribal Arts For Angry Jewish Daughters:
"Touched by an Angel"

In the fall of 2001, *Touched By An Angel* offered a grab bag of stock "Jewish" themes, including Skinhead hate crimes, an alienated Jewish daughter, and a Jewish father who is both (!) neglectful and overbearing. David Margulies portrays a *sofer* (a scribe), Sam Silverstein, who is befriended by a novice angel, Gloria, nicely played by series newcomer Valerie Bertinelli. Gloria is a naïve angel with a computer mind, but this time she gets her information wrong. She meets the *sofer* at a bus stop, and tells him that she knows a lot about Jews, that they are "pigs" and love money, et c., etc.—things she has heard from Skinheads whom she has just met, and dutifully jotted down.

Much to the *sofer*'s credit, however, he realizes that the young woman has good intentions but is misinformed. He is even willing to engage her as a real estate agent, once her celestial supervisor, Tess (Della Reese) establishes this "cover" while scooping her young ward away before the latter can say something else foolish or offensive. (It's interesting that in Rabbinic literature angels are depicted as blabbermouths.)

Another angel, Monica (Roma Downey), is an editorialist at the local newspaper where the *sofer*'s daughter, Rachel "Silver" (Meredith Scott Lynn), works as a cartoonist. Upon meeting Rachel, Monica sees that she has posted at her work station very pointed caricatures mocking her father, who keeps bringing her deli sandwiches and finding other ways to hover about. Monica learns that Rachel has dinner with her parents every Wednesday night because she refuses to visit them for Sabbath dinner, which is "not my thing."

Writers Allen Estrin and Joseph Telushkin, along with David H. Forer, have crowded a lot into this preachy tale. Their intentions are obviously honorable and even noble, but the characterizations, plot and structure impede their goals and their efforts to teach about Judaism and the Holocaust. Since this is television's most serious treatment to date of the subject of women in Judaism, juxtaposed with a first look at the art of the *sofer* in a network TV series, while making statements about hate crimes and the Holocaust, it must be looked at carefully.

The major theme is that a Jewish father, for reasons of "tradition," does not respect the religious impulses of his daughter, thus opening the floodgates to rebellion and maybe even betrayal of the Jewish People.

When Rachel is told that her comic strips must be "grittier," she is provoked to publish one of her caricatures of her father after he nags her and then berates the "hateful cartoons on the walls of your little pretend office."

"You finally had an idea I can live with, Daddy," she says to herself. She decides to call her cartoon, "Chutzpah" (the name the writers chose for the episode).

Sam is so offended by Rachel's comic strips that he leads a protest in front of the newspaper office. When Rachel confronts him, insisting that she cannot be an anti-Semite because she is a Semite, he tells her that sometimes Jews make the worst anti-Semites. When the press asks Sam if he is her father, he responds in her presence, "I have no daughter."

This is all precipitated by a visit from the young rabbi of the local synagogue who slips into Sam's hand Rachel's comic strip depicting Jewish "businessmen" planning to commit arson on their own business for insurance money. The rabbi says that at first the community tried to "show others that we can smile at ourselves," but that this sort of "degrading and mean-spirited" matter "gives fodder to those who already hate us. It's got to stop." Sam confronts his daughter: "I can't live with you insulting your people and your faith. You're doing this to save your job and to insult me. What did I ever do to deserve this treatment?" "If you don't know," she responds, "just forget it."

It is at this point that the father's great sin is revealed to us, the audience, through an angel's eyes. Rachel, a little girl, has drawn and colored a Torah scroll for her father, complete with cute pictures, the "Rachel Silverstein Torah," as she calls it, referring to the Torah being inscribed by Sam that was begun by his father. At first he is gentle with her. The writers do not make him an ogre. He feels, however, he must tell her that her project is "really not a Torah. It takes a long time to do a Torah properly. It must be perfect. It's the word of God we're preserving. There are no pictures in a Torah. Besides, you're a girl and I don't believe girls are supposed to make Torahs."

That event, we are told, is the great trauma that precipitated Rachel's animosity, rebellion, cartoons, and slander of the Jewish community.

There is more that the episode would have us consider. It seems that Rachel's column is admired by the Skinheads whom Gloria had encountered at the beginning of the hour. Since Sam first met the naïve, newly created angel, Gloria, at the bus stop, and saw that this "smart girl" was susceptible to anti-Semitic diatribes, he has tried to educate her about

Auschwitz and Dachau. (We learn that his parents had survived the Holocaust and come to America only to be killed by a drunk driver. Rachel had described them as "good people.") Gloria visits the local Holocaust Museum. The scene in which Gloria emerges with awareness of the horrors that occurred is most touching, due to Bertinelli's performance.

It was, indeed, effective writing to suggest that even a brilliant, newly-created angel can fall for the lies of hate groups. The writers have the angel Monica pay tribute to the Jewish People when she speaks of Moses receiving the Torah at Mt. Sinai and of the People Israel's faith and tenacity in following it. "You don't know their history, the strength of their faith," she tells the fledgling angel. The writers may also be the only ones to date who have clearly stated in a TV drama that mockery of Jews and Judaism by Jews in the media can fuel the cause and actions of Jew-haters.

Toward the end of the episode, Rachel receives a call from Skinheads telling her that they are going to "take care" of the "cruel pig" old Jew who led the protest—namely, her father. Rachel has the presence of mind to call her mother and the authorities. She rushes to the synagogue when she hears that her father is there. The angel Gloria had accompanied him there to apologize for her unquestioning acceptance of hateful lies. They had arrived as the Skinheads were vandalizing the synagogue and destroying the Torah scroll. When the Skinheads try to kill Sam, Gloria reveals that she is an angel, and is joined by her celestial colleagues. Sam blames his daughter for the vandalism; the Skinheads have written "Chutzpah" on the wall. "You…made us less human and that's all they needed."

The drama notes the subtleties of Sam's personality. He is, I repeat, no ogre. (Margulies brings warmth to his nuanced performance.) He does have a sense that it "bothers" his daughter that he believes that a "woman *sofer* is not traditional." He is gentle and even doting with her, but always manages to express his convictions in ways that are hurtful to her. The writers never focus on the real problem—namely, Sam's and Rachel's way of speaking to each other. They attribute the conflict to Dad's stance on women scribes. In general, Sam is kind and helpful to women. He is most patient with Gloria and is gentle with her while she learns about Jews.

Monica takes Rachel to task for her abandonment of "the faith," but not, interestingly, for her vindictive behavior. "If you acknowledge angels," Monica tells her, "you have to acknowledge God. Then you have to acknowledge the faith you left behind."

The writers focus on Rachel's lack of faith in order to indict Sam for a narrow-mindedness that undermines his daughter's connection with

Judaism and with the Jewish People. Monica tells Sam: "You took the letter of the law as you interpreted it and you unwittingly crushed her spirit." Unfortunately, the rhetoric here smacks of the old Christian canard that Judaism is concerned only with the "letter" of the law. Monica's remarks do enable Rachel to express her resentment to her father, "You never finished the Silverstein Torah because you wanted to finish it in three generations of Silverstein men." How can the writers attack Sam's stance without disparaging certain interpretations in the Orthodox community honored by men and women alike?

Monica then explains to Sam that his daughter lost her dream to become a *sofer* on the day he criticized the Torah she made as a child, and that she also lost her respect for him. This is all right, I suppose, as a pop psychology and parenting lecture. Despite its stated concern about how Jews depict themselves in the media, this episode ends up with a very negative portrayal of a Jewish woman as vengeful, self-indulgent, angry and grudge-filled, testing and testy—not unfamiliar images in film and TV.

The bad image is mitigated somewhat by the writers' depiction of Sam's wife, Eva (Carol Locatell, in an affecting portrayal) as gracious yet possessing strength and conviction. "Women like you have a choice to work," she tells her daughter, Rachel, "because of women like me. You've had other jobs [drawing cartoons] before. You can get other jobs again. You've only ever had one father." One wishes that the characterization of Rachel's mother had been more fully developed.

The episode never acknowledges that Rachel's vindictiveness is at least as much a flaw as any she resents in her father. At one point, Tess and Monica tell Gloria that Sam wants understanding (about Jews) from Gloria and that's what Rachel wants from Sam. Here, at a pivotal moment that invokes the Holocaust, the father's mistakes that contributed toward the alienation of his daughter are put on the same level as the hate-filled rhetoric of the Skinheads (which Gloria had at first parroted). Even after the synagogue is vandalized, and the Angel of Death tells the Skinheads that they are not interested in the truth, but only in looking for excuses to hate, he makes a crack about how they will be visited in prison by "another angel," to whom they had "better listen." Is Sam's treatment of his daughter so horrible that even vicious Skinheads must wait for him to be straightened out first? Doesn't Rachel require a stronger angelic reprimand?

In the "resolution," Rachel becomes the hands of her father in the writing of the parchment. (His hands are injured by the Skinheads.) But does that rather pat and predictable ending lead to mutual respect and

understanding between father and daughter, or simply to mutual indulgence? What becomes of the important and real issue of whether there can
be respect for different interpretations of Judaism within one family, or
between different groups in the family of the Jewish People?

Jewish Ritual as Backdrop:
"Unstrung Heroes"

Unstrung Heroes (1995) is such an effective film that it pains us and
yet leaves us completely satisfied, emotionally speaking. It is not only
catharsis, but a controlled total workout for all the emotions, stretching
them and massaging them, and reminding us, through an exhilarating
soreness, that they are there and under-used.

For Jewish audiences, the film is perhaps an added treat, though it will
touch everyone. Based on a memoir about 1950s Los Angeles by sports-
writer Franz Lidz, it is about a Jewish thirteen-year-old (memorably played
by Nathan Watt), whose mother (Andie MacDowell) is dying of cancer and
whose father (John Turturro) is less able than his son to face her death. The
boy's mother is the wise and gracious and beautiful nurturer of both her
husband and son and younger daughter. The father is a tinkerer and an
inventor of oddities, whose own son wonders whether Dad is from another
planet. The father thinks nothing of endangering his children with his
experimentation. He offers neither emotional nor physical security or
safety, and becomes cold and erratic in his grief.

It is hard to tell which scenes are more wrenching: those in which the
boy tries to come to terms with his impending loss (including the heartless
way the news is broken to him), or those in which the father realizes his
helplessness to save his beloved through his credo of scientific experimentation and faith in rationalism.

Enter the boy's two eccentric uncles, Arthur (Maury Chaikin) and
Danny (Michael Richards, "Kramer" of *Seinfeld* fame). Enter they do, in
the strangest way, at the beginning of the film. The boy flees to them at the
height of his sorrows at home, and treks their bizarre but warm and
memorable world. The brothers are paranoid, but are not sure whom they
believe is after them. They mouth some platitudes of the Left, but also wear
yarmulkes and recite "*brochos*" (blessings). They are alienated from family
and community, yet insist that their nephew have a bar mitzvah and
advocate for him at his school. Uncle Danny (Richards), especially, fears

conspiracies everywhere and finds anti-Semitic codes in every popular expression. These uncles rename their nephew Franz, though his father, their brother, begs him to keep the name Steven, that his mother gave him.

While Franz's mother voices the fear, albeit half jokingly, that he might become "one of them," she senses that his uncles can give him something that his father cannot. As she tells her husband, "Maybe there is a God, and maybe some of us want to believe that there is." He responds: "Religion is a crutch. Only cripples need crutches." When she replies that "We're all cripples in some way," he declares "Well, I'm not." Our inventor proclaims that he stands for belief in one's own ability, though it becomes increasingly clear that that belief is his own crutch, and as much of an illusion as his brothers' delusions. Dad's "faith" is no match for the (albeit eclectic) Jewish beliefs that become symbolic of the only reality test and safety net of uncles and nephew alike.

I say, "symbolic," because this film is not about the saving power of Judaism. Now *Unstrung Heroes is* very respectful of Judaism, religion and even of odd Jews who have their own version of Judaism for whatever reason. Director Diane Keaton has provided a warm account of eccentrics in one Jewish family. There is no suggestion here that Jews-in-general or Jewish traditions are odd. There is every suggestion, however, that the sacred rituals are there as a life-line for whoever appreciates them and for whoever would utilize them. As one of Steven's uncles tells him, "We need our rituals to rise above the patterns of History." Few madmen in film are so profound, especially nowadays.

Unstrung Heroes is about the power of preserving memories through objects, experiences, and, above all, "documentation," which in this case means the home movie camera. It is, in the last analysis, a filmmaker's movie about the power of filmmaking. It honors the images of the synagogue. (Some of the beautiful murals of the Wilshire Boulevard Temple in Los Angeles are shown.) It even respects the images of the Jewish cemetery (despite a rather bizarre ritual there on the part of the uncles). Ultimately the "Jewish" memories are only a part, albeit an important part, of memories-in-general, of documentation-in-general, which, according to this movie, is the ultimate comfort and salvation. At the climax of the film, therefore, the "real" funeral for the mother, which brings father and son together, is a celebration of film documentation.

I found myself thinking of Bernard Malamud's last book, *God's Grace* (1982), which was not about God and the Bible, but rather about the power of stories about God and the Bible. It was a writer's meditation on the importance of storytelling. Likewise, *Unstrung Heroes* is not about Jewish memories, but about the power of one's own memories, including one's Jewish memories (where applicable) to bring some comfort and humor to life's tragedies. Who are the "heroes"? Lidz's beloved mother offers the working definition: "A hero is anyone who finds his way through life." Young Steven finds his way through life and loss by means of his movie camera—with a little help from his uncles.

8

MISREPRESENTED PRACTICES
AND SENSIBILITIES

ℰↃ℃ℛ

**Reinventing Jewish Law:
"Saint Elsewhere,"
"Chicago Hope," "The Nanny,"
"Cybill," "Crisis Center,"
"Medicine Ball," "Seventh Heaven"**

B eginning in the late 1980s, television took its cue from certain big screen trends and began featuring Jewish practices, or at least practices of Jews. These "rituals" were tantamount to the reformatting of Jewish Law (*halachah*) and customs (*minhagim*). They began with the bizarre and then "graduated" to out-and-out misrepresentation.

The advent of the bizarre stage was reflected in a 1988 episode of *St. Elsewhere*, the second to the last episode of the series, in fact. The episode, written by Tom Fantana, dealt with the aftermath of the death of the father of Dr. Fiscus (Howie Mandel). Fiscus's mother (Lainie Kazan) is having a difficult time readjusting her life and is lavishing all her attention on her son to the point of making it almost impossible for him to tell her about his plans to do his residency in Nicaragua (!). (Fortunately for the image of Jewish mothers, the teleplay makes it clear that Fiscus's mother is not usually so overbearing, but is going through a difficult time.) In several scenes, we see the mother sprinkling an ash-like substance in many of the rooms she visits—at Fiscus's apartment, at the hospital, everywhere. Finally, at the end, Fiscus asks her about this strange ritual and she says that she is spreading her dead husband's ashes around places that are significant to her and to her son.

True, the rite is not presented as a Jewish custom per se. It is more the sick and silly (albeit therapeutic) ritual of a woman not coping well with loss, who happens to be Jewish. Nothing is said here about such ritual being contrary to the abhorrence in traditional Judaism of cremation or any other kind of maiming, dismembering or immolating the dead body, out of respect for the integrity of God's creation. This is unfortunate, given a previous episode featuring writer Douglas Steinberg's fine use of Jewish rituals of mourning.

Beginning with the mid-1990s, television writing began to speak with authority about Jewish practices which were, in fact, the inventions of the writers. A January 1995 episode of *Chicago Hope*, about the death and funeral of a rabbi, spoke of a ritual called a "pre-*shiva*," a gathering of family and friends before the *shiva* (seven days of mourning at home after the burial). Rabbis around the country received inquiries as to whether a pre-*shiva* was necessary, or even whether it could be an alternative to the *shiva*. But in Judaism, mourning cannot begin until there is proper burial (or formal declaration of death when there is no corpse). Moreover, up to the time of the funeral, the mourners are exempt from many daily rituals and observances out of respect for their disoriented state.

The rabbi had died in open heart surgery. It did not help that a member of the surgical team dropped the rabbi's heart and it slid across the floor. It is instructive, by the way, that the same episode, written by Michael Nankin, featured a eulogy for the rabbi by nurse Camille (Roxanne Hart), Christian wife of Dr. Aaron Shutt (Adam Arkin). Camille speaks after a eulogy in Yiddish and praises Rabbi Taubler (veteran Jewish actor, Nehemiah Persoff) for joking that she was his first *shiksa*—that is, the first non-Jewish bride at whose wedding to a Jewish man he officiated. The implication is clear: The more old world the rabbi (with Yiddish eulogizers yet), the more "Jewish" the interfaith marriage ceremony. This, too, is a misrepresentation of Jewish Law and tradition, which recognizes only a wedding between two Jews (and both can be converts) as a Jewish religious ceremony. Even more misleading than the fabrication of "pre-*shiva*" is the redefinition of Jewish marriage.

Still, the seemingly small coinages of "Jewish" customs or usages have far-reaching effects. *The Nanny* (1993-1999) is a good case in point. In a 1996 episode, "The Tattoo," written by Caryn Lucas, Fran Fine (Fran Drescher) confesses to her mother Sylvia (Renee Taylor) that she had herself tattooed some years before. Sylvia lambastes her: "This time you haven't just defied your mother. This time you defied God. If you have a tattoo, you can't be buried in a Jewish cemetery. And unless you have it removed, consider yourself disowned."

It is interesting that this is the only time in the entire series that Fran's mother took a strong stand, moral or otherwise, regarding her daughter's behavior. Sylvia is actually depicted in one episode, by writer Diane Wilk ("The Cantor Show," April 1966), as sneaking ham sandwiches into the synagogue on Friday nights.[1] The effectiveness of Mom's "stand" is, by the way, immediately undermined by writer Caryn Lucas with a line that quickly follows about Sylvia's intention to keep panhandling for food from the butler despite her rift with Fran. Still, Lucas ends the episode on a touching, if satirical note, with Fran's telling her teenage ward, who plans to become tattooed at age eighteen, that if she does get the tattoo, she won't be buried next to her Jewish husband. When the teenage girl responds that she's not Jewish, Fran whines, "Don't be selfish. You know I live vicariously through you."

While tattooing is prohibited by Jewish Law as an imitation of pagan practice (see Leviticus 19:28) and as thoughtless mutilation of one's God-given body, it is not, nor has it ever been, grounds for exclusion from Jewish burial. Due to *The Nanny* and parallel purveyors of misinformation, some Jews really began to think that tattooing barred them from Jewish burial, and many rabbis were asked about it.

The Nanny even did its part, as a series, to undermine Jewish traditions of dignity and respect at funerals that were lovingly and thoughtfully crafted.[2] After the funeral of an aunt, Fran's grandmother, Yetta (Ann

---

1. The only strong stand that Fran takes is to refuse to cross a picket line, thus embarrassing her boss publicly. Yet in that episode, aired in 1994 and written by Janis Hirsch, she attributes her stance to respect for a dead aunt, not to teachings about justice and fairness to the worker in the Bible and Talmud, the sources of Jewish Law.
2. See Samuel H. Dresner, "The Scandal of the Jewish Funeral," in *The Jew in American Life* (New York: Crown Publishers, 1963).

Morgan Guilbert), comments that she wouldn't want an open casket at her funeral because she doesn't trust anyone else with putting on her make-up. No one mentions, however, that at a traditional Jewish funeral, an open casket is regarded as mockery and as an insult to the deceased, making that individual the object of conversations in which he or she cannot participate. The episode was written by Fran Descher and her husband and producer, Peter Marc Jacobson.

It is noteworthy that in that particular episode, Fran inherits a mink coat from this aunt, but refuses to accept it both because she believes in animal rights, and because she believes she must be a role-model to one of her young wards, an impressionable teenager. At a rather bizarre, *shiva*-like family gathering, Fran's mother takes her daughter into the "privacy" of the kichen and shouts for all to hear, "How can you turn your back on everything I raised you to believe in? This is mink." When Fran asks her mother why *she* doesn't take the mink coat, the latter replies, "I'm too busty." Fran retorts, "It didn't stop you from wearing a tube-top to temple." Her mother answers, "It [the temple]'s Reform." The "It's Reform," which is, I dare say, insulting to Reform Judaism, might have served as an effective disclaimer of the open casket at the aunt's funeral (though Reform Judaism has long been reconsidering the value of traditional Jewish funeral practices), but it could never explain the stricter-than-tradition approach to tattooing.

A contemporaneous series to *The Nanny*, on the same network, C.B.S., *Cybill*, upped the ante a bit on Jewish funeral laws. The series starred Cybill Shepard as an aging actress forced into degrading roles, yet rather self-assured as a mother of two and as the ex-wife of each of her daughters' fathers. One ex-husband is the lovable but neurotic lawyer-turned-novelist, Ira (Alan Rosenberg). In one episode, Ira's teenage daughter, Zoey (a standout portrayal of a bright and spirited youth by Alicia Witt) teases him with the question: "Shoes without socks? Dad, when did you start dressing like a Gentile?" Ira responds that he is dressing to please his new fiancée and hastens to add: "But technically without socks I can't be buried in a Jewish cemetery." Here, the writers introduced (untrue) lore about Jewish burial practices in order to elicit an easy laugh. It certainly was fashionable in 1990s sitcoms to depict Jewish burial practices as bizarre. Could that have been because many involved in the writing and production of these items were realizing that non-Jewish spouses could not be buried in Jewish cemeteries? Are the Jewish laws of burial "discriminatory" or effective at reinforcing in-marriage?

That same year, 1997, a short-lived N.B.C. series, *Crisis Center*, about idealistic social workers, physicians, and lawyers in San Francisco, did try to do some justice to Jewish burial laws. Its principal characters unite in a patchwork agency that doles out quick fix help. The resource person in Jewish beliefs and practices is Jake, an Asian American Jewish young adult whose take-out service keeps the do-gooders supplied with pastrami and egg rolls. We are immediately informed that while Jake's Chinese education consisted mainly of being able to say "Happy Birthday" and "Where's the bathroom?" he did pick up a bit more about Judaism. He and his mother have just returned from attending a cousin's bar mitzvah. Also, we learn right off that Jake and his mother are trying to get the family establishment onto a rabbi's catering list.

The only "in-depth" look at a Jewish theme, and in a slightly sustained way (the best this cartoon series could do) involved case worker Lily Gannon (Nia Peeples), who takes up the cause of a deceased Holocaust survivor, Norma Fisher, a homeless person. Fisher's body was found near the dumpster whose lid dealt her a fatal blow to the head while she was rummaging around. Jake explains to Lily that the numbers on Norma's arm indicate that she was in a concentration camp, and that her entire family was killed in Europe. Though somewhat gratuitous, the invocation of the Holocaust does have some plot relevance here, at least in the mind of the writer. Lily, abandoned as a child to adoption agencies, identifies with Norma Fisher, who had to struggle alone in America. The writers seem unaware of the Jewish social agencies that dedicated themselves to helping Holocaust survivors, and of the success that the survivors had, as a group, in making a living and building a life in America.

Hearing that unless a relative can be found, Norma's body will be seized for cremation or for medical students, Lily resolves to find some blood relation of Norma's, especially after Jake informs her that "It's against Jewish Law to desecrate the body." An opportunity was lost, however. The writers never did get around to defining "Jewish Law" or "desecration," nor did they find the time for Lily to do a little research on her own on the *mitzvah* (commandment) of burial in Jewish Law and tradition.

Two years before, in 1995, another short-lived (Fox Network) series, *Medicine Ball*, dabbled in misrepresentation of Judaism, this time with respect to the circumcision rite, usually at the beginning of the life cycle rather than the end. This ill-fated show about young doctors tried to compete with the popular medical series then in vogue, *Chicago Hope* and

E.R., and attempted to be even more outrageous and offbeat than these series, but with no effect.

None of *Medicine Ball's* young doctors was identified as Jewish. In the very first episode, one of the subplots was about, of all things, an adult circumcision. This particular Judaic theme was chosen in order to get some gratuitous laughs from the circumcision and penis jokes which abounded. The premise here is that a grown man discovered that his birth parents were Jewish, and immediately wanted to be circumcised. There were strange aspects to this story line besides the rarity of Jewish children being given over for adoption to non-Jewish agencies. The writers invented for the occasion a *halachah* (religious law). The adoptee maintains that he must be circumcised within eight days of discovering that he is a Jew. When I last looked, the eight day requirement is a biblical law (Levit. 12:2-3) that applies only to newborns.[3] Also, it is quite improbable that a Hasidic rabbi would co-officiate at the circumcision with a woman physician, whose presence in the room during that particular operation on an adult male would be seen in some Orthodox circles as a violation of Jewish laws of *tzeniyut* (modesty).

It is hard to say whether these wanton revisions of Jewish Law and practice will leave a lasting impression on TV audiences. The immediate effects, however, can be felt. Within days after a 2002 episode of *Seventh Heaven*, a bride asked me with skepticism whether she needs to remove calla lilies from her wedding décor. She had seen the scene in which the rabbi's wife protested to wedding party planners: "I said Lilies of the Valley, not calla lilies. Calla lilies equal death. Lilies of the Valley equal life. We want life. Give me life."[4]

Writer Sue Tenney tied this little soliloquy to another protest by the rabbi's wife: "I heard they're planning on serving pork spring rolls as appetizers. Why don't you go into the kitchen and ask the guy with the

---

3.   According to Jewish Law, a person born of a Jewish mother, let alone of two Jewish parents, is Jewish. This is true of a male whether he is circumcised or not. It is a cardinal *mitzvah* for males to be circumcised according to the *b'rit*, the covenant, of Abraham. If the parents do not carry out this sacred obligation, it is incumbent upon the man upon coming of age. It is considered meritorious for such an individual to be circumcised as soon as possible. But no eight day deadline applies.

4.   I am grateful to Karen Mellman Smith for reminding me of this reference.

yarmulke why you don't serve pork to Jews." In the same segment, the same character also lectures her future in-law, a minister's wife, that Jews don't have wedding rehearsals because "rabbis don't believe that brides and grooms should rehearse." Note that the strange comments about calla lilies and wedding rehearsals, which have nothing to do with Jewish tradition, are sandwiched around an important religious law about the eating of pork. This is, unfortunately, an effective device for giving sanction to misinformation.

Television can be more successful than one might imagine at distorting and even fabricating religious rituals and practices. One hopes that writers on Judaism and Jewish themes will show greater discretion and responsibility in all scenes and dialogue, including the seemingly casual.

Protest Preempts Sabbath: "Beverly Hills 90210"

Whenever *Beverly Hills 90210* trotted out the Holocaust survivor, Grandmother Rose (played only once by Lainie Kazan, and thereafter by Beth Meisler), the purpose was to sanction whatever choices her granddaughter, Andrea Zuckerman (Gabrielle Carteris) believed mandated by immediate circumstance, such as fibbing about residence to stay in a particular high school, or marriage out of the faith. Andrea was supposed to represent the bright and thoughtful student, but she always could count on Grandma to lend an aura of Jewish authenticity to the most impulsive or ethically questionable decisions.

In the opening scene of a 1994 episode about tensions between Jewish and African American students on campus, Grandma Rose is given the opportunity to provide the reference to the Holocaust that sets the tone of the hour. She observed that Andrea's baby (whose father is Catholic) looks like a relative who died in the concentration camp. Then Grandma is quickly whisked off to a Hadassah meeting.

Andrea, who became TV's "role model" of the teenage mother who can achieve it all, goes to the college library to study for an exam, but she is soon told by Jewish activist Noah Levy (Jon Kean) about a troublesome event soon to occur on campus. It seems that the black student organization wants to pay to bring a Rev. Turner to the campus. Turner has maintained that Jews control the banks, were responsible for the slave trade, control the media and the Congress, and "suck the life blood out of black communities." The rhetoric, of course, resembles that which has been used by Louis Farrakhan and his followers. Turner even says that Jews faked Auschwitz so they could get the State of Israel.

The angry and open debate between the black students and Jewish student activist Levy threatens to divide the student council (and, even worse, the episode suggests, to ruin Kelley's photo shoot opportunity and that of the African American woman sponsoring her). All sides believe that student council president Brandon (Jason Priestley), Andrea's other buddy from Beverly Hills High, is not responsive or decisive enough.

Brandon seeks out the dean in order to determine how to diffuse an explosive situation. The dean tells him that he was one of the first black students admitted to the University of Georgia, and remembers the threats and catcalls when he tried to desegregate lunch counters and register new voters. The dean says that he was at the reflecting pool in Washington, D.C., when Dr. King spoke about his dream. "And every step of the way," he concludes, "at every battle that needed to be fought, Jewish people were right there with us. To have it all unravel after only one generation is a very sobering thought."

Not sobering, apparently, for the black students who regard sponsorship of Dr. Turner as a precious right and an exercise in free speech. A black law student tells the Jewish students that Turner might be toning down his rhetoric, and that "they said the same about Martin Luther King and Malcolm X." (Is this the company with whom Dr. King should be lumped together?) One African American student comments that he doesn't trust a "promoter who tells poor people what they want to hear at $10,000 a pop."

Unfortunately, writer Charles Rosin chose not to build upon the latter remark. Had he done so, he might have come up with a more creative resolution of the situation, such as a joint project of the Jewish and African American student organizations in a neighborhood requiring economic and educational development, with the black students offering the $10,000 as seed money to a loan or community improvement program.

The writer definitely has another "resolution" in mind. Andrea determines to attend a demonstration by Jewish students while Rev. Turner is speaking, a protest scheduled to take place on Friday night, the Sabbath. What have the Jewish students decided to do at the protest? To hold candles. In other words, they have decided to pre-empt Sabbath observances and even Sabbath laws about kindling, holding and transporting flames in order to have their protest. Thus, writer Rosin allowed his demagogue Rev. Turner to determine Jewish Sabbath observance!

Grandma Rose has yet another idea. She will change the nature of the protest—or at least Andrea's part in it. For Grandma Rose is upset that Andrea is arguing with her friends, at odds with black fellow-students, and disagreeing with her Hispanic husband. It would seem that Grandma Rose doesn't concur with the strategy of the Jewish student group (named by Rosin the "Maccabee Society"), who demand that swastikas painted on the campus religious center be kept there to show that "it can happen again," or with Andrea's comment to a black student leader that although the swastikas were probably not painted by an African American, the black students created a hostile atmosphere on campus by inviting Rev. Turner. Grandma decides that "Jews must reach out to the anti-Semite who seeks the good of the community"! She says that Jews must "go and bear witness"—in other words, personally attend every talk by every anti-Semite in order to "reach out" if that anti-Semite has some concept of the "good of the community."

This "sage" advice justifies my nervousness every time that Grandma Rose was trotted out in an episode of *Beverly Hills 90210*. Not that the theme of Black-Jewish campus tensions shouldn't have been explored. The topic actually allowed for the interesting subplot of Andrea shaming high school friend David into thinking about what it means to be Jewish. The best Jewish student protest might have been having a regular, spirited, Friday night service outdoors on the other side of the campus, bearing witness to the Creator and to the preciousness of all God's creatures, instead of to a demagogic racist.

The Torah of Vengefulness:
"In The Heat of The Night," "E.R."

Some television writers of the 1990s were intent upon giving their Jews the "right" to be angry and unforgiving. The result was a dangerous and troublesome precedent for nasty and thoughtless characters.

When long-popular CBS series, *In the Heat of the Night*, about life in a small Southern town, offered its requisite "Jewish" episode in 1994, the theme of choice was, interestingly, a Jew's failure to forgive. A synagogue is vandalized by local youths and a Torah scroll is stolen. Just in case the audience doesn't get it that these crimes are bad enough, a murder is thrown in to make the point that only a bad (or at least disturbed) anti-Semite can steal a Torah.

In this episode, Jerry Stiller plays Rabbi Hillel Feldman, who has returned to his home town in the South after spending ten years at a synagogue in New York. "The people were very gracious," he says, "but I never felt at home." He adds: "I missed the South in spite of myself." The rabbi is a widower, and has returned with his daughter, who is affectingly played by Mindy Rickles, the daughter of Don and Barbara Rickles. Stiller, who is laughably miscast as the rabbi, persists in confusing Southern dialect with unnaturally slow speech.

The rabbi has returned to dedicate a fledgling synagogue meeting in a small church building. He must face hostile youth who resent that the synagogue is now "occupying" a former church, suggesting to them that the Jews can "buy anything." He must also face a local entrepreneur who is doing everything possible to buy the church and responds to the rabbi's firm, "I'm not going to bargain with you," with the comment: "Never thought I'd hear a Jew say that." Later, when the synagogue is vandalized, the townspeople make it clear that the Jewish congregation should get no special financial help and that, after all, "This is a Christian community." The father of one of the vandals is more interested in hiding his son until "the whole thing blows over" than in teaching the lad respect for the law and for other faiths.

So far, it would seem, the writers have made a noble effort to discuss anti-Semitism and to shatter certain stereotypes.

Many TV programs about Jews in the South have suggested that "Jews" are interlopers from New York and that there is no tradition of Southern Jewry. This episode deserves credit for setting the record straight regarding the long history of Jews in the South, especially in small communities. The episode also depicts well the hurt that Jews feel when their houses of worship and sacred objects are desecrated, though the rabbi is represented as boasting a little too much about how much the Torah scroll costs (and it is a rather tiny scroll, at that). Also, the writers put undue emphasis on the fact that the Methodist church gave its building to the synagogue, as if to suggest that it would have been *really* vulgar and acquisitive of Jews to have *bought* the church.

Obviously, the story line and dialogue are not without their problems, but in the aspects already reviewed, the episode is innocuous enough, perhaps even helpful. Unfortunately, the writers did not stop there. They add a subplot which really becomes the plot of the episode. It seems that the returning rabbi has it in for the sheriff. "I don't trust the sheriff," he says. "He is ill-disposed toward our people." He tells the sheriff: "Stay away from us. Stay away from our lives."

He relates his concerns immediately to the sheriff's wife, a black woman who was a schoolmate of the rabbi, and is now a town official. The sheriff, of course, is played by none other than Carroll O'Connor, in his second famous and long-running TV role. O'Connor won hearts on this series with his fine acting, his total shedding of any aspect of the Archie Bunker persona, and his mastery of the Southern dialect which makes the viewer forget the old New York borough brogue from *All In The Family*.

What was the sheriff's sin? We learn toward the end of the episode, from the sheriff himself, that he was one of the "bad guys" when the first synagogue in the town was burnt down in the 1960s. Not that the sheriff was involved in setting the fire, but he went along with the police chief at the time who suppressed the evidence against the "upstanding citizen" who led the torching of the synagogue because Rabbi Feldman "supported the Civil Rights Movement openly and courageously." The sheriff confessed to his African American wife that he had kept his mouth shut, and was therefore one of those responsible for the absence of a synagogue in a community where Jews had lived "since before the War Between The States," until forced to attend another synagogue in Jackson.

Again, the writers are to be commended, this time for recalling the real risks that many Jewish leaders, rabbinic and lay, took for their belief in the Civil Rights Movement. Indeed, at the end of the episode, the current police chief, who is black, says that he will remind the town that the rabbi stood up for his neighbors when no one else would. At the ceremony of rededication of the synagogue, the rabbi asks the black police chief to hold the Torah and lead the procession to "reaffirm the solidarity of our peoples." The writers obviously have their hearts in the right place, making a sincere attempt to point to past Black-Jewish alliances in order to heal some current tensions. They find precedent for a non-Jew holding the Torah in a (TV writer manufactured) *midrash* about Alexander the Great and in the Rabbinic principle of *mipne darchei shalom*, "for the sake of maintaining civility and peace."

While I admire their use of the Hebrew expression in order to represent a classical Jewish concept (the most authentic way to communicate Jewish values in film and TV), I do find it interesting that the writers are invoking a rather extreme ritual measure for repair of intergroup relationships when it comes to Black-Jewish relations, which are quite good in this particular case, and not for the broken relationship between the rabbi and the sheriff. For it would seem that the writers would want us convinced that the sheriff has done *teshuvah*, has repented and made amends for his sin of omission of thirty years before. He cannot be considered a racist, for he cherishes and respects his African American wife. He is clearly sincere in his current abhorrence of anti-Semitic acts, for he gives the teenage offenders an eloquent lecture that is beyond the call of duty: "It's your own private affair whether you like people or you don't like them. But if you insult them or offend them or hurt them it becomes everybody's affair."

The pivotal scene in this episode is not this speech by the sheriff (though it should be) or even the dedication of the synagogue in which the procession is led by the black police chief. It is the scene in which the sheriff comes to see the rabbi, who is urged by his own daughter to forgive the sheriff. The rabbi refuses to forgive. At one point, his daughter tells her father, "You yourself said it was old stuff. Can't you let it go?" And the rabbi responds, "No. There are some things I can't let go." The rabbi goes so far as to say at one point, "In my opinion people seldom change."

Hath not a Jew forgiveness? Hath not Judaism a doctrine of forgiveness? Hath not Judaism a belief that people *can* change and begin again? After all, the Talmudic sage, Ben Azzai insisted, "Do not disdain any person...For there is no person who does not have his hour" (*Avot* 4:3) Judaism introduced to the world the Biblical and Rabbinic teaching that one who cannot forgive others cannot expect God to forgive him. It was Judaism that taught that we can recognize genuine *teshuvah* (repentance) in a person if, given the same opportunity to repeat a sin, that person, having confessed it and resolved not to do it again, overcomes the temptation and the opportunity and acts well.

I can't help paraphrasing Shylock's monologue in Shakespeare's *The Merchant of Venice*. For it seems that out of the best of motives, writers David O'Connor and Elyse O'Connor have defended the right of a rabbi to return home to the South and build a temple to a religion that has no capacity of forgiveness. That religion is not Judaism! Even so, it appears that the writers would compare the relationship of the rabbi and his daughter to that of Shylock and his daughter Jessica, who escapes all the anger and lack of grace and mercy at home by running off with a more pleasant and less complicated Gentile. In this episode of *In the Heat of the Night*, there is a telling scene in which the rabbi's daughter and the sheriff's handsome deputy exchange some pleasant words which seem to be the daughter's only relaxing moments amidst all the tensions at home and in the community. The writers entitled this episode, "The Rabbi." It might have been more aptly titled, "The Rabbi As Shylock."

The depiction of Jews and especially rabbis as bitter and unforgiving creatures is bad enough. It is most disconcerting when such mischief is done for the well-intentioned purpose of turning stereotypes on their heads. I was particularly shocked, however, when such antics literally followed me home. In 1996, the staff and crew of *E.R.* actually emerged from the TV and filmed an episode in one of the Jewish cemeteries close to my own congregation. The executive director of the Chicago Board of Rabbis, Ira Youdovin, was contacted and asked to read the Kaddish with Red Buttons, who was playing a bereaved Jewish man who had just lost his beloved wife. Rabbi Youdovin did well. Yet the encounter in the cemetery, as delineated by writer Lydia Woodward, is strange indeed. The series' darling, earnest intern Carter (Noah Wylie) was becoming cranky after having been the most dedicated and sympathetic of young doctors. He began avoiding emotional snags with patients, such as leveling with them or their families, became testy and hypercritical, and preoccupied himself with personal gratification and hopes of a prestigious fellowship. He even spread gossip about beloved chief resident Dr. Mark Greene. Yet all the while, the audience sympathizes with Carter and understands his lapses in judgment as a form of stress. When the character played by Red Buttons, an old show biz type named Rubadoux, discovers that Carter has avoided alerting him to the seriousness of his wife's condition, partly because Rubadoux has been a nuisance and partly because of Carter's ambition for that fellowship, Rubadoux tells Carter off.

When Carter hears of the death of Mrs. Rubadoux, he does feel remorseful, and he shows the strength of character to attend the funeral and to apologize at the cemetery. He tells Rubadoux: "I'm very sorry about your wife. I made a mistake. Not in the way I treated her, but in the way I treated you. I wasn't honest, wasn't fair. I was wrong. And I'm very, very sorry." Rubadoux responds coldly, "This day isn't about you, Mr. Carter." After such a moving, obviously heartfelt apology! Carter even places his hand on the casket, after Rubadoux walks off, as an expression of contrition and of affection for the deceased.

Aside from the question of whether a senior citizen in mourning would use such a 1990s expression at a time when most mourners, of any age, draw upon more primal vocabulary, we do have another instance of a basic inability to forgive that surfaces even—or especially—in the hour of mourning. True, the Hebrew Sages taught that one should not try to engage in conversation with someone when his dead lie before him. The timing is wrong. Yet Carter did speak from the heart, and Rubadoux's gut response was ungracious rebuff. This at a time when TV writers seem to delight in depicting Jews as unforgiving, and applauding them for it. Is there a penchant for revisiting some aspects of Shylock in TV writing circles?

Why did the writers and producers need to make Rubadoux Jewish, anyway? I suppose the rabbi of *In the Heat of the Night* had to be Jewish, but why depict Jews as unforgiving without making them accountable to Judaism's teachings regarding forgiveness?

Religious Stances as "Temporary Insanity": "Seventh Heaven"

After two episodes featuring eldest son Matt's (Barry Watson) whirlwind romance and elopement with Sarah (Sarah Danielle Madison), daughter of Rabbi Richard and Rosina Glass (Richard Lewis and Laraine Newman), *Seventh Heaven* pressed toward the end of its sixth season (2001-2002) by testing and provoking around the theme of interfaith marriage. The engaging series about a minister and his family was clearly poised to push the envelope. The couple keeps their marriage a secret and plans an interfaith wedding in order to involve their families in the union that has already taken place.

Even in the two episodes in which they are not featured, the presence of the Jewish parents is very much felt. One of these, written by writer/creator Brenda Hampton, who introduced the interfaith marriage theme, ups the ante of interfaith romance by pairing off Matt's college-age sisters with two Catholic brothers. The Jewish parents came across from the start as rude and confrontational, in marked contrast with the graciousness of Matt's parents, Reverend Eric and Annie Camden (Stephen Collins and Catherine Hicks). In fact, Matt's dad the minister says early on to the bride and groom, "Have I told you that despite all the shock and surprise of this sudden romance, that I'm genuinely delighted to see my son as much in love with his future bride as I am with my wife?"

One episode provided the requisite Shabbat dinner. This one was given over to writer Paul Perlove who turned up the histrionics. It began with Annie Camden frantically cooking kugel and other kasha once she hears they have been invited to Rabbi and Rosina Glass's home. Though the

Glasses have not asked her to cook, she feels obliged to try her hand at following Jewish recipes.

The entire episode comes across as a study in good intentions leading to disastrous faux pas under emotionally-charged circumstances. The Camden's younger son Simon (David Gallagher), insists on bringing along a "half-Jewish" friend who is "a good student, honest, responsible," and who is intended to be a sixteen-year-old "example that mixed marriages actually work." Much to Simon's consternation, however, this kid cannot tell the Jewish holidays apart. It's hard to know whether this is some sort of commentary on children of interfaith marriage or simply comic relief.

Things really go down hill when the rabbi reveals that Matt is planning to convert to Judaism. Apparently, Matt has not yet found the "right moment" to tell his parents, and in an uncharacteristic fit of rancor, Rev. Camden condemns the "changing of religion like the changing of a shirt," telling Matt, in the presence of all gathered at the Shabbat table, "I know what you are and what you're not. You're not a Jew." The reverend protests that for 21 years his son has had "one, abiding concept" in his life, Jesus, and now he takes one bite of kugel, and "it's not even Jewish kugel, it's WASP kugel, and suddenly no Jesus."

Rev. Camden's anger in that scene was the only moving moment in the entire cycle of the Matt-Sarah saga. He is genuinely concerned about religious integrity. The impression given is that the rabbi and his wife do not share those concerns. The rabbi apologizes that, though he is Reform, his wife keeps kosher because she was "raised that way." Every Jewish home, he adds, observes Shabbat differently. (There are no two Jewish homes that observe it in somewhat the same way?) Rosina Glass leaves the table in tears when the minister's wife says that she put cream in the kugel instead of (non-kosher?) chicken fat. The rabbi seems clueless as to whether his wife is concerned about the mixing of meat and dairy, or, as Rosina later tells Annie, that she is emotional about her daughter's upcoming marriage.

The real question here is whether the rabbi has any sensibilities, religious or otherwise. He has no concept that raising the issue of Matt's conversion at the Shabbat table is insensitive, whether Matt has told his parents or not. The Camdens join Rabbi Glass at the temple later that night, for a "brief service" that is described as a prelude to "more cake and coffee." After publicly welcoming Matt and his family into the Glass family, the rabbi invites the minister to the pulpit to quote Matt's philosophy that "love" transcends churches and temples ("and all other faiths," to be politically correct). Still, writer Perlove entitled that episode "Lip Service," as if to say that no one will live up to this "profound" doctrine.

In the final episode, written by Sue Tenney, Rosina tells her husband, the rabbi, who is having second thoughts about the wedding: "The heart wants what the heart wants. She [Sarah] fell in love with Matt, like I fell in love with you." "But I'm Jewish," the rabbi interjects. Note his wife's response: "And if you weren't, do you really think I would have listened to my parents if they had forbidden me to marry you?" What sort of loyalty to one's religion is this from a partner of the clergy, about whom we hear more than once that her religious commitments are solely the result of how she was "brought up"?

Religious loyalties aside, writer Tenney seemed intent on making Rabbi Glass the most indelicate and pushy character ever portrayed on the series, and actor Richard Lewis was more than happy to oblige. Lewis struggled embarrassingly with the Hebrew, but knew exactly how to keep his rabbi just obnoxious enough. In the penultimate episode, the rabbi usurps the entire "interfaith" wedding ceremony, doling out to the minister the "candle-holding." The rabbi and his wife devalue the rehearsal dinner that is so important to the minister and his wife, yet insist on a kosher dinner in their future in-laws' yard for some 100 Jewish relatives. The rabbi continues to push for Matt's conversion and insists that it be announced at the wedding. (All rabbis I know would regard this as crass and as disrespectful to Matt's parents.) The rabbi declares to Matt that, as a Reform rabbi, he regards *milah* (ritual circumcision) and *mikvah* (ritual immersion) as "optional," and would be happy with a "public pledge" that Matt will enter into "a covenant with God, establish a Jewish home...[and] stay active in the synagogue." Someone has obviously done homework as to the requirements and easements regarding conversion among different streams in Judaism. The reference to "a" covenant inserts a strange relativity into a rabbi's reference to a central doctrine of Jewish belief and practice—namely, God's Covenant (*b'rit*), or pact, with the Jewish People.

While it seems that Matt's parents are reconciled with his intention to convert down the line, his father goes ballistic again when he hears that Matt is considering conversion before the wedding. He is even willing to concede that "our religion" is not better than Judaism or any other, but he cannot in good conscience allow Matt to "make a decision about changing faith so quickly." Matt is attracted to conversion as "maybe" the way to bring him and Sarah together as "one family, one religion."

When push comes to shove, when it comes to what is explicitly called the "battle" over the wedding, writer Tenney is unable or unwilling to depict either the minister or the rabbi as zealous for his religion. Sarah lashes into her father, "If you think he's converting to enter into a covenant between God and the Jewish People, then good. But if, as I suspect, you're only doing this as a last ditch effort to try to cause some sort of drama that might cause my wedding not to happen, then…Abraham himself is not going to protect you from my wrath." So all of Rabbi-Dad's talk of Covenant and God is regarded by his own daughter as empty rhetoric to sabotage the wedding? Likewise, Matt tells his father that Dad's angst is not "about religion, but about not wanting me to grow up." So all of Minister-Dad's concern about religion is not really religious after all? Indeed, in the final episode, the minister himself will attribute his concern to "temporary religious insanity." Yet all of this talk about "growing up" seems disingenuous because the writers all infantalize Matt and Sarah by depicting them in need of the wise counsel of Matt's wunderkind eleven-year-old sister, Ruthie (Mackenzie Rosman).

Here we have one of television's finest family shows (at least until these episodes), a program that offered a few years before one of TV's best efforts at Holocaust education, a popular icon at the height of its powers, telling the public that there are no religious issues. "There is nothing to get worked up over," *Seventh Heaven* declared, "Religion does not matter. Sure, there are 'differences,' but 'family' sanctions religion. Religion does not really shape family. Relationships, in the family and otherwise, 'transcend' religion and religions."

Could it be that, in the wake of the barbaric attacks on America of September 11, 2001, in the name of "religion," all religious stands subsequently depicted on *Seventh Heaven* were dismissed as "Holy Wars," the disparaging title chosen for the "Jewish" wedding episodes? The writers and producers betrayed an aversion to invoking God when they put in the mouth of Lucy, the daughter who wants to study for the ministry (!), the typical New Age phrase, "The universe is not happy with your plan."

The season's final episode, also written by Tenney, is a study in contrasts. Both the rabbi and the minister become worked up to the point that they threaten not to attend the wedding. Both Matt and Sarah tell their recalcitrant fathers that they may never forgive them if they boycott the wedding. Rev. Eric finds good counsel in *his* father to the effect that Matt is not rejecting Eric or his values, but, rather, finding his own way: "As long as he goes out into the world and does some good, does it matter if he's Christian or not?" (I would think that it would matter to a devout Christian, particularly to a minister.) Eric can say to Matt, "My dad taught me forgiveness. I want to be there for you and for me and for Sarah when you convert." The rabbi complains about his parents and clearly regards them as a burden. He, too, will forgive, if not forget, but mainly because of Eric's appreciation of his own father's advice, and only after his wife and daughter have already secured the services of another rabbi.

Is such characterization of the rabbi's—and to some extent, the minister's—pettiness intended to promulgate a belief that all religious loyalties and commitments must be regarded as "temporary insanity" when in conflict with "what the heart wants"?

Jewish Rituals as Sex Appeal: "Gideon's Crossing"

The medical series with the intense but lovable African American chief of experimental medicine, Dr. Gideon, affably but commandingly played by Andre Braugher, featured a male Jewish intern, Dr. Bruce Cherry (Hamish Linklater). Writer Samantha Howard Corbin saw to it that Dr. Cherry found the Gentile woman of his dreams while making a college try to seek out Jewish women.

Though not particularly religious, the resourceful young doctor shows up at the hospital one fine day donning a *yarmulke* (skullcap). When a colleague from Wyoming asks what he is wearing, Cherry condescendingly assumes that "my goyishe friend," as he calls him, is not familiar with *yarmulkes*. Yet the latter makes it clear that he knows what it is but wonders why Cherry is wearing one all of a sudden. "There are Jews in Wyoming," the colleague protests, though it is hard for him to name one when cross-examined by Cherry. It seems that the writer wanted to burst the stereotype that Jews live only in New York or in Boston (where the drama takes place). Yet with the latter exchange she may have undermined her own point.

An African American colleague gets a better line when he asks, simply, "Since when are you one of the chosen people?" It is a legitimate question, especially when one considers Cherry's explanation for his choice to wear a *kippah* (Hebrew for *yarmulke*, a Yiddish word). "I've been playing the dating game all wrong," he confesses. "I haven't been playing to my strengths—straight, Jewish, doctor, no hair on my back." Picking up on

Cherry's artifice, Cherry's Wyoming friend observes: "So you're hoping the beanie will act as a sort of homing device?" The viewer has already learned to regard Cherry as somewhat cynical and as a bit of an operator and manipulator.

So the scenario suggested here is not only par for Cherry's course, but the "Jewish" use of Cherry's all-too-often misguided energies. Cherry tells his friends, "I'm going to temple. A little Torah reading, a little davening, and then I'm in fat city." Obviously, he's ready for samplings of the religious rituals if this puts him at a useful vantage point to meet single Jewish women. When asked, "When was the last time that you were in temple?" Cherry responds: "It's like riding a bike. You never lose it." He goes to the synagogue happy in his expectation that it will be, as a colleague puts it, a "seedy meat market." Yet he is surprised and chagrinned that the temple he has chosen consists of old men who need him to make a *minyan* (quorum for prayer). They have not had a *minyan*, the rabbi says, in ten years!

One wonders exactly what point writer Corbin intended to make. Did she want to make some kind of comment about the larger congregations with singles services—namely, that their "user" mentality contributes to the aging and decline of other congregations? Or is she simply bringing some humor and irony—and poetic justice—to her self-indulgent and self-serving character's uninformed choice of a congregation?

Noteworthy, by the way, is the writer's depiction of the rabbi. She is careful to make him explain some of the mindset of traditional Judaism, having him quibble even over Cherry's use of the word, "temple," as a trivialization of "the importance of the Temple [in Jerusalem]." Later, the rabbi relates to a new friend of Cherry's that the young doctor showed great commitment in attending the service, risking embarrassment but having nobly "kept on" with the rituals. The rabbi is touched that Cherry kept reciting the Hebrew alphabet throughout the service. This is, of course, reminiscent of a story told by the Baal Shem Tov, the founder of Hasidism in the eighteenth century, who spoke of an ignorant shepherd boy who knew only the Hebrew alphabet. The boy prayed that God arrange the letters according to His will—a prayer regarded in Hasidic lore as most pleasing and precious to God. What does our writer do with this story? Is she trying to highlight some hidden piety, or at least a desire to pray or to help the congregation, on the part of Dr. Bruce Cherry? Or is it meant as a kind of rote recitation out of boredom to fill in the time at the service? Why allude to such a charming story without explaining the reference and being clear about how the allusion is meant to have us understand the character?

Ironically, the rabbi relates the story of Cherry's pious (?) recitation of the Hebrew alphabet to a Gentile "floating nurse practitioner," Money Raspberry DuPree, whom Cherry meets while treating a case involving the charming and almost mystic eccentricities of a Caribbean patient. The French-speaking young woman, from New Orleans, is familiar with the patient's concerns and sensitive to them. Bruce is more "rational." Yet they bond almost immediately and the mutual attraction is clearly strong and immediate. "I'm a dark, angst-filled brooding mess, Money," he protests. "You know what they say about opposites," she quips. "They attract, they get together, and eventually they end up trying to beat each others' brains out with shovels."

While preparing to step out with his new girlfriend to explore her cultural haunts, Bruce Cherry runs into the rabbi, who appears to have pursued him in the hospital in order to ensure a *minyan* for the Friday night service. Money graciously prods Bruce to attend the service after hearing the story of his recitation of the Hebrew letters in prayer, but indicates that she will date him on Monday. The writer suggests that Cherry's "religiosity" is attractive to Money, and makes sure to have the rabbi ask at the end, "Is she Jewish?"

For some reason, Ms. Corbin has chosen to utilize Jewish observances and lore not so much to underscore the ambivalences and machinations of her character as to bring some flavor and respectability and maybe even a modicum of likeability to his usually obnoxious behavior. This is, to say the least, a disquieting use of Jewish rituals which, in the context of this hour, serve to frustrate and to pull apart what "spirituality" has put together. The "spirituality" here, by the way, rests in Caribbean customs. This is what brings the couple together when the old time religion and its God would keep them apart. Yet "spirituality" is polite to the old time religion. It kindly allows Cherry to fulfill his obligation to the *minyan* despite the rabbi's (inevitably?) impolite question at the end.

Given the "character" that Corbin (and, one must assume, the writing staff as a whole) gave to the Cherry persona, it was easy for subsequent writers to continue to render him the vain and thoughtless one among the interns and residents. He is, after all, the one who tips off a colleague's father, stricken with pneumonia and lung cancer, to a place where he can smoke. (Writer Eric Overmyer felt compelled to insert that scene into another episode.) The writers definitely want their main Jewish character to be consistently self-absorbed, but stop short of making him careless and slipshod. Obviously the staff expended a lot of time and energy making Bruce Cherry the poster boy for stylized heedlessness.

Flip Gothic Judaism:
"Home Court"

NBC's (thankfully) short-lived 1995-1996 TV series, *The Home Court*, was consistently obnoxious in its Jewish noises. Set in Chicago, *Home Court* testified to the life of a divorced judge, Sydney Solomon (Pamela Reed), who presides over family court during the day and then deals with her four children, one pre-teen, one fourteen-year-old, and two teens, at night.

Reed and the rest of the cast were talented enough, and they might even have been pleasant were they not pressed into a formula where both mother and children were forced at every moment to combine cuteness with rebelliousness. The working mother here was expected to be both maternal and vampy, wise and free-spirited. While society does expect working mothers to be all things, and unfairly, the glaring problem with *Home Court* was that it put its protagonist through every possible awkwardness, resulting in perpetual frustration, and then held up the souped-up, senseless characterization as some kind of role model.

As if it weren't bad enough that the writers didn't know how to handle the subject of working mothers, it is even worse that they couldn't let go of any opportunity to joke about the family's "Jewishness." In an episode with a fairly nice premise—the judge's daughter defying her mother by dating a convict who had been in Mom's court, and learning about a similar act of rebellion by her mother in high school—a vulgar side theme emerges of the older male siblings among the judge's children trying to frighten their youngest brother as he prepares for his bar mitzvah. Writers Larry Spencer and Sy Rosen, and director Noam Pitlik, find a way to hang a sinister edge on the bar mitzvah ceremony which is now a widely understood and oft-attended event by Americans of many backgrounds. Yet the older siblings ask young Ellis, "Aren't you afraid of the secret ritual?" which turns out to be a "continuation" of circumcision. "I thought they did that when I was born," Ellis protests. "That was just the starter course," his brother tells him.

Viewers learn that this little scare tactic is the "Solomon bar mitzvah story," a "tradition" through which the "[teasing about the] scissors" is "passed on to the next generation." But Mother does not seem aware of the family tradition when she innocently comforts Ellis, stating that the "only hard part is having to sing through it." Ellis bolts from the room screaming, "I don't want to be a man." One wants to ask: Where have the writers been? What Jewish child (not to mention many non-Jewish children) does not have a very clear idea of what happens at a bar mitzvah? The writers tell us that at twelve Ellis is "starting Hebrew school soon." No wonder he is clueless. Most American synagogues insist on at least four to six years of Jewish education before bar mitzvah. If the "Jewish" motif of a sitcom does not get across the typical flow of American Jewish education and bar mitzvah preparation, then what is the point of it? The circumcision jokes were already pretty tired on *Cheers* and *Seinfeld*, and these were much better written shows to begin with.

The gracelessness and lack of focus of *Home Court*, both with respect to Jewishness and in every other way, came to the fore in an episode in which son Marshall (Robert Gorman), the 14-year-old, feels profound guilt after "making out" with a girl during a great uncle's funeral. The theme leads writers Larry Spencer and Vicky S. Horwits to write a prayer to God uttered by young Marshall in a moment of remorse: "I probably should have sent you a thank you note after my bar mitzvah. How often does a 14-year-old get to make out with a pretty girl over his uncle's casket? Just don't send me to Hell."

It seems that neither Marshall nor the writers can distinguish, even in the prayers, between worship of God and ancestor worship! In a scene reminiscent of *Carrie*, but not clever enough even to be a parody of it, Marshall lights several candles, *yahrzeit* candles, both as an altar to be able to pray to God and as a kind of shrine to his uncle. The writers insist on the "Jewish" themes so that they can put their characters into bizarre rituals and suggest that their "religious" impulses lead to strange behavior. Yet they allow Marshall's all-wise mom, the judge, to tell him, "We're Jewish. We grieve by eating. You paid your respects at the funeral, right?" All is resolved by a wink and an off-color response. Marshall can honestly tell his mom that, at the funeral, he was "touched" and "felt something," and Mom dispenses brilliant moral instruction in her judicious sitcom way, "You'll know you're ready to have sex when I tell you you're ready." It's amazing what a moment with Mom at the end of an episode can do. Marshall is "cured" of going to school with a *yarmulke*, rosary beads and a Buddha in his knapsack.

Did the writers think they were grappling with serious issues of death and guilt in a "witty" and "New Age" style? There is a near-tender moment here when Marshall's older brother reassures him in an empathic way that "I've done stuff far worse than this and I haven't been punished." Those potentially touching and meaningful exchanges, however, were not built upon in this series.

Home Court suggested that Jews deal with life cycle situations in vulgar ways. The judge tries to divide all of her uncle's property during the funeral, and arranges a drawing or lottery as a weird diversion at the *shiva*. (Note that most of the "Jewish humor" was associated with death.) The writers never got around to explaining where our judge Sydney Solomon, who constantly identifies herself as Jewish, picked up a sister (Meagan Fay) who conveys stereotyped main-line, WASP neuroses, and has a son named "Christian."

In the final episode, Sydney's ex-husband, a brilliant laboratory researcher, visited, and convinced her that a near-death experience transformed him from fussy and anal, to spontaneous and sexually appealing. Sydney resolves to run off with him on a vacation, choosing him over her new, attentive boyfriend, only to discover that he has become too irresponsible. One is reminded of an episode of *Northern Exposure* in which Dr. Joel's Jewish mother was rendered more bearable once exposed to Native American legend, and yet no longer functional. The implication here is that the Jewish ex-husband from Atlanta (at least Jews are not stereotyped here as New Yorkers only) became more interesting, and yet even more neurotic, when confronted by death, which "exposes" the limitations of his own background.

It's too bad that *Home Court* turned out to be so obnoxious. Judge Solomon liked being a Jewish mother. ("Not since Noah built his ark has a Jewish mother been so proud," she says at one point.) She was the only character on TV who prominently displayed Jewish ritual objects in her home; but the writers would not allow us to like the characters—or their Judaism, which was associated with "Gothic" themes of death and castration, and was more silly than scary.

Jewish Ritual Over Jewish Children:
"Family Law"

What happens when an interfaith marriage breaks up over the return to religious roots on the part of both partners, and they battle for custody of the children in order to raise them exclusively in one faith?

This is the intriguing and slippery question explored in a 2001 episode of *Family Law*, a study in a law firm specializing in domestic issues. The episode presents a morality play on ethics, divorce, and religious conflict.

It seems that young attorney Danni Lipton is offered the case she wants to refuse, that of a Baptist father and Orthodox Jewish mother who each want their daughter's soul, or at least full attention, religiously speaking. The parents are played with just the right understatement by James Acheson and Lisa Edelstein. Sashawnee Hall is most affecting as their six-year-old daughter, who is torn and almost driven to atheism because she regards her parents' bitter struggle as the result of their efforts to make her "good."

The hour-long drama is fine at depicting the psychology of both parents, child and lawyers. Writers Bill Chais and Stephen Nathan have tried hard to treat both religions respectfully and to offer thoughtful dialogue. Chais and David Shore came up with the storyline. The writers take pains to convey an appreciation of the theology of both faiths, and even of the doubts and frustration of secularists of both Jewish and Christian background.

At the outset, Attorney Danni Lipton (Julie Warner) asks her client, the mother, whether she discussed religious issues with her ex-husband before they were married. The mother responds, "We were both secular." When their daughter was born, she explains, the husband saw the event as a miracle and reconnected to his fundamentalist church. Moved (or spooked?) by his religious return, the mother came to embrace Orthodox Judaism and to keep kosher and not answer the phone on the Sabbath. She becomes indignant when her daughter tells her that "Daddy says if Mommy doesn't love Jesus, she'll go to Hell." The child's mantra is the fearful question, "Is Mommy really going to Hell?"

The mounting conflict in the courtroom opens a can of worms of ambivalences and religious loyalties in the law firm itself. Danni shows her discomfort with the entire scenario when she asks her colleagues, "Who are my expert witnesses? Moses and Jesus?" A male colleague, played by Tony

Danza, sighs that all the suffering in the world, such as the Holocaust, slavery and AIDS in Africa, indicate that, at best, "God is on vacation."

We are told quite early in the drama why Danni is so ambivalent about the case. She says that she is Jewish but has been raised with a smattering of Jewish instruction and observances because her father, a Holocaust survivor, chose assimilation over being "different." Yet she is reluctant to tell her father that her boyfriend is not Jewish. For most of the hour she proclaims that there can be no justification even for disagreement over religious doctrines. Ms. Lipton tells the parents: "One of you is going to lose custody because of these beliefs. Is it worth it?" Or, as she complains to the head of the law firm (Kathleen Quinlan): "They're both equally decent parents and they're both equally insane."

At one point, her Orthodox client asks her, "You're Jewish, aren't you? Can't you understand [that] it might be important to me to preserve our people, to pass on my way of life to my daughter?" Danni responds by dismissing the question, "Your way of life isn't mine. When the sun goes down on Friday, I'm going to turn on my TV; at a restaurant, I'm going to eat a cheeseburger." The client clearly wants to strike a nerve when she replies, "But you're still a Jew, Ms. Lipton. The world sees you that way. I believe that God spoke at Sinai and gave the Jews a mission, to give values and wisdom to the world." The dialogue here provides a fine interpretation of the biblical notion of the "chosen people." A sacred role for Jews is affirmed in the discussion of Judaism.

There is an impression given here that the more Danni has to deal with her Jewishness, the more she finds herself showing hostility to a female colleague, Randi King, played by Dixie Carter, who is assigned to the case because she is a Baptist and a believing Christian. At one point this colleague tells Danni, "You want to help me bring down my own religion?" Randi admits that the "doctrine of redemption [through Christ] is compli- cated."

The writers' efforts to respect the complexities of both religions are admirable, but some of the old Christian canards about Judaism are given forum without sufficient refutation, while the allegations of a "dark side" to Christianity are given meaningful response. Thus, for example, when Danni's Baptist colleague blurts out, "All the fear and violence comes out of the Old Testament. That's why we needed a new one," nothing is really said to counter the statement. The writers prefer to depict it as a defensive remark when, in fact, it has been used for centuries by various churches as an assault on Judaism. True, the writers decide to "respond" somewhat by having Danni's Gentile boyfriend extol the wisdom of the Talmud which he had studied evenings at a kibbutz in Israel where he had once visited and volunteered. None of these praises of the "Jewish side" are as heartfelt as Danni's colleague's testimony that, doctrines of damnation notwithstanding, "If I do a good thing, it is from love of Jesus." The Talmudic Sages taught over 2,000 years ago that whatever one does, it should be out of love for God, but we don't learn that here.

In all fairness to the writers, I must point out that they do have Danni discover some beautiful laws about compassion in the Talmud. Our attorney does follow her boyfriend's advice. She reads up on Judaism. She is impressed with a law that one must send away the mother bird if one needs an egg from the nest, in order that the mother not suffer distress. (The law is indeed discussed in the Talmud, by the way, but its source is the Torah, Deut. 22:6-7). After her Baptist colleague accuses her of being "vengeful" in the way she responds during a cross examination, Danni does try to show more understanding, and they both laugh about their nasty behavior. The writers do not try to connect Danni's increasing mellowness with her study of Judaism. Her colleague seeks solace and counsel in the church at every turn.

The treatment of judges and of legal issues here is creative, informative, and realistic. The case is indeed a lot for courts to deal with, given a reluctance to cross church (or synagogue)-state boundaries. At first a judge rules that the mother had agreed in her wedding vows to raise her daughter as a Christian. If this is not done, the lawyers worry, the mother is in breach of the custody agreement. Then the judge is swayed by Danni's argument that the mother has a Constitutional right to change her mind on religion and to expose her child to those changes. Danni then requests that the judge withdraw because she is a Christian and therefore "biased." Both counsels agree on a Buddhist judge (after rejecting a judge with a Jewish name, of course). The good news here is that the writers do not allow the episode to become a clearing house for New Age propaganda that Buddhism is a more neutral and therefore "spiritual" (as opposed to "religious") faith. Indeed, the conflict would be just as great were a Buddhist parent determined to ship off a child thought to be a reincarnated lama to Tibet against the wishes of a Christian or a Jewish parent. In fact, there could be deep tensions in a custody agreement between an observant and a non-observant Jew. One can understand, however, why the writers chose to hone in on Orthodox Jewish/Christian Right struggles in the wake of the 2000

Election, in which both groups received much hype due to the respective beliefs of Joseph Lieberman and George W. Bush.

The teleplay does give the Orthodox mother the last word in defending her religious convictions and the social and cultural observations that prompted them. Danni tells her that she has learned a lot about her own Jewish heritage that she likes, but that she prizes her independence, her work, more. The client knowingly responds that Orthodox women can have careers, too, but that "Everything's tighter for Orthodox women. But does that make it wrong, or does it just make us value our lives more?" The writers hold back, however, from depicting the scope of Orthodox Jewish beliefs in the afterlife.

There are indeed a lot of well-taken and well-intentioned twists and turns in this tale of interfaith marriage and divorce. The hour might even be considered a warning to think twice about such marriages, or at least to get an iron-clad prenuptial agreement. It also points to a certain dishonesty on the part of the Baptist father who at first denies telling his daughter that he believes his ex-wife will go to Hell, and then seems to admit having said it, even as he confesses publicly at the trial that he does hold, as Danni puts it, that Buddha, Gandhi, and Jews killed by Christians in the Inquisition and the Holocaust, are in Hell.

From the point of view of classical Judaism, and within the context of the plot itself, the ending is unsatisfying, inconsistent, tragic and most offensive. The (Buddhist) judge threatens to put the child into a foster home unless the parents work things out. So, all of a sudden, Danni becomes a rabbi and invokes the account of Rebeccah in Genesis to exhort the mother to send away her child as Rebeccah sent away Jacob when he was in danger. "She'll always be a Jew," Danni says, "because of you."

While the decision is purportedly Rebeccah's, the "solution" is clearly borrowed from the account of King Solomon and the two women fighting over the baby. The one who is not willing to cut the baby in half turns out to be the real mother. In the Solomon narrative, however, the baby is not given away. In Judaism, the turning over of a Jewish child is unthinkable; it is oppression personified. It is also not necessary in Protestant theology, where performing baptism before the child can make a mature decision for Christ is discouraged. If, as the father said, he sees Christianity as the "fulfillment" of Judaism, then it makes more sense to build up the Judaism in the child first so that there is something to "complete."

Rabbi Samuel Dresner wrote: "If Christianity has been a 'religion of rescue,' concerned with bringing salvation to the sinner…then Judaism has been a religion of inoculation and immunity....But the truth of the matter is that while salvation may be more dramatic than prevention, it may well be offered too late."[5]

Likewise, the Yiddish poet, Jacob Glatstein, spoke of parents and teachers guiding the "blind fingers" of the next generation over the precious sacred literature as over Braille, in order to inoculate children from the outside world. The test for every Jewish child is whether the inoculation holds. Have we come to a generation of Jews (and of Jewish television writers) who believe that Jewishness is "because" of birth and not an inoculation of identity and belief and observance that must be allowed to "take" before being ravaged by outside doctrines and cultures?

---

5.   Samuel H. Dresner, *The Jew in American Life* (N.Y.: Crown Publishers, 1963), p. 77.

9

INVERTED HOSTILITIES

ഉറ

Shema Without Scruples:
"Picket Fences"

In 1994, *Picket Fences*, David E. Kelley's clever, well-crafted and well-acted series, offered an episode that was clearly directed at rabbis like me. It seems that the obnoxious and unethical local Jewish attorney in a small Wisconsin town, Douglas Wambaugh, has been expelled from the synagogue by his rabbi (Barry Primus), who could no longer tolerate Wambaugh's annoying antics and character, as portrayed all too well by Fyvush Finkel. The last straw, as far as the rabbi was concerned, was an impromptu eulogy at the funeral of a temple member in which Wambaugh told a "politically incorrect" joke with a racist punchline insulting to both Jews and Native Americans.

Wambaugh is obviously very hurt by the rabbi's words and actions. Unable to chase ambulances for days afterwards, he pines and sulks and his helper, the sheriff's daughter, cannot console him. (For some reason, Kelley wrote the character of Wambaugh's wife out of the episode, offering the disclaimer that she was visiting a sister. That was interesting because his wife is sympathetically presented and portrayed in contrast to Wambaugh himself. It is almost as if the writer decided to let Wambaugh stand on his own for the purpose of allowing him to accumulate sympathy points.)

Wambaugh determines that he will bring the rabbi to a *Bet Din* (Rabbinic Court). He tells his helper, "I'm a good Jew. I'm a God-fearing man. I've been a religious Jew all my life." He is confident that he can defend himself at the *Bet Din* because he fancies himself a "good rebutter."

The senior rabbi who is in charge of the *Bet Din* is a dignified and impressive figure. He explains that the Rabbinic Court operates on the principle of *peshara*, "fair compromise," and that "Each of you must be prepared to make concessions." He chides the rabbi in Wambaugh's congregation for tones of ridicule, and begins the proceedings with an appropriate prayer from the Hebrew liturgy (which comes across as esoteric because it is not translated).

This episode of *Picket Fences* may well be the most widely seen depiction of a *Bet Din* in the history not only of large or small screen, but of the novel, as well; the most famous such novel probably being Harry Kemelman's first mystery, *Friday The Rabbi Slept Late* (1964). The presiding rabbi wants to know how the local rabbi could expel Wambaugh when Jews who have served time for murder have been allowed into temples. The local rabbi responds that Wambaugh "epitomizes the most negative characterization of a Jewish lawyer," and that this is "in a way worse than murder because his behavior disparages an entire culture." He adds: "Douglas Wambaugh *is* the ugly caricature...." He says that Wambaugh's behavior "fosters anti-Semitic stereotypes."

Unable to contain himself, Wambaugh breaks into Yiddish to vent his protest against what he regards as unfair indignity. (Why is Yiddish always TV's language of anger or vulgarity?) He then observes that the rabbi is advancing stereotypes that Jews turn upon one another (!). Wambaugh insists that his ploys and deceptions as a lawyer must be understood as the manifestations of "Wambaugh the lawyer, the hustler, not the Jew."

Another member of the *Bet Din*, a lay member (and I give the writer credit for showing that in Judaism one does not have to be a rabbi to be regarded as an authority or to play a significant role in ritual), nicely played by Paul Eiding, replies, "That's not the way the people see it....The ambulance chasing shyster is a negative image that has plagued us. My father was a Jewish attorney. He was victimized by that caricature."

Wambaugh is provided with strong comebacks by Kelley, who obviously thinks that his (admittedly) far-from-perfect character has been wronged, both within the drama and by critics of having such a persona on the series. "My father was in Poland," Wambaugh replies. "He died in an oven. Do you want to compare hardships?" (Note that the Holocaust is invoked by Wambaugh as justification.) And Wambaugh continues, "I suppose I could wake up each day and assume…. that the world is full of anti-Semites, but that would make me a bigot. I prefer to presume that the people are enlightened and not prejudiced."

In other words, Wambaugh believes he has the right to be insensitive and unethical, whether consciously or unconsciously, and to try to promote himself at any cost, and to get away with anything and everything he can, because he sees only the good in others and is certain that if they see the bad in him they will still recognize the nobility of the faith he professes. Maybe he is even promoting the faith because fair-minded Gentiles will research Judaism to see if he is for real!

There is more to Wambaugh's (and, I dare say, writer Kelley's) argument. "Integrity," quoth Wambaugh, "has never been mine to settle. I have it….but to get by I become Douglas Wambaugh, the character, the opportunist, the winner." Then, after making a stupid urinal joke and immediately acknowledging the inappropriateness of his own comment, Wambaugh confesses, "I'm a character. I embarrass myself. But I would not embarrass my God or my faith. If I have done so, I am nothing." (The latter sentence is particularly powerful, and forcefully delivered, getting across the point that Wambaugh really *believes* that he is a good Jew, and that being a Jew in good standing means everything to him.)

The pathos of Wambaugh's lines and of his tears is memorable. Finkel is particularly effective in his Yiddish outbursts, and who could be more adept at this than a veteran of the Yiddish theatre? One might speculate that the reason Finkel is so moving here is that he has been hurt by adverse criticism of his persona in columns such as mine, and in letters I'm sure the network has received, and uses his entire arsenal of dramatic skills, which is considerable, to strike back. Indeed, in interviews he has said that Wambaugh's raison d'etre as a character is precisely to show that he must not be identified with Jews in general, and that people who do that, especially Jews (and, one might add, even more so, rabbis) have their own problems of bigotry and of self-consciousness to work out.

In the episode, the local rabbi goes so far as to say that Jews like Wambaugh deter conversion of Gentiles and return to Judaism by born Jews. Such talk leaves Wambaugh speechless, and he who has specialized in crocodile tears cries real tears. (Hath not a stereotype feelings?) Yet the sheriff's daughter comes to the rescue, noting that she has reason to resent him because he defended the kid who shot her brother. She says that "while it's true he'll take any case for a fee, it's also true he'll take a case for no fee," citing copious examples. While it's true he delivered an offensive eulogy, at least he regards it as a duty to eulogize the dead when no one else will, even, on another occasion, a political enemy. He has "never done anything to deliberately hurt a person." She concludes, "Any temple, any faith, should be proud to claim him." Her eloquent defense of Wambaugh, plus a cute note from her little brother who has considered becoming Jewish, sway the *Bet Din*.

The presiding rabbi announces the *Bet Din*'s ruling that the local rabbi should reinstate Wambaugh's membership. He agrees that to assume that the general public attributes Wambaugh's conduct to an entire people is bigotry. Besides, if the sheriff's daughter regards him that well, he can't be hurting the Jews that much, anyway. After jokingly requesting that Wambaugh not stand up at his funeral, the rabbi dismisses the case.

The decision of the *Bet Din* is, of course, the agenda of Kelley and Finkel, but it is beside the point when it comes to the teachings of Judaism. For any religion worth its salt must consider (as much as impressions on other people) the effect of a person's actions on himself and how one's deeds reflect on God. Was Moses bigoted when he told the Israelites: "Observe these laws and norms faithfully, for that will be proof of your wisdom and discernment to other peoples" (Deut. 4:6)? Were the Talmudic Sages promoting bigotry when they interpreted the commandment, "You shall love the Lord your God" (Deut. 6:5) to mean, "You shall make the Lord your God *beloved*. Because of you [of your words, deeds, character] the name of God should become beloved"?

That is the meaning of *kiddush Hashem*, sanctification of God's name, in Judaism. One is concerned about the image of the individual Jew not because of bigots, not to keep Jews in the fold or to bring more people in, but because to truly love God one can't be a pietist at home or synagogue and a scoundrel at the office.

Integrity in Judaism is not, as Wambaugh would suggest, something one either has or doesn't have, but is something one must constantly achieve through worthy deeds. One achieves nothing in the moral sphere without a sense of embarrassment. Abraham Heschel observed that he dreads the thought of any Jew, of any human being, without a sense of embarrassment because it's what makes us human—and religious. Embarrassment, he wrote, "is a response to the discovery that in living we either replenish or frustrate a wondrous expectation. It involves an awareness of the grandeur of existence that may be wasted,...of unique moments missed."[1]

It is, after all, writer Kelley who raises the issue of embarrassment.

How is it possible to have a *Bet Din* of rabbis validate the right of a so-called "religious Jew" never to be embarrassed by behavior he admits is inappropriate, and to confuse an issue of *Kiddush Hashem*, the obligation to represent God well in this world, with a provocative test for human bigotry?

Kelley's work suggests two reasons. First, this episode presents us again with the only thing *Picket Fences* holds sacred—a court scene whose major purpose is to deal with bigotry. The presiding rabbi was simply filling in for the crusty old town judge, played by Ray Walston. It's all the same scenario in Kelley's series: the court scene and prejudices to battle. Ironically, the *Picket Fences Bet Din* makes its decision that it's all right not to be concerned about how Gentiles perceive Jews on the basis of the testimony of a young woman whom the writer is sure to identify as—a non-Jew!

Such confusion is possible, secondly, because this episode was never intended to get into the mindset of Judaism, but to exploit the institution of the *Bet Din* to promote the agenda and mission of this program—namely, to embody anti-Semitic stereotypes in the Wambaugh character in order to provoke people into responding strongly so that they can realize that their responses betray their own assumptions. Yet, according to Jewish belief and teachings, the provocation is itself problematic and offensive.

So we are left with what was definitely a first in the annals of American TV *or* literature—namely, taking up the cause of a self-avowed Jewish hypocrite with the goal of fighting prejudice by making as many viewers as possible feel sorry for him! Kelley actually tries to one-up Shakespeare who drummed up a little sympathy for a Shylock whom the Bard believed to have been locked into vengeance because of bigotry as well as belief. Kelley wants us to feel sorry for a Wambaugh who chooses to be a scoundrel "for the image" even though he has some sensibilities and is surrounded by people who want to like him. The episode actually fights for Wambaugh's right to choose to be irredeemable and to stifle his own awareness of wrongdoing: "Love me. I'm only hateful because I need a

---

1. Abraham J. Heschel, *Who Is Man?* (Stanford, California: Stanford University Press, 1965), p. 113.

provocative image. That's the only reason I purposely offend *people*, though I do love *God*."

I really wanted to like this episode. It uses good Hebrew terms and defines them well. It offers positive Jewish characters—the presiding rabbi, even the fed up local rabbi, to counterbalance less positive ones. It gives a certain dignity to Jewish traditions and even uses the Yiddish language effectively. Its use of Jewish concepts and institutions as its medium is attractive. I can't deny that, but in the last analysis, the medium is *not* the message. The message is the message. What is presented here is Kelley's view of Judaism as a lightning rod to expose bigotry rather than as a teaching to fashion better human beings.

In Judaism, the means of refining human thoughts and deeds is the *mitzvah*, the Divine Commandment, as found in the Torah. Kelley reduces the commandments to rituals with which Wambaugh fortifies his designs as the self-proclaimed town "character."

In a subsequent episode, the judge walks in on Attorney Wambaugh to find the latter wearing a *yarmulke* and reciting the *Shema* (Deut. 6:4) as he awaits word on a case that will take him to the Supreme Court. Wambaugh explains that he uses the *yarmulke* like "an ace bandage" when he's thinking deep thoughts, so as not to "pull a muscle." Actually, Wambaugh is using the *Shema* as a kind of wishing well. Jewish rituals are invoked by Kelley for his own utilitarian purpose—namely, to make Wambaugh more sympathetic, and, therefore, more an object of curiosity.

The *Shema* and the *Bet Din* on *Picket Fences* reinforce Kelley's depiction of Jews (Wambaugh on *Picket Fences* and Drs. Geiger and Shutt on *Chicago Hope*, etc.) as a test of the tolerance and sensitivity of others by virtue of their being strange and clever and "Jewish" and "characters."[2]

---

2.   To reinforce this concept of "Jewishness," Kelley brought Alan Dershowitz into the Supreme Court episodes with Wambaugh as if to endorse Dershowitz's thesis in *Chutzpah* (1991) that old religious teachings that Jews should behave so as to bring honor to God and the Jewish people are obsolete. Dershowitz declared that Jews ought to get beyond rituals and theology in order to develop an in-your-face political activism to preserve Jewish rights and foster justice in America and on the world scene. The problem is that, in the absence of the old religion, Dershowitz affirmed New Age concepts of synchronicity or being "blessed by destiny" in his subsequent volume, *The Vanishing American Jew* (1997), pp. 40-41.

Could there be some reverse bigotry—or maybe just plain bigotry—in this scenario?

The Synagogue as Vicious Cabal: "The Practice"

Producer/writer David E. Kelley took his series, *The Practice*, to the edge in a most outlandish way. He offered a 1999 episode about a popular middle aged rabbi (Michael Tucker, an alum of Kelley's *L.A. Law*) who is charged with raping a twenty-three-year-old African American female. The audience learns from the rabbi himself that he engaged in "forceable but consensual" sex with the young woman. We learn also, from the woman, that while the rabbi made it clear to her that "intermarriage" was unthinkable, he kept asking for "dates" from the time they met as counselors at a drug rehabilitation center. The rabbi also confides to his attorney that he believed that the woman's repeated efforts to break up with him were intended to excite his rage and to provoke "rough sex."

It is clear after only a few minutes of the episode that this is one warped rabbi. Kelley makes sure that the rabbi is branded an aberration when he has his eccentric Jewish character, Attorney Ellenor Frutt (Camryn Manheim) observe: "You know, there are thousands of model rabbis out there. Why is it the ones who come in here are all criminals?" "Because we're criminal defense attorneys," her boss reminds her.

Yet this is a very mild disclaimer indeed when one considers the temper and the implications of the rest of the hour. For here it is not so much the rabbi, as the synagogue board of directors, who are the offenders and the exploiters of people and of the law. The board is depicted with intimidating camera angles as a round table of arrogant power brokerage in the name of fundraising. They want the firm's black attorney (Steve Harris) to defend their rabbi against the black woman, and they have a large "settlement fund" to buy the freedom of the "enormously popular rabbi essential to our fundraising." Kelley envisions these Jews as conducting their meetings in the chapel of the synagogue, and their rabbi meets with his attorney in the sanctuary. (Hadn't the congregation which lent its beautiful facilities to this vicious fare read and discussed the script and the concept of the episode?)

The spokesman for the (all-male) board turns out to be a savvy lawyer, who attempts to coerce the rabbi's African American attorney into the ethically questionable act of trying to bribe the young woman before the

trial begins: "If this goes to trial, you'll know what you'll do to the girl."
Indeed, the emotionally powerful theme of the episode is not so much the
"rapist rabbi," as a member of the defense (!) law firm contemptuously
describes him. Rather, it's the tragedy of an African American lawyer
forced to impugn the reputation of a promising young woman of his own
race, in public and on the witness stand, because of a manipulative
synagogue board that insists on protecting its "popular rabbi" from the
wheels of justice. We learn that once before the board had paid off a
woman who claimed to have been raped by the rabbi. The refrain of
Kelley's depiction of synagogue politics is, "The synagogue handled
it"—namely, the rabbi's getting off scot-free.

When the African American lawyer bursts into a board meeting,
charging the trustees with perverting justice (with money, of course) in
order that their rabbi can keep them in the "best wood for pews" and the
"fanciest temple in town," a Jewish attorney responds that lawyers have no
right to get the whole truth from a client (even a rabbi or a synagogue
board), and that when lawyers take on a case they have a duty to see it
through. He sends the rabbi's lawyer to work on his summation, just as the
D.A. is doing. We've checked you out, he tells the African American, and
know that you will not quit on us—even, he suggests, if that means
destroying the lives of good African American people.

It is interesting that Kelley depicts the acid-tongued lawyer who is the
board's ringleader as the one *not* wearing a *yarmulke*, as if to say that the
others may be more "religious," or at least more demonstrative of rituals
and less forthcoming in their treachery.

Now I'm sure that Kelley intended to depict no more and no less than
an unusually bad rabbi. So why did Kelley depict the synagogue board as
manipulating a black man into compromising himself?

Actually, this episode was the logical culmination of years of Kelley
series. Tucker's old character, Stuart Markowitz of *L.A.Law*, could act up
and destroy his Christian mother-in-law's home at the first sign of anti-
Semitism. On *Chicago Hope* the Jewish doctors were defined by their
ability to act up verbally and to provoke others to act up. On *Picket Fences*
the attorney Wambaugh proclaimed the right of Jews to behave obnox-
iously and even unethically right in the faces of their clergy, as a test of
their own self-worth and of the tolerance level of others; *Ally McBeal* has
already dated a rabbi for shock effect.

For a long time now, Kelley has made it clear that he regards Jews as
a special, funny, perhaps bizarre people. He obsesses on Jews in his series.

What he admires about them are precisely the stereotypes of nervous energy, verbal adeptness, and cleverness in business and in manipulating systems. He associates Jews, as well, with defining but non-debilitating neuroses and stinging one-liners. At every opportunity he poses the question whether these are stereotypes or qualities that can lead either to achievement or treachery, perspective or hypocrisy.

It is almost as though Kelley wants to see his Jews denuded of any of the scruples and beliefs of Judaism so that he can let them demonstrate what they are and do in and of themselves. So Wambaugh of *Picket Fences* can exult in being a "character" without having to improve himself by the standards of Jewish beliefs and practices. The rabbis, however, cannot extricate themselves from Judaism. So they may be skirt chasers or zealots, but they are always talking about vengeance and money and deals and minor points of Jewish Law. It would seem that Kelley sees rabbis in the terms of the most vicious canards about "the Pharisees," and he regards Jews as amusing and colorful to the extent that they break away from Judaism. Why should we not assume that the board in this episode of *The Practice* is representative of how Kelley regards synagogue Jews?

The Synagogue as Vintage Television: "Thirtysomething"

The second season Christmas-Chanukah episode of *thirtysomething* (1987-1991), aired in 1988, remains, in the annals of American television, a significant statement about religion, mainly because it posits a similarity between Judaism (and religion in general), and old television reruns. While, at first, the episode written by producers Marshall Herskovitz and Edward Zwick, appears to ramble in a disjointed manner, as a kind of free-wheeling stream of consciousness, it does in fact have a pretty unified format and theme, though one wonders whether the writers are aware of the full ramifications of their concoction.

Whatever we can or cannot say about the intent of the writers, we can safely say that the hour is a refinement of the previous year's episode about the "December dilemma" of interfaith couple, Michael and Hope Steadman, played by Ken Olin and Mel Harris in their career-making roles. In that first episode, in 1987, the couple argued for the first time after years of marriage about whether to bring a Christmas tree into their home—a disagreement precipitated, as the writer, Richard Kramer, knowingly observed, by the arrival of their new daughter, Janie. The episode was effective at showing the audience that Michael's reluctance to incorporate Christmas into his home does not make him a "Scrooge," but a person who grew up in a different spiritual heritage. Still, Michael had been depicted consistently and unrelentingly as a brooding character, a worry-wart, as contrasted with Hope's upbeat "Protestant" outlook. By the end of that first season, the writers had succeeded in creating some moving moments in their depiction of mixed marrieds, but had offered a rather unoriginal Christmas-Chanukah episode that recycled the familiar O. Henry storyline, having the couple give each other the gift of their respective religious symbols, the tree and the menorah. The statement, while unoriginal, was still radical for television in its unequivocal declaration that religion is sanctioned by love relationships, as opposed to love relationships being sanctioned by religion.

The second year episode on the Christmas-Chanukah conflict gives the impression that the writers had thought about their first season and decided to produce something original and creative and even more respectful of Michael's feelings. They succeeded. The statement that they made in that second episode about the holiday season is, perhaps, even more radical and dismissive of religion, even though it ends up in a synagogue.

The familiar quarrel about holiday observances is prefaced by an opening scene which attests to the solid construction of the episode. Michael and Hope and their friends are playing a trivia game, and one of the gang protests that he is stuck again with questions about old TV shows. "Can't this generation define itself with something other than...songs [from] old television shows?" he protests. Another friend observes that mothers were often dead on the vintage TV shows, like *Bachelor Father, My Three Sons,* and *Family Affair.* These associations provide the psychic garden from which will sprout the dreams and daydreams that seize hold of Michael in the unfolding of subsequent events. His preoccupations also derive from plans to attend the unveiling of his father's tombstone just before Christmas, an imminent event that he obviously finds difficult to discuss. All he can do is mouth a weak joke about unveilings being after a year's time in order to make sure that the lamented is really dead.

Michael is ready to play the smart aleck once again in his annual spat with Hope over the Christmas dinner she is planning. He bargains, half playfully, half belligerently, "I'll give you the star and the three wise men if you agree to no lights outside, presents on at least two nights of Chanukah, and at least a fifty-per cent reduction in medium range ballistic missiles." Hope's response bares the scenario that the writers are determined to make right: "I just want this all to be o.k....Last year you were so sad and obnoxious." Immediately, the writers indicate that Michael is headed for higher consciousness, for he shows instant understanding that Hope is imploring him to give her Christmas, which means a great deal to her. Though he still can't understand her mania for seeking the "perfect" presents, he begins to make peace with her behavior, finding comic perspective for these simple conflicts in envisioning similar discussions on the classic *Dick Van Dyke Show.*

At the office Michael kibbitzes with his friend and partner, Elliot (Timothy Busfield), who brags about his history of "consorting with Jews" and tells Michael that he cherishes "Jewish warmth and infinite patience in the face of adversity." He does add jokingly: "Of course they killed our lord but I forgive them." Elliot fondly recalls losing his virginity to a Jewish girl, who dumped him for a Jewish boy, and then says that he thinks they both became Sikhs. Michael says that Elliot did marry his "own persuasion," whereas he, Michael, "might as well have heard voices" calling to him from the synagogue, "Michael, why did you do it? Why did you marry a *shiksa?*" Yet Elliot is quick to respond that he married within his faith and is now facing divorce—a point that the writers make over and over again, as if to foreshadow the ultimate lifting of Michael's cloud of guilt.

This is where the writers allow legitimate angst to banish guilt. Hope and baby daughter Janie get into an auto accident and, thankfully, escape serious injury, though Hope is quite banged up. As Michael contemplates the blessings and dangers of life, and continues to be exposed to Elliot's marital problems, he continuously seeks perspective in imagining his life as a *Dick Van Dyke Show* episode in which all endings are happy and the only religious presence to complicate life is a non-sectarian Santa Claus who solves all problems, grants all wishes, and demands no commitment of thought or observance and imposes no guilt. The Santa character is played cutely, and with an aloofness bordering on ominousness, by Jack Gilford.

Once reassured that Hope is recovering nicely in the hospital, Michael goes Christmas tree hunting with the help of his cousin Melissa, who is engagingly played on the series by Melanie Mayron. He is still shocked at seeing the extent of damage to Hope's car, so he is somewhat susceptible to Melissa's offer that he accompany her to her temple, which she attends because it gives her a "warm feeling," has a bright rabbi, and is "something to do on a Friday night." Michael is not ready to do that, especially with a Christmas tree on the top of his car. (One suspects that Melissa made her proposal precisely because her cousin is in *that* situation.) Michael does drive her to the temple, after joking that her regular attendance may be motivated by seeking out single Jewish men. Melissa, for her part, quips that the Christmas tree on his car roof may be Michael's punishment for the tree he planted in Israel in the name of Alfred E. Newman.

The nostalgia here is not so much for Hebrew school as for the writers' real Jewish hero, Woody Allen, who joked in *Radio Days* (1987) about Jewish boys in Hebrew School tampering with money collected to buy trees for Israel. In many ways, Michael's character has been built on Allen's jokes about neurotic Jewish males. Ironically, Hebrew School is far more a *rite de passage* for Woody Allen than for Herskovitz and Zwick, who have Michael relate that he could never associate Hebrew School with "Little League, the Beatles and getting girls to go to second." In other words, as a child, he regarded Jewish practices as being a kind of detached black-and-white universe, outside the living color of "real" childhood and teenage concerns. This is the first indication that Michael does not believe that the "Jewish God" can relate to his choices in life.

In Michael's life as in his *Dick Van Dyke Show* daydreams, the pathos of divorce is constantly woven into his ruminations about God and Judaism. Little Ethan, Elliot's son, tells Michael: "Your dad is dead. Mine is separated." Yet, after asking Michael if he is Jewish, Ethan can say, "I'm glad I'm a Christian." Michael can only respond, "People should be glad they are what they are."

His own sage advice, coupled with an obvious desire for comfort in the face of the world's tragedies, from death to accidents to divorce, finally pushes Michael into the doors of the synagogue. As he enters, he witnesses an attractive young couple leaving together. The writers obviously want Michael to agonize a bit more about his own life decisions by seeing a same-faith couple. He also peruses the yahrzeit tablets and museum cases in synagogue lobby, as if to pay homage to the past.

When Michael seeks out the rabbi, he is shocked yet fascinated to find that the rabbi is the Santa Claus of his *Dick Van Dyke Show* dreams. Michael tells the very rabbinic Santa Claus that he has come to see how the synagogue is doing. That question transforms the attitude of the rabbi from gentle solicitude to nasty rebuff. The rabbinic Saint Nick asks: "So how are we doing?" When Michael says, "How would I know, I...," the rabbi turns away, saying, "We're doing fine."

Michael has searched for God and been a believer rebuffed. First *he* rejects the Rabbi Claus. In his daydreams, where, as Rob Petrie (Dick Van

Dyke's character), he is convinced that the Santa is authentic, Michael is rebuffed by the once indulgent Santa, who tells him that his wife is not coming back. Hope does return to the worried Michael, after going out for some prolonged errands despite his concerns about her health and equilibrium in the aftermath of the accident. (Olin offers a memorable performance in his depiction of Michael's torrent of anger and gratitude at Hope's return.) Hope reveals that she has just learned that she is pregnant with their second child, and not suffering from after effects of the car collision, as they had feared. So both Santa Clauses are not only moody, but wrong.

Later, Melissa visits, jokingly announcing herself as "Hanu-Claus," and proclaiming, "Happy pagan ritual, everybody." (After several viewings of the episode, I still can't figure out the purpose of this salutation.) Michael tells the good news in a private conversation, and adds that the accident has made him realize how "incredibly much" he loves Hope, so much that it's "scary." Michael muses: "So we can have this wonderful life, I can give her everything she wants, like Christmas. I can make her happy." He is, however, troubled because, as he puts it, "I believe in God. I didn't think I did, but I do." Michael recalls that his father believed in God and had no problem with such belief, maybe because "he didn't marry a non-Jew." In typical formula for our writers, Melissa reminds Michael that his father got divorced. Regular viewers of the show had the additional associations of Dad having been a philanderer and deserter of the family. So much for the easy, endogamous believers.

Michael suggests that he was unable to find comfort with the "Jewish God" because his wife, and probably his daughter (and new child?) are not Jewish. So he must now ask questions like, "Which God, who God, where God?" Obviously he has had a religious experience, or at least an over-whelming need for a religious experience, in his worry to the point of despair, in his "almost losing hope" (or "almost losing Hope"). He says, "It makes me want to..." He does not finish the sentence verbally, but the next scene shows him in the synagogue again. In the second visit, he unsuccess-fully avoids an encounter with the rabbi. He is disappointed and relieved to find that the rabbi of the synagogue is not the Santa Claus, but a youthful, handsome, stylish young man, like Michael. Yet Michael is beyond shock or relief, and bails out of the rabbi's office as quickly as possible. The scene purges him of his dependence on nostalgia, on black-and-white Santa rabbis, and of his guilt in the awareness that people his own age (like the second rabbi) establish Jewish homes with confidence and dedication.

Significantly, Michael does not rush out of the synagogue, but into a daily service where he recites the Kaddish with comfort but not without defiance. Apparently, this is the first time that Michael has said Kaddish for his father, though the year of mourning is almost complete. (After all, he says earlier that the last time he was in the synagogue was 1967, when he was caught by the janitor "slugging down" Manichewitz wine with a friend.) Michael has found his entitlement to mourn and to find both comfort and gratitude. A milestone point is made in the annals of TV: It does not matter whether the rabbi or congregation is welcoming or not, or whether one has intermarried or not. Michael will choose his own way of celebrating his father's memory, his belief in God, and his marriage. Judaism is an entitlement, his entitlement, to use the synagogue whenever and however he chooses. The writers chose to introduce the Kaddish with a reading from the old Conservative prayer book, by Rabbi Jacob Kohn, that refers to "the unbroken faith which links the generations one to another."

The writers suggest that since Michael is part of "the generations," he is entitled to say the prayer without having to consult with rabbis, who need not be at the service, anyway. The writers are not incorrect. Then again, the impression that one gets from this episode of *thirtysomething* is that Michael's final stop will not be in the synagogue. The "Jewish God" is too narrow and will not prove "spiritual" enough for him. Sure enough, by the Halloween episode in 1990, Michael is finding spiritual direction with ghosts and spirits, which can more easily be summoned by interfaith families, without guilt and without the need to reckon with a Jewish people-centered religion that claims to hold truths for all the world.

Judaism Without Jews: "Northern Exposure"

Northern Exposure (1990-1995), the popular TV series about life in a small Alaskan town, featured a major Jewish character—Dr. Joel Fleischman (Rob Morrow), who is bitter to be "exiled" from New York and "incarcerated" in the polar state while on a work program to pay off his medical school debts.

At the beginning of the 1992 season, writers Diane Krolov and Andrew Schneider had Joel reaching out to his fellow Jews in more than an ethnic, nostalgic way. In an episode about an unemployed former KGB agent, the Russian visitor cajoles Joel into letting him pay his doctor's fee in a "more meaningful way" of compensation—namely, with the dossier of a Refusenik named Fleischman who could be a relative of Joel's. Reflecting on his namesake's being persecuted simply because he wanted to study Hebrew and "evinced some pride in being a Jew." Joel tells young Ed (Darren E. Burroughs), a Native American, "This could easily have been my life—if my grandfather hadn't bribed some *muzhik* 50 rubles to smuggle him cross the Russian frontier in the back of a haywagon."

Joel reminisces that each Passover, while sitting around the table "eating latkes" (actually, latkes are Chanukah food), his family would take a moment to remember Russian Jews. He tells Ed that this Fleischman of the dossier made it to Israel: "You see what it means for a Jew to have his own country? After 2,000 years of wandering he can go home. He can always go to Israel."

Ed reminds Joel that the Russian Jew is freer than he is, as Joel is stuck in Alaska because of his medical school debts. Yet Joel is so fascinated and inspired with the spiritual implications of a Jewish State and of a common Jewish heritage (or so it seems), that he calls the Russian Fleischman in Israel and manages to bond with him over the telephone though they can't really communicate. Joel says he wants to know how things are in Israel.

Dr. Joel Fleischman certainly had his ambivalences about Judaism and everything and everybody else. Most disconcerting was a May 1993 episode about the death of Fleischman's dear Uncle Manny. Joel promises his Aunt Helen that he will say Kaddish for his uncle, explaining to a friend that "Kaddish is a Jewish prayer for the dead." He tells his young friend, Ed, the aspiring filmmaker, that he must have a *minyan*, which Joel defines as "ten Jewish males, thirteen or older—actually, in most places now it could be women, but I'm not really sure how Uncle Manny would feel about that; he was raised Orthodox." When Ed asks why you need a *minyan*, Joel replies, "I don't know.... Nine guys on the field to play baseball, ten Jews in a room to say Kaddish."

When Maggie O'Connell (Janine Turner), the local pilot, Joel's landlord and one-time almost-girlfriend comes to pay a condolence call, he shows her photographs of Uncle Manny and Aunt Helen, especially at his bar mitzvah, for which they purchased his *tallit* (prayer shawl) and *yarmulke*.

Word gets out that Joel needs a *minyan*, and Maurice (Barry Corbin), the town mogul in this Alaskan hamlet who has endentured Joel's medical services in payment for medical school loans, feels that he must help Joel pay proper tribute to his uncle. Maurice calls a town meeting at which he insists that everyone must try to find a Jew. When young Shelley asks why nine besides Joel, Maurice responds, "Do I look like Tevye?" Maurice announces that he will pay $100.00 plus expenses for "any *bona fide* member of the Jewish faith who'll come here and pray with Fleischman." Holling (John Cullum), the local restauranteur, says that he doubts you'll find that many Jewish people within miles of the city. A new African American member of the community points out the importance of finding Joel a *minyan* because it is "so that the mourner doesn't go it alone in …[his] time of grief."

Maurice hands out maps of surrounding areas, and responds to queries about how to tell who is Jewish. At first, he says, "the tip of the penis used to be a pretty accurate yardstick," but "with the proliferation of circumcision" it is "no longer an accurate form of I. D." He shows a slide of a photograph of Hasidim, commenting that most Jews no longer fit this stereotype, and throws in a slide of Kirk Douglas to make the point. The best clue for pinpointing Jews, he concludes, seems to be last names and characteristics: "Your Jewish people are a lot like your Chinese people, only with a sense of humor. They value family, tradition, education. They tend to go toward the professions." Maurice adds that when he was a famous astronaut, he was "happy to have a lot of Goldfarbs and Finkelsteins at the button, though none of them got into a Mercury capsule. Get out there and beat the bushes for a Jew."

Chris (John Corbett), the local radio disc jockey, announces that Maurice (who owns the radio station) is "looking for a few good Jews," notifying the public of an "APB for any and all children of Abraham who can sit *shiva* with our own Dr. Joel Fleischman in honor of his Uncle Manny." Jews are told on the radio that they can "say Kaddish and get the Cicely [Alaska] experience," namely, cash remuneration and free room and board."

The obvious questions that go through the viewer's mind (or ought to) at this point are whether Maurice's stereotypes of Jews will be refuted and whether Jews will be found who regard *shiva* as a *mitzvah* (holy deed, commandment) and not as a good deal. The former task is accomplished; the latter objective is never really broached. As a result of the latter's never being discussed, the entire program degenerates into the most bizarre possible premise, as far as Jews and Judaism are concerned.

The most unusual and diverse kinds of Jews are discovered. Ed finds a lumberjack Jew called "Buck" hitchhiking and wearing suspenders. Protesting that Jews don't do these things, Joel examines Buck and confirms that he's an (albeit unconventional) Jewish boy from Cleveland who knows the *Shema*. A British Jew, a chemical engineer at an oil company who is fascinated with geology, is also discovered, as is a distant cousin of Joel's receptionist, Marilyn (Elaine Miles), a Native American who has converted to Judaism. In an interesting dream sequence, Joel is tormented by a bunch of exotic Jews who all have a contempt for New Yorkers like him.

Writer Jeff Melvoin makes the point that Jews come with all kinds of abilities, interests, and looks, but not so much to break a stereotype. Actually, this theme was not new to the series' writers, as they already brought in a kind and tolerant and pleasant and blond Jewish doctor to substitute for Joel (who doesn't always display these qualities and who isn't blond) during a vacation. Now it seems that even then the point may not have been only to challenge stereotypes of Jews (which Joel had become) but to proclaim that many Jews have absolutely nothing in common and should admit it. In this episode, Joel asks Marilyn, rhetorically, why he wants to pray with those people. When Marilyn replies, "Because you're Jewish," Joel answers: "What does *that* mean? We hold certain theological, ethical precepts in common, we only know a smattering of Hebrew, years ago our ancestors *shlepped* around the Negev, but....Intellectually I appreciate it. Emotionally, I don't know. I just don't know."

Lest you begin to think that this is all intended to be just some honest soul-searching and questioning on the part of Joel and the writers, then consider that all of this *does* come to a definite and deliberate resolution. After most Jews for the *minyan* have been found, and Maurice promises Joel that he'll locate the two remaining Jews even if he has to pay the hourly fees of two highly-priced Jewish lawyers in Anchorage, Joel asks Maurice to call the whole thing off because Joel feels uncomfortable about "hired guns." At the end of the episode, Joel assembles the townspeople, puts on his bar mitzvah *tallis* and *yarmulke*, and explains that the purpose of saying Kaddish is to "be with your community." He tells the assembled townspeople that he now realizes that *they* are his community, and asks them to pray or meditate in *their* way while he says the Kaddish. By the

way, the actress who plays Marilyn announces the commercial break in her
Native American language with a perfection that is conspicuously lacking
in the way that Rick Morrow, as Joel, read the Kaddish prayer.

So there we have it, the deliberate conclusion of Joel—and of the
writers: that you no longer need Jews for a *minyan*, since what does it
matter anyway if Jews are going to respond to a call to Kaddish as "hired
guns?" Hundreds of years ago, the Kabbalists described Judaism as the
individual Jew's spiritual dynamic with God, Torah and the People Israel.
If Jews are not required for Judaism, then what is the value of their Torah
and their Covenant with God?

Yet Judaism is perpetuated or not perpetuated, is authentic only to the
extent that the precious formula of God, Torah and the Jewish People can
be preserved in the individual Jew's spiritual life. Cut out one aspect and
the entire effort to be a Jew and to preserve Judaism crumbles. In a
systematic and wanton way, *Northern Exposure's* writers and characters
hammered away non-stop at all three pillars of Jewish identity.

Cantorial Music as Manipulation:
"The West Wing"

In early 2000, the popular series, *The West Wing*, about the workings
of a White House staff, offered a promising if not fully satisfying glimpse
into interfaith responses to capital punishment. In a thoughtful and touching
episode written by producer Aaron Sorkin, the Catholic president (Martin
Sheen) is under a weekend deadline to commute a high-profile death-
sentence. While the polls are overwhelmingly in favor of the death penalty,
his own staff members, parish priest and conscience, not to mention the
pope, are urging him to intervene against "state killing."

In this mosaic of different religious perspectives, Sorkin gives central
stage to a Reform temple. (Lawrence O'Donnell, Jr. and Paul Redford
contributed to the writing.) When a staffer (Rob Lowe) receives a plea for
presidential intercession, he alerts a public defender that communications
chief Toby Ziegler (Richard Schiff), who is Jewish, regularly attends
temple on Saturday morning. We soon see Toby sitting in his pew, listening
to the rabbi (David Proval) preach against capital punishment. Interestingly,
the writers connect the theme of capital punishment to a pre-Passover
sermon, as if a typical Saturday morning is somehow not occasion enough.
The temple is obviously Reform because neither Toby nor a majority of the

worshippers feels compelled to wear *kippot* (skullcaps), and the organ figures prominently in "funeral rehearsals."

Toby is clearly perturbed when his colleague not only calls him out of services via cell phone, but gloats about how a mutual friend has already gotten to the rabbi. Sorkin very deftly goads the viewers into sharing some of the justified indignation felt by Toby at this scenario, and with equal deftness has Toby (and us) understanding that the rabbi and other involved parties have acted with deep conviction and with enough candor to catch Toby's attention.

The hour presents one of the most significant milestones in the depiction of Judaism in the annals of American television, and for at least three reasons. First, it offers an effective forum for the platform and outlook of liberal Judaism. Toby stops back into the temple to see the rabbi on a non-Sabbath. The rabbi makes sure that the meeting takes place in the sanctuary, ostensibly, to bring the weight of sacred space to his advocacy—and, also, the weight of Jewish sacred music, which a cantor chants in the background, with organ accompaniment, in "rehearsal for a funeral," as the rabbi explains it. This emphasis on Jewish liturgical music is the second milestone.

When Toby gently chides the rabbi for his interventions, pointing out to the preacher that "the Torah doesn't prohibit capital punishment" and that it says, "an eye for an eye," the rabbi retorts with a mini-sermon. The latter insists that the Torah's standards on homosexuality, polygamy, slavery and capital punishment represent, "for all I know, the best wisdom of its time," but "it's just plain wrong by any modern standard." The rabbi concludes that "society has a right to protect itself, but it doesn't have a right to be vengeful. It has a right to punish, but it doesn't have a right to kill."

The writer makes us and Toby aware that this rabbi will pull out all stops in order to promote the liberal theology—including the stops on the pipe organ. Toby suggests that the rabbi has the cantor there on purpose to provide atmosphere for the rabbi's importunations—and the possibility is left open. The rabbi responds only that the cantor is "our communication director." (In this case, the cantor is a woman.) The reference is, of course, to Toby's role in White House communications. Not only does the episode showcase the theology of liberal Judaism, but it also highlights in a very positive way the power of the cantor and synagogue music (though, interestingly, by taking the cantor and liturgical composition outside of the Sabbath service). Also, for the first time ever in a TV series (the third milestone), a particular liturgical composition, the setting for the *Hashkivenu* Prayer ("Grant that we lie down in peace...") by Max Helfman (1901-1963), an outstanding American composer for the synagogue, is highlighted, not only in the synagogue scene, but as a leitmotif and as background for the priest's counsel to the president. The production is most respectful, by the way, of the integrity of the Hebrew phrasing. But the prayer is for evening, not funeral, services.

Of course, the position of liberal Judaism on capital punishment is but one approach within American Judaism, and not the traditional approach. Sorkin does conscientiously hint at this when he has Toby report to the president that the Talmudic rabbis "couldn't stomach" capital punishment, but could not and would not abrogate biblical laws, so they came up with extensive "legal restrictions." One wishes, however, that Sorkin and his character had mentioned that a significant portion of rabbis have declared for two millennia that to abrogate capital punishment in every case would be to "multiply murder in Israel." (Mishnah Makkot 1:10)

Something in the rabbi's pitch to Toby was rather disturbing, and was, hopefully, meant to be such by Sorkin. In an attempt to turn Toby's political stomach, the rabbi admonishes him that he had better get the president to commute the death sentence before the latter talks to the pope, thus "realizing" the "fears of non-Catholics." There is nothing anti-Catholic about this rhetoric. The rabbi begins his statement with a tribute to the Catholic Church's "unimpeachable" position on life—"no abortion and no death penalty." There is, however, something unseemly in the rabbi's spiel even if it is done out of fervent concern. The president's old parish priest, affectingly and memorably played by Karl Malden, is far more appropriate in his rhetoric than the rabbi, though he and the president are both painfully aware that the Chief Executive will probably make a choice not to act (lest court sentences come to depend on the "moods of the Oval Office") and thus to sin in the eyes of the Church. In this most complex and heart-wrenching state of affairs, the Catholic confession is treated with heightened reverence.

Aaron Sorkin has penned a thoughtful episode, and has created a likeable Jewish character, who is obviously at home in the synagogue. One wishes, however, that the rabbi had shown some of the priest's wisdom and restraint, especially when classical Judaism offers no simple answer to the issue of capital punishment.

Postscript

Unfortunately, Sorkin went on, in the second season, to suggest that it is not just a particular rabbi who is ungracious, but maybe Hebrew Scriptures themselves. On one level he appreciates Scripture and creates a president who has a feel for it. In a touching November 2000 segment about Chinese refugees claiming protected status as persecuted Christians, the president applies a biblical test to determine the religious knowledge of the claimants, centering around the ancient password, "shibboleth" (see Judges 12:6). A refugee's knowledge of the term becomes a fine study in the use of biblical expressions for human bonding in faith and trust. This happens, tellingly, on the show only in a Christian context, and may reflect the influence of Patrick Caddell, who was given credit for the story. The "Jewish" context is much different.

More often than not, the Hebrew Bible on *The West Wing* is a lightning rod that provokes the scorn or anger of characters (even rabbis) and perhaps of the writers. TV never featured a more nasty assault on the Hebrew Bible than an October 2000 segment of *The West Wing* in which the president (Martin Sheen) attends a "talk radio" reception and begins to reflect on the impact of call-in shows on national discourse. Soon after starting his talk, he spots a Dr. Jenna Jacobs, a character who would seem to have been conceived out of Sorkin's beef with Dr. Laura Schlessinger. Interrupting his formal remarks, the president greets Jacobs. (The name is perfect, because it can be both Jewish and Christian. So it can be taken as an assault on both the Christian right and on "conservatives" among the Jews.) Soon the president interrupts himself again and asks her if she has degrees in medicine or psychology or theology or social work, and if not, whether her listeners are confused as to her qualifications or lack of them. (I suppose that one could ask Sorkin or any other writer what his qualifications are as human observer and preacher. After all, there were more sermons in *The West Wing* than even Sorkin might spot.)

The president's nasty baiting of Dr. Jacobs is even more vicious than the abuse of the occasion and of power to single out and to publicly humiliate a single individual. When, in response to his inquiry, Dr. Jenna says that *she* does not call homosexuality an abomination, but that the Bible did, the chief executive declares, "I'm interested in selling my youngest daughter into slavery, as sanctioned in Exodus 21:7. She's a sophomore at Georgetown, speaks fluent Italian, always cleared the table when it was her turn. What would a good price for her be? My chief of state insists on working on the Sabbath. Should he be put to death? Should I do it myself?" He goes on to ask whether the Washington Red Skins could play football even though the Bible prohibits touching a dead pig. Could they touch a football if they put on gloves? He concludes, "Can I burn my mother in a small family gathering for wearing garments of different threads?"

Now, by any standards, this is a nasty and pointed segment, especially for television, which had, at least until the 1990s, been a rather polite and tame medium, compared to film. No matter how you cut it, the president's monologue is a wholesale attack on the Hebrew Bible and therefore on Judaism. Interestingly, Sorkin treats it as a moment of righteous indignation in the daily routine of his president, and some of his other characters regard it as a (somewhat justified) blowing of steam.

PART THREE

GLIMMERS OF SANCTITY ON BIG AND SMALL SCREENS: ADMIRABLE AND INSIGHTFUL PRODUCTION EFFORTS

೧೦೧

10

HEART AND SOUL

ℰᗉᏏ

TV's Best Exploration of Judaism:
"Little House on The Prairie"

If I could give an award for the best television episode ever with a Jewish theme, it would be an episode of *Little House On the Prairie*, entitled "The Craftsman." Aired on January 8, 1979, it was a masterpiece of insight into the Jewish soul.

In this hour, Albert (Matthew Laborteaux), the bright, streetwise lad adopted by the Ingalls family becomes fascinated with an old Jewish gentleman, Isaac Singerman, played by John Bleifer, who was a veteran of the Yiddish stage. When Mr. Singerman's son goes East to find a Jewish wife (for once, interfaith marriage was *not* glorified), the Ingalls boy works for the old man and is called a "Jew-lover" in school. Yet he cherishes his friendship with the elderly Jew and learns what a marvelous and inspiring creature a practicing Jew actually is, especially when the Sabbath comes.

The old Jew is honest. He is a coffin-maker, but will not use nails, because he wants to make the best possible product, and regards nails as a sign of bad craftsmanship. Albert learns from him about pride in one's work.

Singerman teaches the boy the meaning of the Jewish concept of compassion or *"rachmones"* (Yiddish for the Hebrew word, *rachmanut*). The word is actually used and the concept nicely explained on the show. He illustrates this Jewish value-concept[1] by taking the little boy to visit an elderly Gentile neighbor whose walking cane was broken by some rowdy children. Singerman brings the man a new cane. Since the neighbor is too poor to buy it, the old Jew "trades" the cane for some worthless article, thus carrying out the Rabbinic teaching that the best way to give charity is to make the poor person feel that he is somehow giving something in return. The boy is most impressed by this object lesson in *rachmones*.

The show depicts anti-Semitism, as well, but does not present it as the core of Jewish concern. It effectively demonstrates the pettiness of prejudice on the part of adults and children. The Ingalls boy learns just how petty such prejudice is when regarded in the light of Singerman's faith, goodness and humanity, and so does the audience.

In 1999, twenty years after first reviewing "The Craftsman," I determined to interview the writer, whom I imagined to be a veteran of TV's "golden age," perhaps quite on in years. I was pleasantly surprised to discover that Paul Wolff is a Baby Boomer who grew up in Brooklyn after World War Two, and attended Hebrew School and high school in the Flatbush area. Always interested in writing, directing and producing films, Wolff was happy to take any job with United Artists, working his way up from the mail room to publicity writer. He started producing his own film shorts, which he was able to sell, and directed the Peppermint Playhouse children's theater.

In 1975 Wolff moved to Hollywood and determined to make a living as a TV writer. His agent asked him which show he'd like to write for, and he immediately spoke the name of the program he liked best, *Little House on the Prairie*. Wolff did not agree with critics who called the series "saccharine." He admired its producer-star-director, Michael Landon, for taking risks and for dealing with controversial topics.

Paul Wolff told me that at the time he met Landon, his Jewish *neshamah* or soul was "dying to come out." He regretted having been too reticent and uncomfortable in giving voice to his Jewish identity. He was searching for a way to proclaim with authenticity, "I am a Jew!" Landon liked the idea of a story about a coffin maker who took pride in his work. Somehow, Wolff got up the courage to add, after his pitch, that he envisioned that character as a Jew. At this, Wolff says, Michael Landon's

---

1.   On value-concepts in Judaism, see Max Kadushin, *The Rabbinic Mind* (New York: Bloch, 1972).

eyes lit up and he said, "A Jew? I'm a Jew!" (Landon's father was Jewish.) Landon chose to direct that episode himself.

I was impressed not only by what Wolff wrote, but by what he refused to write. Landon had asked him to script another episode of *Little House*, aired in 1981, about an interfaith couple choosing to raise one child as Jewish and one as Christian. I reminded him of that program, which I have regarded as one of the worst and most vulgar ever on a "Jewish" theme. With refreshing principle and modesty, Wolff related to me that he informed Landon that he did not feel comfortable writing it. Someone else took that job.[2]

Paul Wolff went on to produce a Mary Tyler Moore series, *Annie McGuire*, and *Life Goes On*. He also became a senior lecturer in the University of Southern California film school. In the late 1980s, he took off some time from show business to pursue Jewish studies at the University of Judaism and with other creative Los Angeles rabbis. He now acts as a *magid*, a storyteller who imparts Jewish values and concepts to all ages. He regularly dialogues with the Jewish elderly at nursing homes, and participates in interfaith seminars. It is a blessing to him and to his audiences that the concepts and concerns he cultivated while writing "The Craftsman" have guided him in creative ventures and in service to the Jewish and general community. The publication of his stories will one day be a major treat.

The Bible and Its Jews: "NYPD Blue"

In the 1997-1998 season, TV's *NYPD Blue* offered its usual fare on Jews, who are depicted either as victims of crime or difficult people. In an episode written by John Chambers, for example, the new squad office receptionist is complaining to her landlord, a Mr. Sigel, about his son and employee rummaging through her underwear drawer! Often on *NYPD Blue*, "difficult" can mean perverted, especially when it comes to the depiction of Jews.

Then there is Jew as victim. Another episode, written by David Milch and Ted Mann (with Bill Clark, Meredith Stiehm, and Nicholas Wooten), dealt with the murder of a Hasidic woman, Hester Rosenblatt, whose body

---

2.   That episode, "Come, Let Us Reason Together," aired on January 12, 1981.

is found near the Brooklyn Bridge. The girlfriend of the (Hispanic) perpetrator explains the crime: "Victor done robberies before at the bridge with no problem. With the Jewish girl it goes wrong. She's heavy, you know, and pretty strong. Fights back. It ends with Victor having to kill her, against his will." The officer responds: "The fat girl had a name, and a family, and a community that's grieving for her right now." The "message" of the episode seems to be that strong, heavy, women should not fight back when robbed, and that they have friends and family like everyone else. The Hasidic aspect is incidental, obviously intended to add a little ethnic spice. Until the end of the episode, that is. There is a touching appendix scene in which kindly Officer Greg Madavoy (Gordon Clapp) sees to it that the woman's remains are released to her father without invasive autopsy, and with the blood, "soil and such" from the area where she died, out of respect for traditional Jewish concerns about honoring the body in burial. Madavoy's partner James Leo Martinez (Nicholas Turturro) tells him: "No one else in the squad would have known to do that."

So the episode about the death of the Hasidic woman would appear to be a writers' ploy to gain sympathy for an already endearing lead character, and to make a point about the worthiness and importance of knowing and respecting the beliefs and customs of others—whether in that order, or putting the motif of mutual understanding first. Either way, a good point is made, and it is nice to see it made with regard to Hasidic Jews, who are being depicted as rather militant and stubborn in most TV spots nowadays. After all, in Hasidism as in all of Judaism, the teaching of *mipne darchei shalom*, helping one's neighbor and showing him compassion, especially in his grief, for the sake of peace and understanding between neighbors, is basic. I wish that the writers had allowed the Hasidic man to make the point that Jews are enjoined to behave that way with Gentiles, and are therefore doubly touched when Gentiles treat Jews in that manner.

The "Hasidic" storyline was in the first part of a two-part episode in November-December 1997. These were *NYPD Blue's* standout segments, both in dramatic power and in the treatment of Judaism, though they featured no Jewish characters. They told the revolting yet compelling story of the disappearance and murder of a young boy. The police suspect that his own father killed him after prolonged abuse, and try to prod the mother into turning in her husband. The father, who is cunning, manipulative and verbally effective, succeeds in deflecting suspicion to a mute, homeless man whom the boy had befriended. The man, Israel, communicates mainly by pointing to biblical passages. Officer Sipowicz (Dennis Franz) is deeply touched by Israel, and urges his colleagues to corner the father before the innocent man is destroyed by incarceration. When Israel hangs himself in desperation, Sipowicz becomes the guardian of his Bible and tries to figure out the significance of the passage to which the Bible is opened.

The episodes, which together were of two-and-one-half-hours' duration, more than movie length, were difficult to watch. The main theme was jarring and disconcerting, and a sub-theme about people selling their limbs for money was also hard to take. Yet, this two-parter was one of the best psychological dramas ever on TV. It is all the more effective because we sense from the beginning that the father has a bright mind but is warped, the suspense consisting in his being unhinged by coordinated and penetrating police strategy. Brian Markinson and Annie Corley are unforgettable as the sinister and pathetic father and the guilt-ridden and self-hating mother. The acting of the principals, notably Dennis Franz and Jimmy Smits, is equally memorable.

What has this to do with Judaism? At the very end of the drama, everyone is torn up: Sipowicz by Israel's death, the mother by her aching guilt and grief, the officers, staff, the father's attorney and, of course, the father, who at one point had invoked Divine guidance in his twisted rationalizations of the murder. It is at that point that Sipowicz simply starts reading the verses from Israel's scriptures—some words from Psalm 119. The words that Israel has left his friend and supporter have an amazing healing force, just by being read. They address everyone's pain, as if individually.

Never have I seen such powerful and meaningful use of the Hebrew Bible on television—or in film, for that matter. While Christians also love Hebrew Scriptures, those scriptures do come to the world through the Jewish People, who are well represented here *in absentia*. One thinks of Heschel's words: "The Bible is mankind's greatest privilege....No other book so loves and respects the life of man. No loftier songs about his true plight and glory, about his agony and joys, misery and hope, have ever been expressed...."[3]

The drama, whether intentionally or not, is reminiscent of stories by S. Y. Agnon, where the plot becomes a metaphor for the role of the Jew and his Scripture in the world. While I admit that it is much more likely than

3. Abraham J. Heschel, *God in Search of Man: A Philosophy of Judaism* (N.Y.: Farrar, Straus and Giroux, 1955), p. 239.

not that the writers did not set out to do this, there is certainly an association here between Hebrew Scriptures and that name, "Israel," but what sort of Israel do we have here? He does, after all, commit suicide and leaves the interpretation of his Scriptures to others.

Are the writers telling us that the Scriptures maintain their power and beauty even without Israel, or despite his despair and confusion? Or are the writers assuming that one can quote Hebrew scriptures and invoke the name, "Israel," without raising metaphorical associations with the Jewish People? If the sad, latter scenario is the reality, then maybe TV writers ought to operate under it, anyway, for it obviously enables them to communicate the spiritual treasures of Judaism better than when they get bogged down in their stock depiction of "Jewish types."

Relating to God:
"Ben Casey"

The last major depiction of Jews and Judaism on the popular *Ben Casey* series, about a brilliant maverick medical intern, is theologically interesting. In "A Nightingale Named Nathan" (1965), Howard DaSilva is most effective playing (and even shmaltzily overplaying) Cantor Nathan Birnbaum, who comes into the synagogue, finds that another cantor has taken his place, and then takes out his anger on the congregation and on God before being stricken at the *amud* (cantor's podium). Written by Chester Krumholz and Arthur Dales, and directed by John Meredyth Lucas, this episode fascinates the viewer with a portrait of a cantor, a figure of interest in Hollywood since the first *Jazz Singer*, who, like Rabbi Levi Yitzhak of Berditchev (but out of anger instead of Levi Yitzhak's loving devotion to God and his people) argues with God.

Nathan sees even his sickness as a contest with God ("Dr. Casey and me, we'll beat Him at His own game") whom he cannot forgive for his wife's suffering and untimely death, and who now "afflicts" him with a tumor on his vocal chords. For all his talk about God, and for all his pleasant banter with the hospital staff and fellow patients, however, the cantor is a very inconsiderate man. He expects his daughter, who is already marrying late in life after devoting many years to her invalid mother, to postpone her wedding until *he* is able to sing there, even though he knows that his daughter wants to marry immediately so that she can accompany her fiancé on a new job in Paris. The daughter is depicted as frustrated and under stress because of her father, and as justified in her complaints.

If the Jewish woman receives sympathetic treatment, her fiancé is painted as somewhat of a nebbish and her father as a stubborn, selfish and angry man. After a while everyone becomes sick and tired of the cantor's anger. When he tells Ben Casey, "Help me beat Him (namely, God)," the doctor responds: "Nathan, don't involve me in that struggle of yours." Then Nathan is told: "Your daughter was right. Your daughter was right. You lost your wife in a terrible way. Well, that's sad. But you never let your God, your friends or anyone ever forget it."

Still, in this episode, the thoughtless Jewish men are capable and worthy of being saved by their redeeming qualities. The daughter's fiancé looks like he *will* make it with his bride's help. The cantor seems to grow in self-understanding; and in becoming aware of his own selfishness he seems to gain a better understanding of God. He helps a young black patient (memorably played by Don Marshall, later of *Land of the Giants*) to pray, even though, at first, he enlists that young man ("Hey, old man, tell Him for me, too") in his "vendetta" against God ("Look around. What do you see? God's charity? Or His sublime indifference? You see all the trouble? What are you doing up there? Watching television?"). The cantor offers a moving prayer for the young black man, but he still insists on bargaining with God by telling God to take his life instead. Yet he comes to realize that arrogance and selfishness alienate people not only from God, but from each other and from their better selves. The cantor attains true piety when he realizes that one must feel for God, too—an insight which Abraham Heschel, by the way, held to be at the heart of Jewish mysticism. "Ay, what a *meshuggener* I am," says Nathan Birnbaum. "I've been waiting for a sign from Him, and it looks like He's been waiting for a sign from me. Maybe even *He* needs love."

This episode showed that serious religious questions could be raised on television with sophisticated theological response and memorable characterizations.

Covenant Affirmed:
"The Plot Against Harry"

There's something very special about *The Plot Against Harry*. Even the saga of this "1989" release is unique. Writer-director Michael Roemer began shooting the film in 1968 with then partner, producer-cinematographer Robert M. Young. When he held a private showing for friends and colleagues from Yale, he saw, much to his dismay, that no one laughed. So he shelved it for over twenty years, until 1989, when he put it on videocassette as a gift for his children. Then everyone was laughing, from the technicians who worked on the conversion to videocassette, to those who have attended some prestigious film festivals, to many who paid the price of a ticket to select theaters, where the film was shown. The price of the tickets or of videotapes is well worth it, well spent on this remarkable, crisply-written, funny and touching film, which is all finely acted, though not all the principals are professional actors.

It seems that Harry Plotnick (Martin Priest), a Jewish numbers racketeer, has just been released from jail. From the moment he is picked up in his fancy limousine by his loyal flunky, Max (Henry Nemo), nothing seems to go right. Even his numbers business appears to have passed him by as African American, Hispanic and Asian competitors, some of them once his closest associates, have decided that the changing neighborhood calls for a change in bosses.

Almost from the time he leaves jail, events conspire to bring Harry in contact with his long lost family. He literally slams his limo into another car, only to discover that the justifiably irate driver is his long-lost brother-in-law Leo, and that the other passengers include his ex-wife, a daughter whom he hasn't seen in years, who is now pregnant, her husband and their small daughter. As it turns out, Leo works for a synagogue-sponsored catering business, and later is most amenable to Harry's becoming his silent partner in that business. Harry's ex-wife is cordial but cautious, his daughter is sweet, and soon gives birth to a boy whose *brit* (circumcision) Harry attends. Harry even learns that he has another daughter, who models lingerie for a large company owned by a big shot at the synagogue. The synagogue leader's wife uses Harry as a resource person for her sociological study of the bookie game, and it is while attending her heart fund telethon that Harry will give new—and classic comedic—meaning to heart attack.

Harry is no angel. He does a lot of immoral things, and tries to do more. He even contemplates violence against a competitor. He doesn't seem to have any strong feelings or family ties, even toward his own daughters. The only person who exercises any moral authority over him and of whom he takes care is his sister Mae, but he feels he must keep her completely in the dark about his criminal activities and jail terms in order to maintain their "close" relationship.

What is remarkable, however, is that no one harbors any grudges or hostility toward Harry—not his brother-in-law, ex-wife, daughters. Even after he appears on television when dragged before a State Crime Commission, even after his son-in-law, a new father, is interrogated by the police because of innocent remarks he made during a conversation with Harry, the family, while angry and hurt and far from perfect themselves, becomes Harry's network of repentance, atonement and redemption. The synagogue catering business, it should be noted, secures his redemption.

The Plot Against Harry is one of the most "Jewish" films I've ever seen. Not so much because Harry likes Jewish foods and hums Yiddish lieder, but because the film affirms, in a most creative, entertaining and sometimes moving way, basic Jewish values. It affirms *teshuvah*, repentance, the ability to turn around one's life, sometimes in spite of oneself. It says that you can go straight and still make a living. It shows that even going through the gestures of repentance without meaning it can be a beginning in the right direction if others are willing to help. It affirms the Jewish family, and by and large, represents the Jewish woman as strong, sensible, attractive (especially in the character of Kae, Harry's ex-wife, who is not the Jewish mother stereotype of the Sixties).

There are some typically late Sixties touches here that besmirched the family portrait somewhat and that now seem gratuitous, if not in poor taste. At that time one almost had to represent the beautiful younger daughter as pregnant before marriage, and it was regarded as "comedic irony" to depict the respectable son-in-law as taking nude pictures of his wife—just between them, of course, and only if he happens to be a camera buff. Thankfully, these annoying touches do not ruin this film.

This is a very "Jewish" film, also, in the way that it offers a critique of American Jewish life: gently, lovingly, with a reverence for Judaism. It pokes fun at an outrageous bar mitzvah candle-lighting ceremony while still getting across something of the emotional and spiritual power—and family bond—of bar mitzvah. It does the same for circumcision and weddings. The synagogue officer, while a little too curious about gambling, is respectable. It even shows a rabbi, priest and minister without making fun of any of them. The contemporaneous sacred cow, *Fiddler On The Roof*, had, after all, made terrible fun of the rabbi in the name of "tradition."

Above all, *The Plot Against Harry* is a truly "Jewish" film in the way it speaks about Jews and, ultimately, in what it suggests about them. An

Italian mobster tells Harry as a kind of threat, "I thought Jewish people were supposed to be smart." After Harry appears on television, a Jewish woman in the elevator tells him, "You're a disgrace to the Jewish people." Yet as soon as the elevator operator hears that Harry is Jewish, he feels a kinship with him. Harry can do no wrong in the eyes of his flunky, Max, but Max distrusts the synagogue officer's wife because she is not Jewish. In other words, there are a lot of different attitudes about Jews here, from chauvinism to moralism. But the sense here is that Jewishness is special even though Jews are no better—and no worse—than others.

The bottom line is the sense of decency, of right and wrong—the sense of Covenant, if you will[4]—that must be at the heart of any discussion of the meaning of Jewishness. The only tragedy in this fine comedy is that those who didn't laugh in 1968 set back by twenty years the direction that "Jewish" themes in film (and television) should have taken.

Bar Mitzvah as a Gift to Parents: "The Dick Van Dyke Show"

Perhaps the most memorable bar mitzvah in television history is the episode of the Dick Van Dyke Show (1961-1966) called "Buddy Sorrell—Man and Boy." First aired on March 2, 1966, it has been seen by several generations in reruns. Pixyish and lovable comedy writer, Buddy Sorrell (Morey Amsterdam) has the first mass media "adult bar mitzvah." Decades later, Armond Hammer and Kirk Douglas would follow suit. Writers Art Baer and Ben Joelson, together with story consultants Sam Denoff and Bill Persky, and producer Carl Reiner, started a trend of sorts.

What is remarkable about this episode is that the theme was treated, as producer Art Baer expressed it to me, as a "mystery." A straight bar mitzvah was not exotic enough. Buddy had to make a secret of it, and thus arouse the superstition of co-writers Rob Petrie (Van Dyke) and Sally Rogers (Rose Marie). Faced with Buddy's hushed phone calls and tense and evasive behavior, and bold-faced lies about visiting his mother, Rob and Sally decide that Buddy is seeing another woman. A strange message

---

4.   On characterizing authentic "Jewish" literature, or, for that matter, film, as "covenantal," see Cynthia Ozick, "Toward A New Yiddish," in *Art and Ardor* (N.Y.: Knopf, 1983), especially pp. 164-5.

left for Buddy from a Dorothy alerts him to her husband's return home at five o'clock.

The writers do a good job of juggling comedy, mystery and even a bit of foreboding. Soon we see Buddy, who has never had a harmonious relationship with his wife, Pickles, tell this younger, attractive, and pleasant Dorothy that he regrets he ran into her in Florida: "If I hadn't of seen you, this whole thing wouldn't have started." She replies: "Buddy, you can't just walk out now. This whole thing was meant to be. I can't believe our bumping into each other was just an accident."

Not long afterwards, we learn that Buddy has been sneaking off to meet with Dorothy's husband, a rabbi, to study for his bar mitzvah. When Dorothy asks her husband, in Buddy's presence, how the bar mitzvah candidate is doing, the latter replies, "He's doing fine, darling. The only problem is that he started thirty years late." To this Buddy quips, but with seriousness in his voice: "Well, it isn't my fault. It took me that long to save up for a blue suit."

The writers have brilliantly removed the mystery from the audience so that the attempt at "intervention" of Buddy's friends is totally absurd and hilarious. At the end of a work day, Rob stays behind to lecture Buddy on marital fidelity. Hearing Buddy's explanation, Rob is at first so shocked that Dorothy is the rabbi's wife that he is totally resistant to hearing the truth. "When I was a kid, I missed out on my confirmation," Buddy explains. He adds that his mother "never forgave herself" for his not having had a bar mitzvah ceremony. He knew Dorothy when she was a little kid; she "used to go around with my brother," but married a man who "turned out to be a rabbi."

When Rob asks Buddy why he couldn't just come right out and say that he was having a bar mitzvah, he explains, "Well, it was kind of a nice thing to do and I didn't want to ruin my reputation as a rat. If Pickles knew I was doing something nice for my mother, she'd want me to do something nice for her." Rob wants to know whether he should say, "Shalom," and Buddy teaches him the more appropriate term, "Mazal tov," which he translates as "Congratulations."

At the end of the episode, the show's ensemble of characters gathers in the synagogue to witness the ceremony and Buddy's heartfelt speech: "Mama, you waited a long time to hear this: Today I am a man." The rabbi calls Buddy by his Hebrew name, Moshe Zelig. The *kvelling* (gratification) of Buddy's elderly mother is heartwarming to the audience, as is the entire episode, which is all the more effective because of its enjoyable comedy of errors.

I have felt free to give away the plot and the gist of some of the dialogue because I am certain that this cannot do violence to the production. Someone seeing it for the first time, who has also read this synopsis, would not miss out on the joy and benefit of that earliest viewing. The structure and dialogue are so fitting and exquisite that there is an element of surprise in this half hour no matter how many times one may see it. The episode is, in sum, perfect, textbook TV writing. Particularly enjoyable is an encounter between Buddy and a bar mitzvah boy who is the standard age. The rabbi explains to the thirteen-year-old student that Buddy is an "unusual case" because his family was very poor when he was thirteen and "he had to go out to work and help support them. Now, as a special present for his mother, he's finally going to be bar mitzvahed."

Analyzing this episode today, we find in it some worthy features that were, unfortunately, cast aside by later bar (or bat) mitzvah treatments on TV, as evidenced by the first section of this book. True, Buddy's furtive approach to bar mitzvah may reflect more than his own uneasiness. He may represent a reticence about discussing Judaism on the part of most writers and producers, and of the general Jewish community of the time. The very tastefulness of the episode may lie in its bashfulness. Instead of using Jewish traditions and vocabulary as a butt of the humor, as virtually all later depictions of "Judaism" have done, this episode pokes fun at the secrecy about Judaism, at the Marrano mentality which was prevalent and even largely unshakable at the time. That's what made the "mystery" motif so courageous, as well as outrageous.

It would be a mistake, however, to overanalyze this episode. Writer Bill Persky told me that *The Dick Van Dyke Show* appealed so much to the viewer's sense of humanity because "everything in the show was based on something that happened to somebody." Thus, it could tackle important issues of race and family in a gentle but realistic way. Persky sees in this particular episode a sense that "Buddy's not being a bar mitzvah never let him really be comfortable. It was a rite of passage that he had missed." There was "a step along the path [of life] that he didn't have and was supposed to [have had], and as much as he did it for his mother he wanted to have that moment."

Indeed, the episode itself began as a mother's suggestion. Writer Art Baer, who drafted the episode together with his late partner Ben Joelson, told me that he had never had a bar mitzvah, and that his mother had always been after him to do so, and suggested that it might be a good idea for an episode. While leaving a production meeting, Baer mentioned his mother's idea to Carl Reiner, head writer and producer, who was immediately taken with it and encouraged Baer and Joelson to go ahead with it. Baer says that he never had a bar mitzvah because his folks could not afford the Hebrew lessons and the party afterwards, and that he had not been so keen on it, anyway. He believes that Denoff and Persky, together with Reiner, added the nice touch (and good mystery ploy) about Buddy and the rabbi's wife being childhood friends. Baer's father and mother both saw and enjoyed the episode as a kind of surrogate bar mitzvah for their son.

Persky identified with the scenario in that his own parents could barely afford his bar mitzvah in Newark, one of several places he lived as a child due to his father's itinerate auctioneer work. He recalls the small Orthodox synagogue where he had his bar mitzvah after six months of training, with hard candies thrown at him. (The throwing of candies, a custom that has returned to many synagogues, represents the hope and prayer for a sweet and fulfilling life, informed by the Torah, God's teaching, which is described in the Psalms as "sweeter than the honeycomb.") Persky says that, to him, the episode was not so much about Judaism as about "caring for parents, trying to respect them." Buddy wanted to have a bar mitzvah for his mother "before she died." The show was about "family feelings, family values and tradition."

To be sure, the writers are in accord as to the episode's two salient points: first, that Buddy is having the bar mitzvah in order to do something nice for his mother; and secondly, that he did not have a bar mitzvah at thirteen because he could not afford the suit. Is there in this episode a critique, however subtle, of the emphasis on the party and on financial status in synagogue life? Audiences who never knew the Depression may well regard the show in that way. To the generation raised in the 1920s and 1930s, however, the story line was a page taken from the lives of acquaintances who either had to work or whose parents could not bear the shame of not being able to dress their children for a sacred milestone. As if to defend the synagogue, the writers did put in the mouth of the rabbi himself that Buddy did not have his bar mitzvah because he had to go to work to help his family. Implicit in such dialogue is a message to younger generations, who grew up on this show, to appreciate their style of living and to take advantage of their opportunities for religious instruction.

Contemporary audiences may also be startled by the episode's tacit praise of having a bar mitzvah mainly to please one's parents. Today, the emphasis is put almost exclusively on personal commitment and interest, even in the instruction of thirteen-year-olds. The Talmud, however, notes that the honoring of parents is a precondition to the honoring of God. "Great is the commandment to honor parents since the Holy Blessed One attached to it greater importance than the honoring of Himself. It is written, 'Honor your father and your mother' (Exodus 22:12) and also 'Honor the Lord with your substance' (Proverbs 3:9). With what do you honor God? With that which He has bestowed upon you, as when you observe the laws of the forgotten sheaf, the corner of the field, tithes, charity to the poor, etc. If you possess the means of fulfilling these commandments, do so; but if you are destitute, you are not under obligation. With the honoring of parents, however, no such condition is given. Whether you have the means or not, you must fulfill the commandment, even if you must go begging from door to door." (Jerusalem Talmud, *Peah*, 15d)

Sam Denoff had the most extensive Jewish education and background of all the writers. His parents were active in the congregations to which they belonged. He grew up in a Reform congregation in Brooklyn (Ahavath Shalom or Avenue R. Temple) which did encourage Hebrew education and bar mitzvah. Later, when he was out of high school, his parents moved to Great Neck, Long Island, and joined Temple Beth El there. He has clearly had since his youth a genuine appreciation of his parents' two rabbis, A. Alexander Steinbach and Jacob Philip Rudin, both of whom were gifted preachers and writers. Perhaps because Denoff experienced bar mitzvah out of a context of involvement in synagogue life, he does not speak of the episode as a surrogate Jewish experience. He is more impressed with its "mystery" elements, which he helped to craft.

The bar mitzvah episode on *The Dick Van Dyke Show* demonstrates how the different kinds of Jewish experiences of TV writers can combine to shape a multifaceted gem of writing that highlights Jewish practices but also provides "family values" such as "Honor thy father and thy mother" which resonate in different ethnic cultures but at the same time hark back to biblical teachings.

11

REDEMPTIVE JEWISH OBSERVANCES

ଛୁଓଷ

Meaningful Bar/Bat Mitzvah Ceremonies:
"The Wonder Years," "Archie Bunker's Place,"
"Hotel," "Bill: On His Own"

It seems that a bar mitzvah can be quite a ratings-getter. *TV Guide* reported that a 1989 episode of the popular ABC series, *The Wonder Years*, which featured a bar mitzvah, was the highest rated episode to that point. The show's young protagonist, Kevin (played by charmer Fred Savage) becomes jealous of all the attention and even of the rituals that highlight the bar mitzvah of his friend Paul (nicely played by Josh Saviano). Throughout their childhood the boys had celebrated their birthdays together, but now Kevin finds it difficult to accept that, for Paul, this birthday is different from all other birthdays. At first, Kevin feels left out. Then he feels cheated out of a special family tradition. (When he asks his parents what his family origins are, he finds out that he's a "mutt," like "so many Americans.") Then he must deal with his own resentfulness.

While Kevin is getting hold of himself, and learning, with the audience, about the meaning of bar mitzvah, we get insight into what bar mitzvah means to Paul and to his family, the Pfeiffers. The Pfeiffer family is first presented to the viewers through the eyes of Kevin, when he visits them for dinner. Paul's father is an optometrist; his mother is a "mom extraordinaire," who loves to stuff food into the children. True, Paul's parents and sister all wear strange glasses (perhaps because of Dad's profession), and Mom does overdo it with the food. They come across as nice people and good parents, who care about their children, their neighbors, and about their heritage. There's nothing offensive in the depiction of the Pfeiffers, and one oughtn't cry "stereotyping" just because familiar and rather uncolorful types are presented. After all, Jews have their salt of the earth, as well.

The most colorful character in the Pfeiffer family is the grandfather (effectively played by Philip Sterling) who recounts that he was grateful for the gift of a chicken at *his* bar mitzvah. (The line is too good not to come from some writer's family history.) In a very beautiful and touching scene, the grandfather gives Paul a gift that his father gave to him—a prayerbook. He charges Paul with the words, "My grandson, you are on the verge of becoming a man. You are about to inherit the love, the joy, the bitterness of our People, the tradition. From *my* grandfather to my father to me to my son and now to you. Mazal tov."

It's a nice charge and certainly gives the TV audience a sense of the meaning and responsibilities of bar mitzvah. We more professional theologians would have liked to have seen some mention of the "Covenant," of the belief that the People Israel entered into a pact with God that entails commitment to certain teachings (Torah) and to religious practices rooted in *mitzvot* or Divine Commandments. Getting across some of *these* concepts with dramatic grace and theological authenticity would certainly be a challenge to any writer.

Our episode of *Wonder Years* does offer many refreshing directions to TV depictions of bar mitzvah which one hopes will be followed and improved upon by future programs on the subject. First, the emphasis on the gifts is appropriately underplayed here—a big step beyond the vulgar money tree in a bat mitzvah sequence some years before on *Archie Bunker's Place* (see below). True, some of Paul's friends, along with Kevin's rather obnoxious brother, speculate on the school bus with obvious envy that Paul may pull in as much as a thousand dollars in gifts. When pressed, Paul raises the issue of the gifts. But the episode makes it clear that the speculation about loot is puerile, and that the rootedness in a spiritual tradition is far more interesting and even enviable.

The episode also features some chanting of the Torah (very well done by Saviano). It thus demonstrates that the major aspect of becoming a bar mitzvah is the acquisition of skills and of knowledge in a language and a tradition. Even though writer David M. Stern sometimes distracts the viewers with a lot of talk about Paul "becoming a man" without really explaining that "religious maturity," or responsibility for religious observances, is the key issue, the emphasis on skill and learning is quite strong here, especially because Grandpa's gift is a *siddur* (prayerbook).

Also of great significance, I think, is that the bar mitzvah, because it is presented through Kevin's eyes, is depicted as a ceremony in which Gentiles can find meaning. At the end of the episode, Kevin says: "I ate more than Mrs. Pfeiffer could have dreamed possible." Then he adds: "And in a funny way, when I look back on it, I sort of feel that it was *my* bar mitzvah, too." What we have here is more than politically correct interfaith rhetoric. There is a genuine feeling throughout the entire episode that the Jewish emphasis on mastering and being responsible to an ancient tradition, in order to find God through one's People's ancient Covenant with God, is something admirable and lends a seriousness and a meaning to life. Too often bar mitzvah ceremonies have been presented on TV merely as "comic relief." The *Wonder Years* episode goes a long way toward getting across to a general audience—not to mention, to many Jews—the significance of bar and bat mitzvah with humor and thoughtfulness.

There were other impressive bar or bat mitzvah depictions earlier in the 1980s. One thinks of a 1981 two-part segment of *Archie Bunker's Place*, Norman Lear's continuation of *All In The Family*. Archie Bunker's niece, Stephanie, whose mother was Jewish, wants to have a bat mitzvah. There were aspects of this segment that were disturbing and confused (as are aspects of American Jewish life). Stephanie's non-Jewish father and Archie, her non-Jewish guardian, vie for the honor of making a speech at her bat mitzvah ceremony. The emphasis at the ensuing bat mitzvah party is on the presents, especially a "money tree" on which cash gifts are displayed. It is not clear whether the party is held on the Sabbath or later on. One senses the contradictions in American Jewish life in the very fact that the writers do not feel uncomfortable with the concept of a "money tree" on the Sabbath, when currency is, according to Jewish Law, not held, lest one do business on the holy day.

There were, however, many redeeming features in this depiction of bat mitzvah, written by Mark Fink and Stephanie Miller, and entitled "Growing Up Is Hard To Do." When Archie insists that the party be held at his bar (his "place"), and Stephanie's Jewish grandmother demands that it be held at her ostentatious Long Island country club, Stephanie decides that it should take place at home. It was delightful to see a young woman so intent on having a bat mitzvah, and a great pleasure to hear the young Broadway actress (Danielle Brisebois) chanting the *haftarah* (prophetic reading) trope with accuracy and feeling, and thus highlighting the classic beauty and cross-cultural interest of the ancient cantillations.

This bat mitzvah scenario provided interesting background to an agonizing situation, namely, Stephanie's dad's being desperate and base enough to steal her money from the bat mitzvah tree, and Archie's being indignant and unrelenting enough to expose it. Yet in the end Stephanie's maturity and graciousness underscore the real meaning of bat mitzvah, transferring the focus from the rather vulgar money tree concept to the "Tree of Life," the Torah, "whose ways are ways of pleasantness, and all its paths are peace." (Proverbs 3:17)

Two treatments of bar mitzvah ceremonies in the 1980s were among the most inspiring ever in the mass media. In the 1983-1984 season of the series, *Hotel*, a landlocked version of *Love Boat*, a great uncle (played by veteran actor Bernard Hughes) sits down with the bar mitzvah boy and describes the service as the most important thing. So much for my fears that a ritzy hotel location could only degenerate into vulgarity and over-eating a la the wedding reception scene in *Goodbye Columbus*.

Then, the great uncle notices in the hotel lobby the Nazi war criminal responsible for the deaths of many Jews, and for the sterilization of many Jewish women, including this Jewish great-uncle's wife. Again, I braced myself for the worst: A Nazi loose in the hotel might mean another exploitation of the Nazi-hunter theme. Again I was pleasantly surprised. For the episode made the point—quite well indeed—that the great uncle's second "bar mitzvah" was being able to confront his former Nazi tormentor without killing him. Writers Bill LaMond and Jo LaMond did an excellent job. The final confrontation scene was most effective, and the entire episode, despite the requisite parallel subplots, managed to be moving.

For the most touching bar mitzvah ever shown on TV, I nominate CBS's *Bill: On His Own* (1983), written by Barry Morrow, the fine sequel to the 1981 film, *Bill*. Mickey Rooney returned to continue his Emmy-winning portrayal of Bill Sackter, a retarded man confined to a Minnesota state institution for forty-four years after he had been presumed insane. Sackter discovers that he is Jewish, and decides to have a bar mitzvah.

The image of him studying with the children, learning the blessings over the Torah as best he can, drives home the message that bar mitzvah is an important act of identification with Jews and Judaism at any age, for any person. It is not a privilege of youth, but of commitment. *Bill: On His Own* says this well.

Mourning Becomes Bar Mitzvah:
"Touched by an Angel"

In a rather good edition of *Touched By An Angel*, aired in the spring of 2000, Kirk Douglas portrayed the grandfather of a boy, Aaron (Shawn Pyfrom), who is preparing for his bar mitzvah. The grandfather, a health club mogul, Ross Berger, lost his faith around the time of his own bar mitzvah when his father, a pious Jew, became permanently disabled after being run over by a milk wagon. Though Ross's son, Alan (Dennis Boutsikaris), a philosophy professor, and a religious Jew, is prodding *his* son (Aaron) to study the Torah portion for his bar mitzvah, the grandfather is coaching the boy in his own philosophy of life: "Saying a bunch of stupid words doesn't make you a man. You've got to be a fighter. Never put your guard down. Protect yourself. Never depend on anybody." It is clear that Aaron would rather spar with his grandfather than practice for his bar mitzvah.

Alan wants his dad to participate in Aaron's bar mitzvah, but Grandpa is entrenched in his opposition to religion. He brags that he ate a ham sandwich after his own bar mitzvah—and liked it—and never said a prayer again. Alan understands how his father's attitude can be attractive to the boy. After all, he tells his wife, Ross is "everything I'm not. He's focused, ambitious, financially shrewd. Aaron can learn a lot from him." Still, writers Allen Estrin and Joseph Telushkin clearly indicate that Alan is the admirable one: He has a close relationship with his wife (a rare warm TV portrayal of a marriage between two Jews); he has the esteem and love of his students; and his religiosity is sincere and thoughtful. We see Alan saying a prayer when ambulances pass, teaching his son to care about others and to find genuine and profound concern through faith in God. The depiction of Alan's wife, Connie (Melanie Chartoff) is a positive image of a Jewish woman.

The viewers learn almost from the beginning of the program that Alan is ill, that he is, in fact, dying of a brain tumor. When Ross finds out, he wants to spend money to find "better doctors." He says, "Prayer did nothing for my father and won't do anything for my son." Yet when Alan is hospitalized, he wants his father, Ross, to bring in the *tefillin* (boxed scriptural passages strapped to the arm and head in morning prayers, in fulfillment of Numbers 15:37-41) that Ross inherited from his father. Alan gets Ross to put on those *tefillin* and to pray. There is a fine camera shot of

Ross's agonized prayer, which begins with the *Shema*, "Hear, O Israel" (Deut. 6:4). This is, to my knowledge, the only television program to have highlighted the use of *tefillin*. (The camera shots for this scene were most effective and artistic.) Aaron enters the room and, seeing his grandfather praying, leaves in disgust at the elder's compromise of his "principles." Later, when he is questioned by Aaron about his moments of prayer, Ross says he is not sure whether he meant to pray or not.

Seeing the angel of death, Alan recites the *Shema* as he dies. (I don't recall another moment on television where Jewish rituals of dying were featured.) Aaron then becomes more and more convinced that prayers do no good. He tells some people who are helping him make a video about exercise and stroke victims, "You can't depend on someone else to give you what you want." One of them responds, "God is not someone else." Another asks at a different time, "What bothers you the most—that your son is dying or that he's looking to a greater power than you?" Needless to say, these "people" are the resident angels, Monica and Tess.

Indeed, all three of the show's regular angels get their best lines ever in this hour. The heretical old Jew keeps them hopping. They get a taste of the classic Jewish arguing with God (and with God's messengers) that began with Abraham and Sarah. And they have to be on their toes. Monica (Roma Downey), the Irish angel, has to think on her feet even after she reveals herself to Ross in a flood of heavenly light: "Who are you rebelling against if you don't believe in God?" She adds: "You are used to getting the last word whether you're listening or not." Even then Ross has to get in the last word: "I don't like you," he tells her.

I never cared for these angels, either, but this time, I must confess, they did some good service to Judaism. The angel of death moonlights as Aaron's bar mitzvah tutor. (Are the writers getting back at one or two Hebrew School teachers?) He gives Aaron pretty good insight into the meaning of *mitzvah*: "A lot of people think that *mitzvah* just means a good deed. But it actually means Divine commandment. And a commandment is like an obligation, and being a man means that you're ready to accept those obligations, those responsibilities. You do things not because they're nice. You do them because they're good and they're right and they honor God and your family. By the time you're thirteen you should be ready to accept these responsibilities, and if you're not, then you're not ready for a bar mitzvah." This sounds particularly authoritative coming from a bona fide TV angel, as does the credit given to Judaism (in what also must be a TV first) of blessing its faithful with a real sense of peace.

Unfortunately, not all the angels get good lines. Tess, the angel played by Della Reese, mouths a rather inadequate definition of *tefillin*, considering the essential role that these objects worn in prayer play in the plot. (The addition of just a few words about what is in these boxes connected to straps would have made a big difference.) Likewise, Tess's spiel about ritual, which tries to be respectful of Jewish theology while attempting to fit into the overriding spiritual homogenization of the series, should have been cut. She tells us that "all of these traditions that humans have—the bar mitzvahs, confirmations, weddings, sitting *shiva* ... [as opposed to God-given traditions?] are all designed to bring people together in times of joy, in times of need." Is each religion seen as having its own "designer" practices? Is "togetherness" the only purpose for rituals?

Della Reese, as Tess, is made to mouth what the writers and producers regard as the moral of this episode: "God asked His children to do just two things—turn to Him and turn to others in love. And these humans do that best when they have the humility and the faith to use God's resources. And that's what makes a man—or a woman." Are commandments to be regarded as "resources" and reduced to two? Since there are other lines in the hour that make a better case for human humility before God, and since it is disrespectful to set a general agenda for religions to follow, I think it would have been best had most of theses comments been eliminated. Tess could have added a few words to her inadequate definition of *tefillin* to the effect that wrapping oneself in one's faith and in words which speak of love are a time-tested Jewish way of engendering or reinforcing love of God and of human beings. Period.

I would quibble with a few other aspects of the script, though these are relatively minor concerns. At one point Aaron acts inappropriately but understandably at the *shiva*, venting his grief and anger. He condemns the *shiva* as a party. Unfortunately, there is little effort to explain the practice beyond Tess's general comments about "human traditions"; hence, "party" is the lingering impression of the *shiva*. Also, Aaron's dad is depicted as a philosophy professor who is rather infatuated with Pascal's concept of faith as wager—a notion more rooted in the Apostle Paul than in Hebrew concepts of faithfulness in covenant, which are diametrically opposed to the "wager" terminology. It would have been a fine and even artful flourish to have contrasted Pascal with a Jewish philosopher. I know that this suggestion pushes the envelope on TV writing.

Despite these small annoyances, the episode does a fine and creditable job of providing insight into Judaism and bar mitzvah. The whole issue of "being a man," with certain classical Jewish concepts contrasted with "manhood" of the weight room variety, is pedagogically and dramatically effective, and certainly catches the interest of young viewers. My chief concern, however, is the catch-as-catch-can approach to the bar mitzvah (or two?) at the end. For in Judaism, certain traditions and customs are very much time-bound, despite the baggage and emotions and circumstances that beset individual Jews. Somehow, that aspect of Covenant and of *mitzvah* is left out of the formula in this production's depiction of Judaism.

Rosh Hashanah and Friendship:
"Our House"

In its first, 1986-1987 season, the charming series, *Our House*, broached the topic of the High Holy Days. The series starred Wilford Brimley as Gus Witherspoon, a strong-willed grandfather who takes his widowed daughter-in-law and her three children into his home. It was a well-acted and moving show.

Gus's neighbor and close friend, Joe Kaplan (Gerald S. O'Laughlin) was a beloved and important figure in the series. Joe would occasionally advise Gus on how to relate to the mother and three children now sharing his roof, and on how to get along with people in general.

In this particular episode, Kaplan describes the ten days in between Rosh Hashanah and Yom Kippur. He says that during that time "the Lord writes in the book of life for the New Year," and that "by Yom Kippur it's too late to say you're sorry." It is a time to go to one's friends and to ask if you've done anything offensive or failed to do anything in the past year. Come Yom Kippur, he concludes, "you do not have to confess to committing mischief or raising a little whoopee or what have you even if you were a bad boy in Las Vegas one weekend. That's not the issue....The real question is, Did you diminish anyone's humanity, yours or anyone else's, knowingly?"

Fasting, according to Kaplan, "is just to get you in a good one-on-one basis with your Maker without any assistance or crutches or anything like that...so that you can take a real good look at yourself without fibbing."

One might quibble with Kaplan's insistence that "by Yom Kippur it's too late to say you're sorry." Actually, the tradition extends that opportunity through the Sukkot festival that follows soon after Yom Kippur and then, in many ways, throughout the year. Yet Kaplan certainly captures the intensity and the spirit of the High Holy Day season.

What's significant is the way that Kaplan applies these teachings to help Gus with his own relationships. Joe tells him that to prevent one's relatives from solving their own problems, either by playing the martyr or by being overprotective, or both, is a diminishment of one's humanity and of theirs.

This fine episode, written by Peter Tauber, is a rarity in television. The insertion of the Jewish angle is not treated as the usual diversion, intrusion or invasion.

I called Mr. Tauber in 2002, thinking that I was about to interview a pioneering television writer, with a yeshiva background, now in his Seventies. It was a pleasant surprise to find that the author of this classic episode, so respectful of Jewish elders and their cronies, was a Baby Boomer. Tauber told me that the Jewish concepts of forgiveness and repentance have always fascinated him, and were his "hobby horse" at the time the episode was written. He added that he could have just as easily written about Chanukah, but, in retrospect, was glad that he didn't, because he did not appreciate it at the time. I found this humility and self-awareness refreshing.

Tauber, who had a typical Hebrew School education and attended public schools in the Bronx, has been mainly a journalist and a novelist. Two of his books, *The Sunshine Soldiers* (1971), which he wrote in the Army during the Vietnam War, and *The Last Best Hope* (1977) were so highly regarded for voicing the concerns and insights of the Baby Boomer generation that they became required reading on high school and college lists, and are being reprinted by popular demand. Tauber's father, Abraham Tauber, taught linguistics at Yeshiva University while a professor at City College and Bronx Community College, and also ran Jewish summer camps. His mother, Rhea Tauber taught in the New York public schools, and then became a respected voice for Jewish seniors through weekly columns and a book, *Rhea's World.*

Minyan as Sanctuary:
"Naked City"

One of the best known phrases in American popular culture in the late Fifties and early Sixties was the concluding line on the *Naked City* television series (1958-1963), "There are eight million stories in the Naked City." The show was largely the work of its reflective and resolute producer, Herbert B. Leonard, who told me, "We never treated it like it was television. It was always little movies for us."

One of the most moving episodes on *Naked City* was the one entitled "Bringing Far Places Together," with a screenplay by Howard Rodman and the story credited to Nate Esformes. It is, by any standard, an exquisite parcel of writing and acting.

First broadcast in 1963, the hour presented Alejandro Rey as Jaime, a recent Puerto Rican immigrant with no knowledge of English struggling to find a job, any job, in New York City. Jaime's utter "greenness" and inability to communicate only exacerbate his difficult situation. His frustrations are compounded by the full burden of livelihood falling on him, as his wife, in the final months of a difficult pregnancy, is bed-ridden in the dormitory-like tenement where they barely manage to keep shelter. Rey, in one of his earliest roles, brilliantly conveys the pathos of a desperate, isolated new immigrant.

Against the background of Jaime's personal struggle, viewers are given a sense of the disillusionment of the Hispanic neighborhood as a whole. As soon as community members see the police chasing anyone through their streets, they believe they must close ranks and lash out, and there is a full-blown riot, with neighbors flinging anything they can, from windows and rooftops, at the police. The hour begins with one such riot in which a young policeman, chasing vicious robbers who have shot neighbors, is felled by a brick or stone thrown from a rooftop and is badly hurt, perhaps even blinded. The riot scenes on *Naked City* are highly-charged and frighteningly realistic, and convey how dangerous rock-throwing is for police and for citizens alike.

Director Irvin Kershner spoke first about the riot scenes when I interviewed him about the episode. He recalls that he had to do all the preparations for the show, from casting to finding a location, between a Thursday and a Monday (he was called from California on the Wednesday), with the script released by producer Leonard and writer Rodman on a day to day basis. Since the episode could not be filmed in Harlem where it was set, it was shot in Jersey City (within seven days), in buildings slated for demolition. The cast and extras and crew almost froze to death (it was winter), and Kershner had to shoot above the snow on the ground. He recalls the brilliance of Rey, who spoke only two words in the drama,

"Sweep up," and had to convey his emotions mostly with looks and gestures.

A native of Philadelphia with a good Jewish background and an impressive list of achievements in academia, music, photography, and motion picture and TV directorial work (including the film, *Raid on Entebbe*, which the Israelis applauded for its accuracy, and TV's first, hard-hitting news magazine, *Confidential File*), Kershner told me that the riot scenes were all too true to life, as some of the Puerto Rican extras, seeing the police uniforms, actually threw real bottles and bricks, causing some injuries. His work on the episode brought him honorable mention in the television awards at Cannes. He later learned that the show was unanimously nominated for first place, but was vetoed by the Russians on the grounds that the Americans had already won twice in a row.

Toward the end of the first riot scene, the action cuts away to an old man who has suffered a heart attack at the nearby "Jewish Home for the Aged, Blind and Infirm." We witness bearded sages standing, swaying and praying as one of their own passes into death. The home's director, a bottom-line type who also feels for the elderly men, tries to hold back the tears at losing yet another constituent, and comments on the fragility of life.

Meanwhile, Jaime has, in desperation, given his money to a member of his own community who promises to broker him a job. Realizing that the man, Patillas, has lied to him and robbed him, Jaime seeks redress of his grievances but is unable to communicate with the police. When he sees Patillas, he goes for a choke hold, but the "good neighbors" pull him away and then cover his mouth when he tries to complain to a policeman. Later, an old Jew, Aaron (Zvee Scooler) emerges from the home and walks around in a silent search. The old man peers into the faces of the assembled neighbors, as if searching for the right kind of soul. Soon he comes upon the extortionist, Patillas, but gives him a strange look as if to question his suitability. While the Hispanic men obviously find the old bearded Jew to be a strange sight, it is only the heartless extortionist who openly mocks the old sage by asking what he is seeking, and then mocks his answer, both factual and pointed, "I am looking for another man."

The old sage is drawn to the countenance—and, indeed, to the soul—of Jaime, and tells him that he needs another man to help recite the "Prayer for the Dead"—that is, the Kaddish. He explains that ten men are required for the quorum of prayer (*minyan*), but there are only nine men available. (Obviously, the man who just died had been the tenth. The remaining residents want to recite Kaddish for him.) He adds that if ten Jewish men

are not available, they may use "nine Jewish men and one who is not."
(This is not true of Jewish religious law, but it makes for an interesting plot
line.)

Jaime is anxious to get back to his pregnant wife, who, it turns out, is
in the throes of childbirth, but the old man convinces him to spare a few
minutes "for one now dead to all eternity." The latter even offers Jaime five
dollars, but Jaime's campaneros bargain the fee up to ten dollars, thus
advocating for him in a way that they failed to do when he sought to redress
his grievances with the police. Nelson Riddle's music adds mightily to the
drama, brilliantly blending Yiddish and Hispanic motifs.

Esformes told me that in his original story line, the scouting sage,
Aaron, is blind and is attracted by Jaime's name. Esformes chose the name,
which he came upon while working as advertising manager for a large New
York Spanish-language newspaper. His intent was for Aaron to choose
Jaime after hearing it, believing it was the name, "Hymie" (used as a
Jewish name because it sounds like *Chaim* or "life"). Aaron was then to
touch the man's facial features and to conclude that he was Jewish.
Esformes was, however, happy with the changes made by Howard Rodman
and Herbert Leonard.

As Jaime enters the *bet hamidrash*, the house of study and prayer, an
elder puts a yarmulke on him and it is announced in Yiddish, "We have a
minyan." There are authentic sounds of the traditional afternoon liturgy, in
the old Polish style. While the old men are swaying ("*shuckling*") in prayer,
obviously immersed in their devotions, a chord is struck in Jaime's soul, as
well, and he pulls his crucifix and rosary out of his pocket and prays.

When the largely blind *minyan* realize that Jaime is not Jewish,
someone suggests, "What difference does it make how he says his prayers.
Do you think the dead worry about it?" A blind man gives Jaime a gold
watch as a present, saying that he can no longer use it, anyway. (The actual
translation from the Yiddish is: "This is for the Gentile child. I don't need
it anymore.") The sage who recruited him says that it is for "*su muchacho*,"
for his son-to-be. Jaime is overcome by tears at the generosity of the group
and by the concern for his child which they have shown. He and his future
child have been acknowledged and thanked by a group of men in the New
Country. In gratitude, he gives Aaron, the *baal tefillah*, the leader of the
prayers his crucifix and rosary. The latter is not quite sure what to do with
them, but accepts them graciously, explaining to the others (but in not too
much detail), "He's giving us his gift, what he's got."

Upon emerging from the Home, Jaime is fingered by the scheming Patillas, who is afraid for his own skin. The police grab Jaime, and the sight unleashes another barrage of rocks and bricks and whatever else the neighbors can throw down. Jaime is hit, and dies, a victim of a cold world, of an inhospitable country, and of neighbors of the same ethnic background who are not concerned about his frustrations and grievances because they have so many of their own.

The episode is engaging, touching and haunting—but also strange. It certainly has an "ecumenical" spirit, as Esformes described it to me. Herbert B. Leonard told me that he regards it as presenting the "universal theme of the brotherhood of everybody." When I asked director Irvin Kershner if he found the message strange, he said that he "went along" with it, but found it odd that the episode got on TV in the first place because the subject was "grim" for a medium designed to sell products and formatted to be so "happy" and "sentimentalized" as to be "untrue to life." He regards the hour as evidence that "tragedy can be very uplifting." If, as Leonard told me, the episode rises above the "normal story about two sects," then this is, I think, because it offers more than the "brotherhood" fare. It does not declare, in the current New Age spirit, that all religion is interchangeable and that there is a higher "spirituality" than religion.

Jaime's gift is so touching to Aaron because it comes from the heart of one who has been embraced by the community of aged Jews and by their prayers. They had found comfort in the presence of an outsider helping them pay tribute to their dead co-religionist. In turn, Jaime's inclusion is so moving to him because the elderly Jews are a community loyal to their own traditions and are functioning totally within its ageless structure. He therefore feels validated by that structure, which produces a climate of generosity, such that he receives a meaningful gift and wants to give what is most valuable to him. Without those perimeters of tradition, he would not feel so welcomed.

There is a sense that this praying community, though a frail, dying community, is rooted enough in particular time-honored practice to provide moments of sanctuary to someone so completely uprooted.

What did the writers intend to convey? Nathan Esformes conceived of the story and passed it on through an enthusiastic friend to the producers. Descended from a Sephardic family that recalls its fourteenth century journeys as if they were personal experiences, Esformes told me that his father, Judah, immigrated from Salonika to Brooklyn, where he met his wife, Sara, also Sephardic, who became a union organizer and a pioneer in

Montessori schools. Young Nate, like his older brother, went to Hebrew
School and became a bar mitzvah among Orthodox East European Jews. He
knew Spanish and witnessed the immigration, after World War Two, of
various Jewish sects who were refugees from Europe.

Esformes had acted in films and on television (later, for example, he
would co-star on the Western, *The High Chaparral* with Alejando Rey, and
have a role in the film, *All The President's Men*), and was breaking into TV
writing. His concept was given over to veteran TV writer Howard Rodman
(1920-1985), staff member on *Naked City*, who, according to Esformes,
rewrote it completely, retaining most of the plot and the exact wording of
the narration.

I interviewed Howard Rodman Jr., who is also a respected television
and film writer, articulate and Jewishly aware. The younger Rodman has
definite recollections of the episode, which he saw at age thirteen. His
father had grown up in Bronx and then Flatbush, in a proudly Jewish home
that was not religiously observant, but respectful of the Orthodox community all around. He was educated at Brooklyn College and at the University
of Iowa. In 1953 and 1954, he lived on Orchard Street, on the Lower East
Side and later told his son that he came to appreciate the Orthodox "spirit"
that engulfed him. Rodman Jr., whose mother, interestingly, is of Sephardic
background, describes this episode as "the most literal incarnation of that
spirit" imbibed by his father. He regards it as reflecting his father's concern
not so much with the ritual of the *minyan* as with "finding a good man."

Does the episode portray the Jewish community as a dying community?
In some ways, it does. The prayers, we are told, are "for the dead," even
though the liturgy is the regular *minchah* (afternoon) service, which only
concludes with the Mourners' Kaddish. True, in many synagogues the need
for mourners to recite the Kaddish is a great incentive to ensure the regular
daily services. The over-all purpose is not to recite prayers for the dead as
much as to parallel the daily offerings outlined in the Torah.

Esformes and Rodman were not out of line to emphasize the Mourners
Prayer for the purposes of plot and of challenging the viewers. After all,
death is not limited here to elderly Jews. It takes a young Christian man, an
expectant father, who is the victim of human apathy. As the episode turned
out, the baby is born and cries for the first time as Jaime lies dead outside
the window, with the pocket watch from the Jews, perhaps his only legacy,
beside him.

When Jaime enters the prayer room, Aaron tells the others in Yiddish
that they must pray right away, as the man's wife is expecting. He tells

Jaime that he should go to his wife soon, for "death must give way to life." Fittingly, the name, Jaime, sounds like the Hebrew, *Chaim*, "life," echoed by the name "Hymie." The ancient practices of Judaism provide sanctuary to all who would cling to life and affirm the sanctity of life even as death, whether from old age or from dangerous streets, stalks people of all ages and backgrounds.

Yom Kippur Brilliantly Applied: "Northern Exposure"

The theology and rituals of Yom Kippur, the Day of Atonement, found in Leviticus 16, were given center stage in a Fall 1994 episode of *Northern Exposure*. Dr. Joel Fleischer, who is stuck in Alaska and resents being away from New York, has had a moody *erev* (day before) Yom Kippur. He fires his receptionist Marilyn Whirlwind (Elaine Miles) because she leaves him for a few days in the middle of a hayfever epidemic to attend her boyfriend's family reunion. He refuses to help rebuild the home of a patient who is now literally out in the cold because the man burnt it down while disobeying Dr. Joel's medical orders. Actually, we note, Joel's "sins" are not terrible and irredeemable; he has a right to be upset in both cases.

There is significant dialogue in this thoughtful and even touching episode by Jeff Melvoin. Joel is "carbo-loading" at the local inn in preparation for the Yom Kippur fast. (Sociologists tell us that fasting is still a given for most Jews.) Young Ed Chiglak (Darren E. Burroughs), a Native American man, is fascinated with the upcoming observances, especially since his shamanic mentor has told him that he needs more comparative religion. Ed asks whether the fast is a "vision-quest thing." Appropriately, Joel responds that "It's not that mystical... We fast so we can concentrate on being better people and stuff like that."

Joel goes on to describe Yom Kippur as the time "when God supposedly decides what's going to happen to everyone in the coming year. What happens is you have basically ten days between Rosh Hashanah and Yom Kippur to reverse the call....You examine your soul, you atone for your sins." He also describes part of the ritual of the High Priest, reenacted in song and poetry on Yom Kippur, in which the *Kohen Gadol* (High Priest) would "symbolically place all the sins of the entire community on the head of a goat and send it off into the desert." Joel adds—and correctly—that he believes that this is where the term "scapegoat" comes from.

Joel's fine explanations of Yom Kippur to his friend, Ed, make for good TV dialogue, historically and artistically speaking. For the first time, not only on *Northern Exposure*, but virtually anywhere (except one 1979 episode of *Little House on the Prairie* by Paul Wolff), Judaism is meaningfully and accurately explained by a Jewish character depicted as knowing something about his faith and heritage and even cherishing it. And Rob Morrow as Dr. Joel has never been so—well, likeable. Not even *A Stranger Among Us* (1992), the movie about an Irish cop undercover in a Hasidic community, used the opportunity to explain Judaism as well and as engagingly and pleasantly; but there is more of significance that happens in this episode.

Ed is very impressed with Joel's explanation of Yom Kippur. He says it's a "great story," "right up there" with other cherished spiritual stories. I couldn't help thinking that after years of making Judaism appear *less* endearing or interesting than Native American and other nature-centered beliefs, *Northern Exposure* had finally at least put Judaism on the same level, but more happened here. Instead of the usual "Joel-Jewish" storyline running parallel to one or two other co-plots, the Yom Kippur motif is carried into *two* storylines—Joel's visitation by his boyhood rabbi, and Ed's attempt to relieve Holling (John Cullum) of a deep guilt over his rift with his older daughter. In an unorthodox hunt sequence which is fox-less because of local animal rights concerns, Ed volunteers to become the "scapegoat," in the Yom Kippur tradition, on which Holling can cast his guilt. Though Holling protests that the idea is foolish and that Ed could get himself hurt that way, the writer makes it clear that the whole concept is deeply compelling to Holling, who wants to go through with it and does, and even accedes to Ed's request to place his hands on Ed's head as the High Priest did on the scapegoat.

This scapegoat sequence is one of the most significant events for Judaism in the history of mass media, including novels. For it is the first time that Jewish atonement concepts were presented as more compelling and therapeutic for non-Jews than Christian or other symbols or rituals. Though Christian missionaries have, down through the ages, tried to recast the rituals of the Hebrew Bible in Christological terms (and with most bizarre results), this episode of *Northern Exposure* suggests that the old Yom Kippur ritual offers Holling everything that he needs. Not that this isn't a bit bizarre, as well. There are very gross aspects to this "application" of the Yom Kippur ritual, mainly the suggestion of a *human* scapegoat, and, even worse, of a human being becoming a scapegoat not only for a friend (at what point do the demands of friendship or the gifts of friendship themselves become unethical or masochistic?), but for a fox! One hears the radical animal rights chorus in the background, "Let people choose to endanger themselves before they endanger innocent animals."

Yet the scapegoat sequence is not the only Yom Kippur storyline. The other (and perhaps main) theme in this episode is a sequence in which Dr. Joel Fleischman (Rob Morrow) is visited by his childhood Rabbi Schulman (Jerry Adler). Both men play their roles perfectly. Writer Jeff Melvoin has given us much valuable material for consideration.

Joel's Rabbi Schulman visits him, and reviews his notes for the Yom Kippur sermon. "You know how it is [with] Yom Kippur," the rabbi says. "Essentially you get only one shot at the entire congregation for the year. What a headache." A rabbi can certainly identify with *that* line. I must confess, though, that at first I was rather put off by writer Melvoin's decision to cast these segments in the mold of Dickens' *A Christmas Carol*. The concept seemed to be a cutesy poor excuse for not doing one's homework and finding a model from Jewish lore. It seemed disrespectful to Yom Kippur to frame its message in such a way. I still feel that way. Yet the writer also does many things that are moving and that have a Jewish authenticity to them, including the dialogue I have cited so far. The best way to respond to these sequences is the old Jewish way: to offer line-by-line commentary on key passages.

1. Joel asks, "What's with the cloaks?" The Rabbi responds, "The Pharisee look." The New Testament used "Pharisee," a term for a group of Judaism's greatest Rabbis and Sages, as a term for hypocrites, liars and self-righteous fools. Is the term used here [a] for shock value, [b] as an in-your-face mockery of this slander, or [c] for an easy laugh, or perhaps [d] all of the above? The fact that we have to ask shows a flaw in communication.

2. The Rabbi says that he must rush Joel through the tour of Yom Kippur Past, Present and Future because "I'm only an intermediary, Joel, and I have a sermon to give in three hours." A better term than "intermediary," truer to both the storyline and to Jewish theology, is "messenger" (*shaliach*).

3. The Rabbi shows Joel videos of some of Joel's nasty and insensitive comments. Interestingly, those are some of the very attitudes and

statements that the series, at least in the early seasons, presented as Joel's "New York Jewish attitude." Joel protests that the comments are out of context. The rabbi responds that whatever the context, or lack of context, the attitudes and comments require repentance. *This is the first time on* Northern Exposure *or anywhere that an authoritative Jewish character has chided another Jewish character for behavior unworthy of Jews and inconsistent with Judaism.* (When, the same year, the rabbi took obnoxious Jewish lawyer Wambaugh to a *Bet Din* (Rabbinic Court) on *Picket Fences*, there was a bit of a nod in this direction, but only to use the chief Rabbinic judge to validate writer/producer David Kelley's position that Wambaugh has the right to behave like a shyster in public and to be "pious" in private.)

4.   The Rabbi offers a fine observation about repentance: "Repentance is not like washing your hands, you know. It takes time, devotion, pain even." On Yom Kippur, Jews are commanded to "afflict" their souls (Leviticus 23:27) These words are spoken to Joel before the latter is dragged to tour "Yom Kippur Present." Joel's response, "Do we have to?" and, indeed his reactions to the Rabbi at every turn, are among the best humor ever on the series and the best work of Morrow, whose facial expressions are perfect. These responses were also a major turning point in the series because it was no longer suggested that Joel must learn *mentschlikhkeit* (considerate behavior) through relationships with Maggie O'Connell, or the townspeople, or exposure to Native American spirituality.

5.   The segment on "Yom Kippur Future" was significant because Joel is not threatened with a vision of his own grave, but with the grave of someone whom he is failing to help now. He was not jolted by what people said about him after his death, but by what they will say once he leaves town. This is in and of itself a worthy Jewish response to the outlook of Dickens himself. I wish that the writer had elaborated a bit in the dialogue. I thought of Abraham Heschel's observation, "The world to come is not only a hereafter but a herenow."[1]

---

1.   Abraham J. Heschel, "Reflections on Death," *Conservative Judaism* (Fall 1973), p. 9.

6. The episode ends with a meaningful rush to the Gates of Prayer and the sounding of the *shofar*. These dream sequences parallel an actual English-style "fox" hunt taking place outside Joel's window (the race in which Ed is the "scapegoat"), and the writer makes it clear that the Yom Kippur reflections in Joel's dreams and in Ed's running are far more important that this empty exercise of vestigial British royalty. It is gruff and feisty elder stateswoman Ruth-Anne Miller (Peg Phillips), local storekeeper, who voices contempt for the latter. Unlike the series, *Babylon 5*, which would not declare a kung fu match to be an unworthy parallel plot to a *shiva* (see above), this *Northern Exposure* episode did have the courage to state a moral preference, and by more than suggestion. It also concludes by showing something rarely, if ever, before seen on TV, a Jew in deep individual prayer, namely Joel, reading the words of the Ne'ilah (Closing of the Gates) Service at the end of Yom Kippur, "Open Thou the gates, for, lo, the day waneth....Let us enter Thy gates." It is only by completing the prayer that Joel begins to break the fast by peeling an orange, albeit with a bit too much daylight still, but, then again, Alaska days *are* different.

Yet it is instructive to compare Joel's dream about the rabbi with his vision in an episode by Diane Frolov and Andrew Schneider, of living in Manhattan instead of in Alaska. The latter was induced by Ed's shamanic potion. The former seems to be a Yom Kippur reverie, induced by "glucose deprivation" (?), but announced by a totem pole. The shamanic vision was not merely a dream, but an out-of-body experience with a parallel world. The visit from the rabbi turns out to be more of a dream, for even the images of "Yom Kippur Present" turn out to have been exaggerated.

Comparing the visions of Moses and the Prophets with that of the gifted Gentile prophet, Balaam (Numbers, 22 ff.), the Talmudic Sages said that while God communicated with the latter only in dreams, the Divine will was communicated to the Hebrew Prophets while they were awake and fully conscious. It would seem that the opposite was true of *Northern Exposure*. The Jewish visions were mainly while the head touches the pillow (except when Joel stood near totem poles), and the shamanic visions break down every barrier between wakefulness and sleeping. Was there a sense here that shamanic magic is more compelling than Jewish mysticism? Or were the writers merely trying to be respectful to Judaism and Jews by allowing the mysticism to function within more "normal" boundaries?

Portraying Jewish Piety:
"A Stranger Among Us"

In *A Stranger Among Us* (1992), writer Robert J. Avrech and director Sydney Lumet place a tough, street-wise female cop, Emily Eden (played nicely by Melanie Griffith), in a Hasidic community where a young Hasid in the diamond business has disappeared and is soon found murdered. The film, distributed by the Disney Studios, contrasts the morals and crime-filled streets of the wider New York scene with the peace and piety of the Hasidic community where prayer and Torah-study and the laws of *tzeniyut* (sexual modesty) prevail. The film says that there is something in that Hasidic life that is missing from the wider world, and that has notable appeal and integrity. That message comes across loud and clear, breaking a long-standing pattern of things Jewish in major motion pictures. After all, it is easier to get gratuitous laughs by dressing as a Hasid and prancing around in the "real world," as Woody Allen has done many times a la *The Mad Adventures of "Rabbi" Jacob* (France, 1974).

What Avrech and Lumet attempt here is admirable. In both the humorous scenes and in the sad scenes they depict the sense of the sacredness of human life and deeds, which are so central to Hasidic teaching and to Judaism in general. It is amusing, but instructive, to see a young Hasidic woman covering the policewoman's arms and legs so she can show the proper modesty before the rebbe and community, a modesty expected of the men as well as of the women, by the way. It is touching but illuminating to hear a Hasidic woman explain to Emily, when they attend *shiva* for the murdered Hasid, that Jews take off their shoes in the house of mourning to show that the loss of life impoverishes the entire community. That explanation causes Emily to express her astonishment at how much the people care about one another.

Needless to say, in order to qualify as a mainstream blockbuster, the film had to have some romance and some violence. The violence is delivered, as Hollywood formula demands, in shoot-'em-up car chases and in a save-the-hostage scene, both found toward the end. The crime-resolution is hardly suspenseful or perplexing. In fact, for most of the film, for about seven-eighths of it, the audience is so engrossed in the Hasidic world as seen by the policewoman that, were it not for her taking out her gun on occasion, or some switches of scene to Manhattan, the murder "mystery" would have been forgotten.

Right after I saw the film I felt that the murder "solution" was so silly that it would have been better to have had a more low-key criminal, maybe the bus driver who drove the Hasidim to the diamond district each day. But it soon hit me that, whether intended or not, the film became a parody on the endings of most crime films, and qualifies as a kind of social commentary.

As for the "romantic" element, it seems that our hard-as-nails policewoman develops quite a crush on the rebbe's handsome stepson and heir to leadership, Ariel, memorably portrayed by Eric Thal in his professional debut. Some critics have complained that "nothing ever comes of the romance," but the attraction and mutual concern are all the more powerful because Ariel has such a strong sense of his duty. Furthermore, Thal always communicates Ariel's authentic spirituality, which includes a genuine concern for the policewoman and admiration for her. Indeed, women in this film are treated with a respect in the Hasidic world that is not found in the outside world—a direct challenge to claims to the contrary within the wider Jewish community itself.

Also, *mirabile dictu*, the Jewish woman is depicted here not as shrill or spoiled or shrew, but as knowledgeable and knowing, attractive and spiritual, devoted yet indomitable, especially in Mia Sara's low-key but effective portrayal of Ariel's sister, Leah, with whom Emily rooms. Mia Sara is able to communicate the classical quality of *Yiddishe chen* (pronounced, *"khayne"*), graciousness and understanding, traditionally extolled in Jewish women (see Proverbs 31) but cherished in men and women alike. In the person of Ariel's fiancée, the daughter of a French rebbe, who is not only beautiful and French-speaking and elegant, but is presented as Ariel's spiritual and intellectual soul-mate, this film does something that I don't remember any other film doing—namely, suggesting to Jewish males that Jewish females are a diverse and international lot, and ought not to be stereotyped or regarded as somehow limited. (The same is true, by the way, of Jewish males.) After years of films and television programs that suggest that the Jewish man can only grow and find redemption and happiness with an understanding Gentile woman, this *is* a radical statement. Why, this film even communicates the old concept of *yichus* (religiously distinguished lineage), not through lectures but by giving the audience the sense that the rabbi's daughter from France is a worthy wife for Ariel, as was Rebeccah for Isaac in the Bible.

The only scene that did not ring true to Ariel's character was a climactic moment at the end in which he visits Emily's apartment to console her (and himself) that they can never be together, and ends up dancing cheek to cheek with her, though she is scantily clad. It seems to me that the writing should have had Emily throw on some extra clothes even in her sadness, in the spirit of the comical scenes at the very beginning, and that the dance would have been more romantic, perhaps more sensual, had they danced without touching, assuming that a devout Hasid would ever have gone to the policewoman's apartment in the first place.

A Stranger Among Us does get across the flavor of Hasidic life, the Shabbat, the rituals for every aspect of life, the emphasis on Torah study and community. (These are, of course, important to any expression of Judaism.) The Hasidic outlook, however, is not sufficiently explained, nor its place in Jewish history. Nor are the explanations for *kashrut* (the dietary laws), which Leah starts to give Emily, up to par. For Hollywood consumption, the Kabbalah (Jewish mysticism) was reduced to a few sayings about sexuality and women's tears (the latter expressions coming from the Talmud more than from the Kabbalah literature). In a film which not only allows for explanations of Jewish beliefs and practices, but is enhanced by them, one would have hoped for better commentary. (Viewers will still have to turn to Martin Buber's *Hasidism and Modern Man* for perspective.) At least the writer tried.

While I was watching *A Stranger Among Us*, I thought of David Mamet's film, *Homicide* (1991). For *Homicide* also offered a policeman, a Jewish policeman, becoming absorbed in a Jewish world, yearning to find his way back to his heritage. Yet in that film, *Homicide*, the more this Jewish policeman becomes involved with Jews, the more he is betrayed, forced to be disloyal, alone. In contrast, Lumet's *A Stranger Among Us* presents a policewoman from a broken home, whose own father says it would be his greatest honor to see her have a policeman's funeral (as if her being a policewoman were not honor enough). She finds in Hasidic life a world where human life matters more than anything else and where a family's hope and pride are children and grandchildren, and where ancient spiritual commitments permeate every aspect of life, and enable people to care about strangers, as well, about "the stranger among you," to use the biblical phrase (Exodus 12:49).

Exploring Suburban Jewish Spirituality:
"Homicide"

A 1997 episode of the TV series, *Homicide*, was the first in TV history to offer a nostalgic look at post-war Jewish suburban life in a way that highlights aspects of Jewish religion and Jewish peoplehood. Such a treatment was long overdue in American television.

The complex episode, entitled "Kaddish," was scripted by Linda McGibney, and built upon story concepts by Julie Martin, James Yoshimura, and Ron Goldstein. The episode may be far more complex than the writers intended. It is, however, quite redemptive that this milestone in media history should have taken place on the show produced by Barry Levinson, one of whose major film statements about growing up Jewish in suburban Baltimore, *Avalon* (1990), managed to sidestep Jewish religion and Jewish communal life altogether. (See the above chapter on *Avalon*.)

In the *Homicide* episode, Detective Munch (Richard Belzer), who had been, in the main, a Jew-by-suggestion, comes upon a murder scene only to discover that the victim whose death he is investigating is a high school classmate, Helen Rosenthal (played as a teenager by Kennen Sisco), on whom he once had a deep crush. The episode was touching on many levels. It hits home with Baby Boomers, on matters of heritage, matters of familial and neighborhood attachments, and on issues of crime and loss, of unrealized dreams and broken marriages.

Munch learns from Rosenthal's daughter (an affecting portrayal, by Joan Louisa Kelly, of a Jewish teenage girl) that after Helen and her high school sweetheart were divorced, Helen moved in with her mother and began to attend the synagogue regularly. Until then, the only religion in the home was "watching Rudolph on TV." Helen's husband was Protestant, and so, the dialogue implies, anything more "religious" in the home would have exacerbated what was already a difficult marriage with an alcoholic husband, whose drunk driving, we later learn, led to the death of their other child, a son. In recent years, the daughter tells Munch, her mother found comfort in the synagogue. She "liked the routine, the ritual." Apparently, the *shiva* period and mourning rituals are supportive to the daughter, as well, for she says that she can now understand how her mother found comfort in her Judaism.

The daughter asks Munch if he is religious. "The only thing I have in common with Judaism," he replies, "is that we both don't work on

Saturdays." (Maybe that's not the best line the writers could have devised, but it does get the point across.) Yet when the daughter wants Munch to be part of the *minyan* (the quorum for prayer) at the *shiva* (the "seven" day mourning ritual at the home), he reluctantly agrees, knowing that it is not only religiously meritorious to do so, but also respectful and comforting to the mourners. There is no repeat here of *Northern Exposure's* suggestion, in one episode (see above), that a *shiva minyan* should be abrogated if one can't find the Jews of one's own choosing. Rather, there is a sense here of an abiding and continuous sanctity of tradition, faith and comfort that is compelling to Jews on the quiet, split-level lined *culs de sac* of suburbia, as in the *shtetls* of Europe. That awareness is reinforced both visually and musically, though it is already fostered quite well in the plot and dialogue.

The specific focus on a place, Pikesville in suburban Baltimore, adds to the authenticity and the overall effectiveness of the episode. Pikesville is also an appropriate locale for a milestone look at suburban synagogue life from the perspective of American Jewish history. From the time, in the late 1940s, that the Baltimore Hebrew Congregation commissioned architect Percival Goodman to design one of America's first major suburban temples, a new era in religious art and architecture, as well as religious expression in general, was born. During the 1960s, the suburbanization of Jewish families and even religious institutions, began to be dismissed as a purely secular and bourgeois phenomenon. Yet there were dedicated parents, grandparents and religious teachers at work. If Jewish belief is to be taken seriously, one must factor in a sense in suburbia, as in all Jewish history, of a Higher Power at work in Jewish communal life. It is most welcome to have a TV episode that reckons with Jewish religiosity and spirituality (which are one and the same) in suburbia. Many Baby Boomers somehow grew up to believe that there was more to being a Jew than they could articulate or understand, and enough people turned back to synagogues and temples like the ones in which they were raised to suggest that those institutions, while imperfect, offered something. The story of American Judaism, from colonial days to communities built by World War Two G. I.s and their families, to the present time, is fertile ground for dramas and documentary films on spirituality and worthy human achievement.

If ever there is a trend in depicting the positive and enduring aspects of suburban religious life, and I hope there will be, it would do well to consider a few guideposts that emerge from the complexities of this episode.

First, and much to be respected, is the decision of one of the writers or directors to focus on the old *Union Prayer Book*. It is only right and accurate to acknowledge the role that Reform Judaism played in creating positive Jewish feelings and genuine religious devotion. The contributions of all the streams of Judaism should be acknowledged in the gamut of any genre of films and TV shows on suburban Jewish life.

Second, there has to be a sensitive but assertive way of getting across the point that Judaism is best preserved through Jewish marriage, which means Jewish spouses, not out of contempt for non-Jews and for their worthiness as marriage partners, but out of devotion to sacred Covenant that transcends but enhances all times and places. I was more than a little uncomfortable with a subliminal message in this episode, "Munch may have been a geek as a high school student, and maybe his marriage didn't work, but perhaps if Helen had gone to the prom with him she would have avoided a disastrous marriage to an alcoholic Gentile and the tragedies that went along with it, including being strangled by an object associated with that tragic marriage." There are implied stereotypes of Gentiles in this episode, and, concomitantly, the Jews themselves are stereotyped in the process.

This issue of stereotyping brings me to my third point—namely, that television writers have to overcome a fear or avoidance of clustering Jewish characters, especially in episodes with Jewish themes. The episode about Helen Rosenthal on *Homicide* was significant because it was in that hour that the series made a definite declaration that Detective Kellerman is *not* Jewish. Munch and police photographer Brodie (Max Perlich) spend some time in that episode trying to explain Jewish customs to Kellerman ("What's a *shiksa*? What's a *shiva*?") whose medical examiner girlfriend, when asked by Munch how she knows so much about Jewish funeral laws, knows enough to respond, "I'm no ordinary *shiksa*."

As heartened as I was to see a nod of respect toward suburban Jewish religiosity, I was also saddened that the blond, impulsive Kellerman (Reed Diamond), who seemed to have been depicted as Jewish in an episode about black Muslims, was now dubbed (I believe for the first time) "Irish." Yes, "Kellerman" can be an Irish, as well as a Jewish, name, and Munch and Brodie were interesting enough, though they came across, at best, as variations on a stereotype. (True, Brodie proved himself well in a nice Tom Fantana script, against the threats of a college student thug whom he believed to be "not exactly kosher" when the latter's roommate was murdered.) Kellerman would have offered another type of working class

Jew who is rarely seen on TV. (Around the time this episode first aired, there had been publicity that Yaffet Kotto, who plays the African American/Italian captain of detectives, is Jewish, and often used his fists to defend his Jewishness while growing up on the streets of Harlem. How sad that Kotto did not get to play a black Jew on the series.) *Homicide* does deserve credit for giving us creditable Jewish characters in Munch and Brodie, which is two more Jewish cops than *NYPD Blue* ever offered as recurring characters.

Kellerman-the-Irishman's best line in the *Homicide* episode about Helen Rosenthal is his exclamation, after Munch pulls him off a mourner's stool at the *shiva*, "There's a lot of rules in this religion." The scene then cuts to a service in the Catholic church, where another detective seeks answers in the face of marital and religious problems, and where a small group of the faithful confess their beliefs and participate in the rituals of the Mass. I suppose that the juxtaposition of scenes is a kind of response to Kellerman's crack by showing that other religions have a lot of rules and rituals, too.

I would suggest, as my fourth and final point, that TV writers have to get away from the "We'll-depict-one-religion-only-if-we-can-cut-away-to-another-religion" unwritten rule, and respond to questions raised about a particular religion (in this case, Judaism) by focusing on *that* religious community, and not on another.

12

DIGNIFIED JEWISH LIFE
AND IDENTITY

໒໑໔

Authentic Jewish Healers:
"Fight For Life," "Ben Casey"

J erry Lewis and Patty Duke were very moving indeed in the 1987
television movie, *Fight For Life*, which offered the warmth and flavor
of ethnic fat or schmaltz, together with a serious and poignant topic. In this
fact-based presentation, Lewis portrayed Dr. Bernard Abrams whose six-
year-old adopted daughter suddenly develops a form of epilepsy that can
be treated only by a medication available in England, but not yet legal in
the United States, except on a limited, "compassionate use" basis. Abrams
and his wife (Patty Duke) decide that as long as the Food and Drug
Administration have not approved the drug for all children, they must seize
the opportunity to bring the matter to the attention of the public and even
risk prison in order to procure the drug for others.

Such is the serious and poignant story behind the schmaltz. In this film,
the schmaltz itself is serious—a real Jewish schmaltz, conveying an
authentic Jewish lifestyle where Jewish beliefs and practices and concepts
inform all of life and offer perspective in trying times, and even provide a
vehicle for the ventilation of anger and frustration with God Himself.

This is one of the rare occasions on television where you'll see a Jewish
family observe the Sabbath and have a menorah in the living room, and

look forward to a bar mitzvah as a spiritual rather than social occasion. Yet the film, like life itself, makes the point that these things have no magic powers and are not insurance against trouble and suffering (one of the child's major attacks occurs at a Sabbath dinner), but offer insight and perspective and even suggest a plan of action for dealing with life's trials.

Not since the 1979 episode, "The Craftsman," on *Little House on The Prairie*, written by Paul Wolff, has any television production mentioned and taught Jewish concepts with such effectiveness and meaningfulness. The key word of this film—and of the true life story it's based on—is *mitzvah*. In a very effective and moving scene, Jerry Lewis as Dr. Abrams walks out on a tennis game and weeps in the locker room that raising the baby was a *mitzvah* that he and his wife cherished. When a family friend and tennis partner, a priest, asks what a *mitzvah* is, Dr. Abrams defines it as a "commandment," an "opportunity" given by God to do good, and adds that raising a child not one's own is one of the greatest of *mitzvah*s (the plural form in Hebrew is *mitzvot*). Later on, when Dr. Abrams can't sleep because the precious drug that might help his daughter will be available to him in this country only because of his own financial and medical connections, which themselves might not cut through the red tape quickly enough, he urges his wife to allow him to publicize their plight by taking their child to England, because they will thus perform the *mitzvah* of helping other children. These points are well-made and well-taken, and the term *mitzvah* becomes known and respected in the process.

In addition to exploring the concept of *mitzvah, Fight For Life* returns to the sources of Jewish thinking and feeling in other ways. Twice Jerry Lewis quotes the Talmud in his role as Dr. Abrams, and the citations add effectively to the plot and theme. Especially creative and moving are the scenes in which father explains to son the meaning of the boy's bar mitzvah *Haftarah* (prophetic reading), so indicating that a *Haftarah* is not just a rote exercise in memorizing syllables, but an opportunity to master and to personalize the passion and teachings of the Prophets of old. In this film, the words were those of Isaiah: "Comfort ye, comfort ye, my people," words that spoke to a family that needed reassurance in their cause and their struggle.

Through the bar mitzvah preparation scenes, the film depicted well the feelings of a son whose parents must give much of their attention to the epileptic daughter, and who matures even before the bar mitzvah rites by understanding the situation and realizing that his parents are sensitive to his needs. (Jaclyn Bernstein and Sean Roberge offer creditable performances as the children, and Roberge learned his *Haftarah* very well!) The bar mitzvah motif is even carried into Laurence Rosenthal's fine soundtrack, which utilizes modes from the ancient *haftarah* trope with effectiveness and beauty, emphasizing crucial points in the drama with far more subtlety and creativity than the stereotyped Yiddish tunes long used in films to identify Jewish characters and themes.

Because the characters are so authentically Jewish, in their concerns and in their outlook, they come across as real people with whom any viewer can identify. Because one of Abrams' best friends is a priest, the dialogue allows for discussion of issues instead of the stock priest and rabbi jokes, which appear here only once as comic relief. When Jerry Lewis's character breaks down in the locker room scene to which I alluded, the priest is the only one of the tennis partners prepared to handle the issues of faith. He observes that when catastrophe strikes we ask: "Why me?" when we could just as easily ask: "Why not me?" Abrams counters that his question is: "Why her?" Why his *mitzvah* baby? How could God place the child in his hands only to afflict her? To God he shouts, right in the locker room: "Are you crazy?"

The priest looks on with what might be described as a horrified understanding. (Gerard Parkes is wonderful as Father Robert Hunt, and his reactions and expressions are just perfect.) He may not fully comprehend the old Jewish *chutzpah* with God, but he can appreciate the strong emotions and the familiarity. The priest suggests that we must look for God's plan even though we may never find it. Abrams vows to God right then and there that the child will survive. He'll worry about his side of the covenant and expect God to do His part, as well, or reserve the right to consider God crazy.

And it is precisely the affirmation of life that makes the interfaith exchanges in this film realistic and so uplifting. We won't find the bromide here that all religions are basically alike and differences are unimportant. The film says that while differing beliefs and observances are to be respected, religious belief should lead to decency and affirmation of life and offer courage in facing the ordeals that life thrusts upon us. Abrams observes: "It isn't often that an Orthodox Jew, Catholic priest, black paraplegic doctor and British doctor get together." It is precisely the spirit of shared hope and life-affirmation that makes it all believable, in this film as in life. *Fight For Life* is the real life *Wizard of Oz* scenario, where the hopeful, the hope-givers and the savants all find unity in the affirmation of life, humility before its mysteries, and purpose in its preservation. It is that rare kind of film where words like God and *mitzvah* become very real and very meaningful to the viewer of any background.

The theme of a Jewish physician teaching reverence for life through Jewish vocabulary had played effectively on television before. In a 1965 teleplay for *Ben Casey*, "The Man from Quasilia," written by Oliver Crawford and Arthur Dales and produced by John Meredyth Lucas, the character of Dr. Abe Goodman is proudly and clearly identified as Jewish. Goodman, engagingly played by Ned Glass (who unfortunately associated himself with the *Bridget Loves Bernie* series not too long afterward), speaks with a slight Yiddish accent and not only uses, but embodies, Jewish expressions and values. He is the only major physician at the hospital willing to give a poorly-trained South American doctor (Nico Minardos), who has flunked out of neurosurgery, the opportunity to learn about internal medicine (Goodman's own department) so that the latter can return, with useful skills, to his native land, where doctors are scarce. This may be television's first nod at an "affirmative action" program.

Only Goodman is sensitive enough to realize that since so few physicians are trained under such conditions, the hospital must overlook its own standards to serve that country's few doctors who are willing to remain. Goodman insists that the hospital staff must have *rachmones* ("compassion") and uses that Hebrew/Yiddish expression. He calls everyone "*chaver*" ("friend") and challenges his fellow doctors with tact, humor, and common sense: "All we can do is help him [the South American doctor] do a little better. With our own patients too often, a little bit better is the best we can hope for." To the South American he says: "Well, *chaver*, do you suppose we can pick up the batting average a little?"

Goodman is depicted as being a top-notch physician who is friendly, down to earth, and straightforward, keeps up with the most current medical literature and is more open-minded than most of the other doctors, including Ben Casey. Citing a medical journal article, he opens Casey's mind to a case where twins claim to share the same pain. As a result of this conversation, Casey anesthetizes one twin while operating on the other. The depiction of Goodman is one of the period's finest and most authentic representations of Jewishness, particularly because Jewish concepts such as *rachmones* are cited and defined for the viewers.

The Goodman character is all the more remarkable because Casey's mentor, Dr. Zorba, was played by Sam Jaffe, a Jewish actor (with roots in the Yiddish theater), and no one dared at the time to have a Jewish character as a recurring, leading persona. The writers did seem to feel an obligation, however, to refer to a "Dr. Greenberg" in order to show that more Jewish doctors can (and should) be on a hospital staff.

Shabbat Beyond Vandalism: "The Trials of Rosie O'Neill"

One of the brightest spots of television in the early Nineties was *The Trials of Rosie O'Neill,* which starred Sharon Gless in the title role of a recently divorced public defender from a privileged background. Gless offered a remarkably complex and sympathetic portrayal of one person talented and dedicated and effective at her profession, who has faced adversity and vulnerability in her life and who has a fine sense of humor but has known sorrows. The consistently well-written scripts interspersed interesting legal cases with Rosie's interaction with her therapist (usually in the prologue), her sister, her mother, her co-workers, and others. The cast was impressive in both individual and ensemble work. The music by Ron Ramin was especially fine.

Quite remarkable and noteworthy in this series is that one of the main characters is a religious Jew who constantly wears a *kippah* or skullcap. The gentleman is Ben Meyer, pleasantly played by Ron Rifkin, who directs the department of public defenders. From the first episode I wondered whether his Jewishness and obvious religious commitments would be highlighted. Early in the 1990 season these were indeed underscored in a hard-hitting and thoughtful episode.

In that episode, entitled "Shalom," a Jewish cemetery is desecrated, and Rosie is assigned the defense of the clean-cut and seemingly affable young man who is accused of being one of the vandals. After the office discussion of the case, Ben offers to drive Rosie to the cemetery of Temple Beth Shalom, which, he points out, has been his congregation for twelve years. Rosie wants to photograph the damage while seeking possible evidence for the defense. Ben agrees to take her during the lunch hour, when they can get "spiritual nourishment" instead of food.

The desecration of the cemetery is appalling, with swastikas drawn on the stones and on the grass. The hateful vandalism is powerfully presented by the camera. Rosie tells Ben that she is sorry, and asks if he is all right. He responds with resolve: "You know, three thousand years ago, if one could have looked into the future and asked oneself who's going to survive the longest, the Jews or the Babylonians or the ancient Romans or

Egyptians, one would not have bet on the Jews. But we're still here." He says he is fine. Yet Jewishness to Ben is not mere stubborn survival. It is also an important aspect of his identity. He reminisces that when he was a young boy, he wore the *kippah* (Hebrew) or *yarmulke* (Yiddish) every day. Once a week he went across town for a piano lesson, for which his parents sacrificed financially. For the five blocks that he had to walk, the neighborhood kids threw stones at him or beat him up because of the *yarmulke*. Once he decided to remove it, he found that the kids did not even notice him. He tells Rosie that although he had thought that he had it all figured out, it took him 25 years to realize that he had allowed hateful kids to take his identity away from him. The dialogue is a moving glimpse for a general audience into memories of harassment because of one's religion.

I have to admit, however, that I was a little disappointed with a line of Ben's dialogue in which he attributed his wearing the *yarmulke* to his being from an immigrant neighborhood. Actually, most immigrants dropped the *yarmulke* immediately. Was this episode to provide no insights into Jewish spirituality as it had provided eloquent testimony to Jewish survival and to the battle for positive Jewish identity in the face of anti-Semitism?

I am delighted to say that this episode came through admirably in exploring further dimensions of Jewishness and in discussing Jewish religious observances and depicting Jewish spirituality in ways that television rarely explores. Rosie is actually permitted by the dialogue to ask why Ben wears the *kippah*. Better still, he is allowed to answer, and in a way that highlights Jewish spirituality. He responds that he wears it for two reasons: "It gives me constant awareness that there's something above me—God. Also, it lets other people know that I'm very proud of who I am." This is a fine explanation by any standard. The emphasis first on Jewish spirituality is particularly important, for there are still many fundamentalist Christians who believe that Jews "do not know God."

At this point in the dialogue, upon leaving the cemetery, Ben comments that he will soon be going home for *Shabbos* dinner with his family. (*Shabbos* is the East European pronunciation of the Hebrew word *Shabbat* or Sabbath.) He asks Rosie if she wants to join them. Then, much to the benefit of the audience and to the delight of the audience and of this reviewer, we experience part of the Friday night meal at Ben's home. Ben does a very fine *Kiddush* (the prayer over wine that inaugurates Sabbath sanctity). It's a pleasure to see an actor chant Hebrew nicely. After asking Rosie if she is hungry ("Is the Pope Catholic?" is her response), Ben says the *ha-motzi* (blessing over bread). He even sprinkles salt on the *challah* (Sabbath bread)—a reminder that the table replaces the priestly altar of old.

The entire scene allows for explanation of the prayers while maintaining a sense of sanctity and spirituality. It is nice to see the way the family comes together for the Shabbat meal, and the way the children help their mother in serving the dinner. Ben's wife and children are depicted as likeable and responsive; his son is given a long-haired look to suggest free-spirited individuality which is not compromised by Shabbat observance. Ben's wife is openly upset that Rosie is defending the accused cemetery vandal, and asks Rosie if she realizes that Ben's mother is buried at that cemetery. The remark, though accusatory, is understandable and offers a sense of the tensions created by the incident, though, in this one case, I think the writers brought Ben's usually gracious wife to rudeness.

The other sequences in the episode deal with Rosie's clean-cut, "all-American" looking client who complains that he is beaten up in prison. Rosie feels sorry for him until he goes berserk in the courtroom, spouting vicious epithets at the African American judge. After it becomes painfully clear that he spearheaded the vandalism of the cemetery and the beating of a 64-year-old black security guard with a metal pipe, Rosie argues that he should be treated as someone who is mentally warped, and suggests that a stint as a volunteer at a Jewish nursing home would cure him of his prejudice. Fortunately, the judge does not agree and sentences him to six years in jail, even as the young hate-monger indicates to Rosie that he is not insane. The show makes the point well that the clean-cut look can be deceiving (even as the "long-hair" look of Ben's son can go with good family life) and that Rosie, while well-meaning, is not always wise in her suggestions, even though she is competent, diligent and resourceful in her work.

This episode is one of the most effective ever in the genre of exposing hate crimes. Not only the sheer offensiveness of the pictures of the vandalism, but the insights into Jewish sensibilities and the viciousness of the hate-mongers make for a taut and knowing drama. True, as in all programs and films in this genre, the writers feel they must get the audience to identify with hatred of Jews by linking it with hatred of blacks and of others and with violent crime to further emphasize its evil. In the scene at the cemetery, the audience was prodded to identify with desecration of Jewish graves because Rosie herself connects with this when she sees the name "Rose" on one of the smashed headstones. Yet this program is most impressive and significant in that it allows a committed and devoted Jew to speak and to share his responses and to emerge as a good and religious person who has genuine spirituality as well as ethnic pride. At the end of the episode, his *kippah* or *yarmulke* becomes a symbol not only of his Jewish spirituality but the inspiration for a touching human bonding between him and a black colleague. The point that is made so well in this episode is that being a good Jew is a good way to be a good human being, and that Judaism adds to the life of the religious Jew a unique and precious perspective and dimension. For getting across this point so well, writers Nicole Yorkin, Dawn Prestwich and Joe Cacaci deserve much credit, as does producer Barney Rosenzweig.

TV's Best Chanukah: "Big Brother Jake"

Big Brother Jake is one of the most pleasant TV series ever. At its best, it manages sentimentality without sappiness, cuteness without cutesiness, and some very good and refreshingly wholesome laughs. This sitcom ran on the Family Channel (formerly the Christian Broadcasting Network) from 1990 to 1994. Jake Steinfeld starred as a thirtyish Hollywood stuntman who returns home to Brooklyn to help his recently widowed foster mother raise several children in an interfaith and interracial household. Steinfeld, already well known as a personal trainer to Hollywood stars and for his exercise and health program on the Sports Network, took with ease, grace and notable talent to the sitcom genre, which showcased well the sincerity and earnestness he has brought to other aspects of his career. The cast of this program is, in fact, uniformly excellent. Seldom has such an ensemble of affecting and gifted children been assembled on one program. The timing and delivery of the youngest and more mature actors alike are impressive.

The show offered fine treatments of the grief of widowhood, children's need for trust and support, neighborhood squabbles—all within the standard sitcom boundaries, to be sure, but with a bit more depth and imagination than usual. It wasn't until the third episode that Jake used Yiddish words like "*oy*" and "*kvetch*" and referred to his bar mitzvah, and reminisced about the time that a nun who was "a few beads short on her rosary" had given him a St. Christopher medal.

I was uneasy about the very concept of a Jewish boy being raised in a foster home that was not Jewish. Traditionally, Jewish children are adopted by relatives or sent to Jewish homes. I couldn't help thinking that the fondest dream of many an evangelist throughout the centuries was to "save" the Jewish child by somehow freeing that child from "indoctrination" by the parents. In this century, such associations took on both noble and horrible dimensions during the Holocaust. Many Christians—including priests and nuns—courageously rescued Jewish children at risk of execution by the Nazis, yet there were myriad cases of attempts to convert Jewish children, or at least not to discourage such conversion if the children somehow got the idea.

I had a feeling that *Big Brother Jake* would make some kind of significant statement around Chanukah and/or Christmas-time in its first season. I was not wrong. What occurred, much to my surprise, was a full-blown episode on Chanukah, perhaps the only one of its kind on television in 1991.

That episode began with a cute segment on the grab-bag tradition in the foster home of each person buying only one gift for someone chosen at random. Yet that segment, in which one of the kids observes that the simple holiday grab-bag tradition is turned into a "hostage crisis," is only the side theme. The main theme is definitely Chanukah. Jake announces at the outset that he celebrates Chanukah, and recalls impishly that when he was a kid he exploited his "ethnic heritage" by insisting on eight gifts. Was Chanukah, was Jewishness, to be presented as mere "ethnic heritage," with no spirituality?

Toward the beginning of the episode, one of the older children, Lou (Josiah Trager), receives a Chanukah card from his father, and Jake, noting that Lou is upset, follows him as he studies the card which plays Jewish songs and which is from a father who can't be with him but sends him $100.00. Jake asks Lou why he never told Jake that he's Jewish, and Lou, who at the beginning of the show was reserving the TV for his favorite cartoon Christmas special, answers that he never thought that his Jewish background was important enough to mention. He is more interested in the silliest and most exploitative Christmas special about magical animals who assist shoppers. Jake asks Lou if they can celebrate Chanukah together, and Lou says that he usually goes along with the rest of the family and celebrates Christmas. Jake rightly insists that Chanukah is not Christmas, and when Lou asks why "they" put the two holidays so close together, Jake correctly dismisses it as coincidence. In a conversation a little later on, Lou (who often feels "different" enough because of a weight problem) becomes testy and says to Jake: "What makes me Jewish? The fact that my father is?

It's not a lot to go on. Personally, I don't need another way of being different." (Nothing is said of Lou's mother.)

In another scene, Jake explains the Chanukah story to the two restless and mischievous twins in the household. The lads find a silly use for the *menorah* (candelabrum) and show no interest in the story except to quip that it "didn't happen in Brooklyn." While Jake relates the story, his foster mother (engagingly played by Barbara Meek) who is Christian and African American, fills in all the many details about Chanukah that Jake cannot remember. What's nice about Jake's explanation is that he speaks not only about the battles of the Maccabees, but of their desire to worship God. Spirituality as well as ethnicity is highlighted.

When upset with young Lou, Jake complains, "I don't believe him. You just don't turn your back on something this important if you're mad at your father." Jake's foster mother replies: "What's your excuse?" Jake responds: "I'm no rabbi, but I'm a good Jew." She says, "You don't have to be a rabbi, Jake. You just have to know what you believe. I don't think that you do anymore." Jake admits that he got out of the habit of doing things like going to temple, and that he may not be as qualified to teach Lou about Chanukah as he might have been some years back.

It is at this point that we get the story of Jake's entry into the foster household, and a moving story it is. It seems that Jake's parents trusted their good friends and neighbors to be his guardians in case anything happened to them. His foster mother says that Jake's parents, who were killed in an accident, trusted her and her husband with the most precious thing in their lives, and they raised him as his parents would have wanted, with Hebrew School, having a bar mitzvah ceremony, making sure that he was part of a community that was important to them. "It's sad to see that you turned away from that," his foster mother says, and, referring to the Chanukah story, adds: "No one sent an army or burned your home down [to remove you from Judaism]." Her words seem to hit home, at least to the extent that Jake makes a crack about her having the "Jewish guilt" thing down "pretty good"—a gratuitous crack, by the way, which is out of place here.

At the end of the episode, the family discovers that Jake has "gone to Temple." Jake describes his experience of sitting alone in the back, following whatever he can, when all of a sudden a "little guy" in his sixties comes up to him and says: "You're Joel Rosner's son," telling Jake that he looks exactly like his father. The man and his wife help Jake to follow the service. "There's nothing like walking into a place and with no questions asked and just belonging," Jake concludes as Lou listens carefully to what might be television's first depiction of the value and emotional power of synagogue ties. Not surprisingly, Lou asks Jake to show him how to light the *menorah*. Better still, Jake recites the blessings very well in Hebrew, and, in a move that separates the men from the boys (or the women from the girls), takes the lit *menorah* to the window to fulfill the custom of proclaiming God's miraculous deliverance. The episode, clever and well-written by Chris Auer and Jeffrey Sweet, ends with a fine setting of a Chanukah song.

Chanukah and Interfaith Marriage: "Commish"

Set in a suburban New York community, *Commish* starred Michael Chiklis as the police commissioner of a smaller city with big city problems. The program deals with every possible issue and theme, from the homeless to child molesters, from overzealous police to euthanasia, always offering intriguing twists in the writing and unique perspectives and knowing observations.

In its earliest segments, the series presented a Jewish chief of detectives, Irv Wallerstein (nicely played by Alex Brushanski), as a close friend and loyal colleague of the commissioner. When the police commissioner is threatened, we hear a concerned Irv quip that he would not want to see his boss killed because the next commissioner would probably not give him two days off for Rosh Hashana. For some reason, however, the writers decided to kill off Wallerstein. They made it clear, however, that his was a traditional Jewish funeral. His children wear knitted *kippot* (Hebrew plural for *kippah* or skullcap), demonstrating personal interest in ritual observances, and even the commissioner dons a *yarmulke* (the Yiddish word for *kippah*).

Especially significant about this series is that it was the first, and, as of the publication date of this book, the only program to have dealt tastefully with the issue of raising children as Jewish in interfaith marriage. For, as it turns out, the Commish's wife, Rachel (affectingly played by Theresa Saldana), is Jewish. Rachel is portrayed as intelligent, kind and supportive to her husband and young son. She is also presented as a competent and dedicated special education teacher. In one episode that effectively explored the conflict between her own professional dedication and dangers created by her husband's profession, Rachel's educational methods and concern for her students were highlighted with great detail and attention.

Just as *Commish* focused on the unique problems of families of police commissioners, so does it grapple tastefully with the challenges of mixed marriage. It is refreshing that in this series a decision has been made as to how to raise the child; and it is more refreshing still that the decision was made to raise him as a Jew. In the "December Dilemma" episode, first aired around Chanukah and Christmas, 1991, Rachel is concerned that she is losing her "grown" son because he is going to his first boy-girl Chanukah party. (It is noteworthy that the party is strictly Chanukah.) Yet her son, David, is worried that his dad may miss having a Christmas tree. He asks why they don't have one since some of his Jewish friends have trees. His mother tells him that it was very important to her that he be raised Jewish, and elaborates: "When other people, the majority of other people, have something, it's only natural to want it, too, and to feel like you're missing out. We have a beautiful tradition, and your dad and I wanted you to be raised in it, with as little confusion as possible." After kissing David, Rachel adds: "Don't worry, I don't think he misses the tree at all."

That is a brave soliloquy to have in any popular TV series around Christmas time. Writer Stephen Kronish does this brilliantly. When you think of it, it is only fair that TV drama take into consideration interfaith families where the child is being raised Jewish. Such forthright dialogue does not promote intermarriage (already a reality), but it does encourage those who are trying to raise their children as Jews. Given *thirtysomething*'s now classic glorification of the inability to decide and the inclination to spin jokes and stereotypes at Judaism's expense, *Commish* offered a most welcome and balancing approach to interfaith marriage. Even an episode about Rachel's ne'er-do-well (that is, *shlemiel*) brother, which could have degenerated into a stereotype of Jewish brothers-in-law, managed to transcend any ethnic labeling with a truly heartwarming approach to the issue of respect for human dignity despite personality clashes.

Sexual Mores:
"Touching"

The Arts and Entertainment cable network presented in 1989 a unique production in its *Shortstories* series, entitled *Touching*. The film is an account of a summer school meeting of an orthodox Jewish girl and a non-orthodox Jewish boy. The two young people, Dalit and Barry, winningly played by Lisa Edelstein and Barry Mann, two gifted and good-looking young actors, are instantly drawn to one another, as the viewer learns from the glances they exchange when their chemistry teacher observes of certain chemicals that they attract like man and woman. When Barry suggests that they go out, Dalit responds that there would be no point to their dating because they couldn't marry, anyway, since she is orthodox. She adds that this is, in fact, her first time taking classes outside of an orthodox school. When Barry proposes that they study for their tests together, however, she gladly agrees.

This film is labeled as a production of the New York University Institute of Film and Television, in the undergraduate department. One can only marvel at the fine writing, directing and editing by the young filmmaker, Robert Goodman. The cast selection is also impressive. The film-maker creates a realistic atmosphere in the classroom, at Dalit's home, and in the indoor and outdoor settings where the two study and talk. The pacing, the expressiveness of the actors which enhance the interesting dialogue and lend a compelling realism to the story—these all demonstrate the remarkable talent, even sophistication of the film-maker.

I was particularly fascinated with the warmth of the young couple and the sincerity and depth of the conversation. The most important dialogue in the film is that in which Dalit explains to Barry the traditional laws against *negia*, or touching between unmarried men and women. Barry is aware that Dalit has missed a study session because of a date. He is shocked to learn that she was out until 5:00 a. m. just talking, that, in fact, she has never even touched the hand of a boyfriend on a date. He says that he has orthodox friends but has never heard of *negia* before, and wants to know where in the Torah these laws are found. Dalit admits that they are not in the Torah, that they are traditional regulations that emerged among the ultra-pious, and that not all orthodox Jews observe *negia.* She adds that her parents don't observe it. Barry unnerves her—both in the sense of making her defensive and in the sense of challenging her beliefs—when he asks her how she can choose this restriction without having even experienced such touching. He adds that touching is not like tasting pork. He raises the question of whether touching is not more important than sex. The clear implication, both of Barry's queries and of the film, is that Dalit has imposed certain stringencies on herself which orthodox practice does not require.

The filmmaker certainly picked an unusual theme. He has created likeable characters and an interest in Jewish traditions. The question is what his purposes are. At the end of the film, Dalit tells Barry that she *wants* to hug him, and almost does. Barry tells Dalit that he wants to see her. He says that he kept hoping that she'd "break" and hug him, but that he is now happy just knowing that she *wants* to hug him. He adds that he doesn't know what kind of relationship he can have without hugging, but it's better than not seeing her at all. His declaration touches her so deeply that she *does* hug him—right at the end of the film. The last words in the film are Barry's: "Girls. Can't figure them out," he says gently to Dalit.

Films. Can't always figure them out, either.

What is Goodman's purpose here? Is it simply to create a "love conquers all" type of story? Dalit's religious values seem too genuine and respected by the film-maker for that to be his purpose. Yet the film finishes on a fine line between compromising one's religious principles and rethinking them while remaining loyal to the religion. Unfortunately, it fails to define that fine line, even to mention it, and ends flippantly. Yet much of the dialogue and the concept itself convince the viewer that Goodman did not intend for the ending to be a parody on the film itself.

It seems to me that there are two trouble spots in the movie which led to the unsatisfactory ending. First, a key dialogue between Dalit and her father fell flat. It is clear that her father is religious. He is studying a sacred text when they begin to talk. This lends him religious authority, as does the convincing portrayal by Marvin Brenner. But the dialogue does not. When Dalit expresses her doubts about her self-imposed regimen of *negia*, her father says: "Do you know what I believe? The Scriptures say that there are certain things that you just don't do. You don't kill another human being. You don't engage in incest or adultery, and you don't worship idols before God. Everything else, if you're that hungry, so you eat." By *that* argument, dear old dad could encourage premarital sex and eating pork! It is clear from the context that he doesn't intend to do *that*. When Dalit complains that Barry isn't kosher and doesn't "keep Sabbath" (a new Hebraism?), Dad replies: "So, you'll convert him." Obviously, Dad sees the need for some "conversion."

In his speech, Dad mentioned the three cardinal sins for which the Rabbinic Sages recommended martyrdom rather than infraction. It is ridiculous to suggest that in Judaism, or in any spiritual regimen we take seriously, the rule is, "If you're that hungry, you eat." This was the place for Dad to explain to Dalit—and to the viewers—the distinctions between

Jewish Law and certain *chumrot* (personal stringencies) which are not required under changing social circumstances. The dialogue should have emphasized the beauty and blessing of Jewish Law. Instead, the stringencies were defended and then debunked. The result is that Dalit seems fickle. Jewish Law appears to be burdensome to the point of defeating its own purposes, and one wonders what Barry could "convert" to and why it is necessary at all.

The other troublesome scene—though not as critical to the theme—is Dalit's "date" with an orthodox Jewish pre-med student. It is clear that her boyfriend is concerned only about grade point averages and professors' recommendations to medical school. When Dalit asks him whether he has ever dated non-orthodox women, he replies: "I honestly don't think I've ever been introduced to a girl who wasn't orthodox," and then immediately goes on to describe the "recommendations" he hopes to receive. The implication here is that Dalit's date's orthodoxy is rather unthinking, and that he is chiefly concerned about career and upward mobility. The problem is that there is nothing in the film that presents more thoughtful Jewish observance. Also, why should Dalit's feelings for Barry be affected one way or another by anybody else? Why can't the chemistry of their characters and their mutual respect for one another be enough of a reason for their feelings? Why does an "orthodox" Jewish boy have to look bad in order for Barry, a "non-orthodox" Jewish boy, to look good?

Despite these problems, *Touching* is a worthwhile endeavor of an exceedingly gifted young film-maker. Yet all would-be filmic portrayers of differences within the Jewish community will have to recall that the audience, both Jewish and non-Jewish, must be given some insight into Jewish Law and Jewish belief in general in order to appreciate any specific differences or disagreements.

Jewish Marriage Affirmed: "Crossing Delancey"

Crossing Delancey (1988) is a pleasant, intelligent, romantic comedy, cleverly and tightly written and winningly acted, which presents some very old Jewish—and by now universal—values in a most refreshing, contemporary way, blending humor and pathos, wit and romance. It affirms the traditional values of marriage and companionship without being preachy, moralistic or corny.

The drama centers on Isabelle ("Izzie") Grossman—a lovely performance by Amy Irving—who insists she is content with her job at a New
York bookstore where she organizes literary soirees for outstanding writers
and publishers who rely upon her. Izzie also enjoys visiting her "Bubbie"
(an Anglicization of *bubbeh*, Yiddish for "Grandma"), a delightful
performance and debut on the big screen for veteran Yiddish theater actress
Raizl Bozyk, who refuses to believe that her 33-year-old granddaughter is
happy as a "single." At one point Bubbie tells Izzie that she lives "alone in
a room like a dog." To no avail does Izzie explain that that "room" is an
enviable rent-controlled apartment and that she is perfectly content with her
friends and fulfilled in her work.

Bubbie summons a *shadchan* (matchmaker) in her Lower East Side
neighborhood. Needless to say, Izzie is not pleased with Bubbie's *Fiddler
On The Roof* tactics, and is downright hostile when she meets Sam Posner,
a pickle salesman, who turns out to be uncomfortably charming and
sensitive and attractive to Izzie. The seeming contradictions in his
personality, and the fact that he is so poised and is such a stable character
despite those "contradictions," rankle Izzie all the more: He always has his
hands in pickle barrels, yet is well-read and well-educated; he plays
handball but attends the morning *minyan* (prayer-quorum). Peter Riegert is,
by the way, the best possible choice for the part. He and Amy Irving get
across the point well that there *are* such creatures as nice Jewish boys and
nice Jewish girls, and that there is a lot of common experience and
background and values to commend such beings to one another. One can
even—and should—assume from this film, despite negative images of
young Jewish men and women in films since the late Sixties, that Jewish
young people in general fit this bill.

With such an "ethnic flavor," all the way down to the pickles, and with
such a clear contrast between Izzie's Manhattan and her grandmother's
Lower East Side, the film could easily have fallen into stereotypes, but it
doesn't. Likewise, it could have been so self-conscious that its characters
might have lacked any flavor or authenticity at all. Fortunately, it isn't. This
is not to say that the characters aren't, shall we say, "exaggerated" a little.
But herein lies the fun of the film and its effectiveness at getting its points
across. Bubbie's histrionics enable her to walk the line between wise
concern and devious plotting and make her even more lovable. Matchmaker
Hannah (Sylvia Miles) belches and eats like a glutton, yet somehow earns
the respect of her clients, if for no other reason than because of her noble
calling. Izzie is rendered delightfully human (in a vulnerable sort of way),

and still more sympathetic, when, out of vanity and naiveté, she develops an awkward crush on an irresponsible novelist.

Not only does *Crossing Delancey* get the most out of the main characters by approaching them with a certain sympathetic playfulness, but it also uses secondary or supporting characters in a way unsurpassed by any film. Co-workers, old high school friends, strangers at park benches or hot-dog stands, even a singing street lady, enhance the main characterizations immensely. The only time that a main character could have made a better showing is a scene in which Sam walks into one of Izzie's literary gatherings and exits before he has an opportunity to hold his own. His leaving, although understandably motivated by a desire to be alone with Izzie, appears too much like running away. One hopes that he would have stayed five or ten minutes more and made his mark. Yet in the same segment he does take hold of events by finding a way to divert Izzie's bearded, unhappily married occasional houseguest.

Crossing Delancey is rich in ethnic—or better, Jewish—traditions and terms. Yet somehow these "Jewish" aspects seem to lack effectiveness or spiritual impact. This is especially true of one scene where Izzie attends the *brit* (circumcision) of the baby of an old high school friend. Somehow the spiritual significance is lost in standard *brit* jokes which even the baby could have written. (The baby ad libs, anyway.) The writer seems hell-bent on making the point that Izzie's friend has had a baby to raise "on her own" only because her "biological clock" was winding down, and that the friend's main concern is that the baby be profitable and pay his own way by becoming some kind of Gerber or other ad model.

It is heartbreaking that some of the truly beautiful and authentic allusions to Jewish traditions will be lost to the general audience due to lack of explanation or at least translation, such as Sam's reference to attending the daily *minyan*. The most moving and romantic line in the entire film is Sam's line that he was so happy to see Izzie that he made a *brocho* (blessing) for the occasion, reciting the first blessing that came to his mind, one having to do with trees. We can forgive him for not thinking of the *shehechiyanu* prayer recited on special occasions, and we are most grateful to the writer and producers for leaving the line in the film. Authentic Jewish characters must use authentic Jewish terms in films; but the writers must find ways to explain those terms creatively.

The film does miss opportunities. Its sentimentality is so solid that a little schmaltz, an extra dose of sentimentality with a slight nod toward corniness, would not have hurt. A good old-fashioned wedding scene, with *chuppah* (wedding canopy) and all, would not have been out of place here. It's obvious that the writer and producer wanted the film to end in the contemporary key of "maybe," or even in the higher key of "probably." I suspect that many viewers would have preferred it to have ended with a definitive "*mazel tov.*"

Director Joan Micklin Silver has observed in an interview that star Amy Irving pushed this project even though film companies had serious doubts that anything so "Jewish" could win the hearts of so many viewers. Despite some of the criticisms expressed in this review, *Crossing Delancey* aims for a Jewish authenticity that most films on "Jewish" themes just do not have, with the exception of Silver's previous film, *Hester Street* (see below). This, even more than the fine acting and witty writing, makes *Crossing Delancey* unique and precious. Written by Susan Sandler and based on her original play, this film broke new ground and posed worthwhile challenges for film-makers who seek to explore Jewishness.

Explaining Jewish Marrying-In:
"Our House," "Buck James"

In the spring of 1988, the pleasant and good-natured family series *Our House* offered the most significant television exploration of Jewish-Gentile relations to date, presented with a rare sensitivity and depth in an intelligent teleplay ("Two-Beat, Four Beat") by E. F.Wallengren and Jerry McNeely.

It seems that Joe Kaplan (Gerald O'Loughlin), wise and concerned neighbor and best friend of Grandpa Gus (Wilford Brimley) is not admitted into Grandpa's club because he receives one negative vote in what must be an unanimous election. Gus and Joe are stunned by the rejection, and Joe cries anti-Semitism. Gus responds that he would not belong to a club closed to Jews or to anyone else, and that there are already four or five Jews in the relatively small organization. Joe insists that the members are concerned about "too many Jews" taking over, and is certain that one member of the committee "doesn't like *yarmulkes* (skullcaps) around." If the cause of the dissenting vote is not anti-Semitism, Joe adds, then "you're telling me I'm rejected because of a character defect." Either way, Joe is hurt and stops seeing Gus because Gus remains a member of the club. "Forget it, I don't wanna *be* in that darn club anyway," Joe shouts, betraying his deep hurt in a most childlike, primal way.

Gus decides to investigate. He wants to find the one member who voted against Joe. His first stop is the office of a successful Italian American gentleman who sympathizes with Joe's hurt. This gentleman recalls his father saying that there are things that his children shouldn't expect to attain in American society because they are Italian. "I was enraged—at him for believing it; at everybody else if it were true," he tells Gus.

Certain that the blackball does not rest here, Gus visits a friend, Irwin, who repairs vacuum cleaners and other items. Gus tells Irwin that he is determined to find the guy who did such a "weaselly" thing as to blackball Joe. Irwin protests that this was not a "weaselly" thing to do and that the rules do not call for the members to explain their votes. "Rules or no rules," Gus says, "...I think the fellow who did it ought to be able to stand up and say so." It becomes clearer and clearer in the course of the conversation, to Gus and to the viewer, that Irwin is the one who voted against Joe. Finally, Irwin admits it, saying that he is no bigot and has good reasons for not wanting to see Joe in the club. Gus tells him that he should explain his reasons, observing that "you let a fella be humiliated and now you haven't even got the gumption to tell him why....To me that's the worst kind of bigotry."

To Gus's surprise—and to the viewer's—Irwin responds that he voted against Joe because he believes that Joe is a bigot. "Bigotry goes two ways, you know, Gus," he says, adding that he's changed his mind and would be happy to tell Joe to his face why he voted against him. Gus arranges a time and a place for Irwin to air his grievances before Joe and him.

It turns out that about ten years before, Kaplan's niece was staying with him while in college, and she fell in love with a boy names Dennis Clifford, who happened to be Irwin's son. Dennis was deeply in love with her, as well. Irwin says he voted against Joe because Joe broke Irwin's heart by telling him that his niece couldn't see him anymore because he isn't Jewish. As a result of Joe's interference, Irwin says, his son Dennis was all "torn up inside," and even flunked out of college. He was so hurt that it took him a "couple of years to get his life together again." Irwin asks Joe Kaplan: "Are you proud of what you did?"

Kaplan recalls the incident, and responds with compassion and respect to Irwin's accusations. "In my opinion," Joe says, "the most precious thing in a person's life is his or her religious beliefs." He explains that his niece was from an Orthodox family and was deeply in love with Irwin's son, but decided that she couldn't marry him because of her religious convictions. She didn't have the heart to tell him. "So," says Kaplan, "that's where I came in." He adds: "I backed her up then and I'd do it again. But if I hurt your son as much as you say I did, I'm sorry. I'm truly sorry. And I guess that's about all there is that I can say." Joe then quietly leaves the room.

"That's a pretty good man, you know." Gus tells Irwin after Joe leaves. "And one of the most honest I've ever met in my life." That's one of the most honest and straightforward conversations on a controversial issue that you will ever see on television. The issue of Jewish separateness has been a subject of discussion and controversy ever since the ancient Gentile prophet Balaam described the Jews as a "people that dwells apart, not reckoned among the nations." (Numbers 23:9) The ancient Greeks regarded the Jews as misanthropic and mean-spirited for not intermarrying and eating and worshipping with peoples around them. Indeed, in the ancient world it was the Jews who were regarded as bigoted and intolerant because they recognized only their God. The Jews could only respond with the teachings of their prophets and sages that being "chosen" does not mean thinking Jews are "better," but refers to keeping the Jews' side of the Covenant with God which entails holiness or "separation" by beliefs and rituals and family relationships.

Gerald O'Loughlin as Joe Kaplan certainly gets across the pathos of the struggle of a committed Jew to preserve his or her distinctiveness and yet to be part as much as possible of general society and to cultivate meaningful and cherished friendships with Christians and others.

I would, however, take issue with two points in the dialogue. First of all, who says that only "Orthodox" Jews are concerned about their religious commitment and about intermarriage? This is, of course, a concern for all devout Jews. Secondly, it does seem cowardly and cruel of Joe's niece to have refused to have faced her boyfriend and told him herself why she could not see him anymore. Joe was put into a position—and was wrong to let himself be put in a position—that no one could handle with sufficient finesse, let alone grace and gentleness.

Still, this episode should serve as a paradigm and standard for any future explorations of Jewish-Gentile relations on television. It gets beyond the issue of bigotry (which is an important issue, but not the be-all and end-all of the discussion) and explores in a simple, straightforward way, some very complex facts of life—of Jewish life; and of contending with Jewish life, by Jews and non-Jews alike.

That same season, in early 1988, another excellent treatment of Jewish in-marriage was aired, in a series set in the Southwest.

Though in the main a strong, competent and thoughtful Jewish woman, Dr. Rebeccah Meyers (Alberta Watson) persisted in asserting that one can best be Jewish in New York. Though entitled to her opinion, she kept throwing it into the faces of colleagues in Texas, in rather rude fashion. Also, she was unwise in her relationships, somehow linking up with married men, and uninformed about her Jewish history, unaware of an old and continuous Jewish presence in Texas.

The character of Dr. Rebeccah Meyers was central—and sometimes even focal—to the *Buck James* series. (Dennis Weaver played the senior surgeon with the title name.) Significantly, the very last episode aired in the first-run cycle of the series centered on a visit from Rebeccah's Jewish grandparents. It happened to offer one of the most sympathetic and authentic depictions of Jews ever broadcast on television, and perhaps the most thoughtful and decisive television dialogue on the topic of interfaith dating. The episode was written by David Abramowitz. It is deeply moving, as well, in the way it deals with problems in the pregnancy of Buck James' daughter. This episode, like all the others in the series, was enhanced by Barry Goldberg's fine music.

Theodore Bikel and Thelma Lee are endearing as Rebeccah's grandparents, who come across as sweet and genuine people. The grandmother is considerate of Rebeccah's financial situation (she would rather stay at a cheaper motel than have her granddaughter spend money on an expensive room) and she is generous and loving, deriving great pleasure from making lovely dresses and other clothing for Rebeccah. Her skills with a needle clearly match Rebeccah's skills with a scalpel. In her own way, Grandmother is at least as strong and outspoken as Rebeccah. Before the end of the episode Grandma will have ridden a horse for the first time!

When Rebeccah tells Grandma that she is dating a "very fine man" who is not Jewish, Grandma responds that the Pope is a fine man too, "but I wouldn't want you dating him, either." Grandma is aware that Rebeccah's friendship could easily become love: "He's a nice man. I could love him if he were Jewish. And if I could love him, you could love him, too." Grandma also has moral standards and is protective of her husband's sensibilities. When she discovers that Rebeccah's boyfriend has been spending the night, she discourages her from following this practice during their visit. "Don't do this to your grandfather," she says. One would have liked to have seen Grandma take a stronger stand in her own right, as well.

Theodore Bikel offers, as Grandpa, the most affecting performance I have ever seen him give. When he visits the hospital where Rebeccah works, he asks the hospital administrator whether Rebeccah is a *mentsch*. When it is clear that the administrator does not understand the term, Grandpa defines it by asking, "Does she see a human being behind the pain or just another body to be mended?" The best way to represent authentic Jews and authentic Judaism on TV is to *teach* Jewish concepts—with dramatic skill and creativity, of course. At this task, Bikel's characterization succeeds eminently. The administrator is touched by the question and responds that Rebeccah is in fact a *mentsch*.

In a nice scene, Bikel as Rebeccah's grandfather meets Dehl Berti as Buck James' Native American ("Indian") foreman. Grandpa, a butcher, admires the way the foreman is preparing meat (though Grandpa, a kosher butcher, cannot partake of it) and he asks if it is true that Indians say a prayer before taking the life of the animal. Grandpa is sensitive to comparative religion and is a thoughtful man, conversant with Aristotle and Plato, and quotes Spinoza in his discussion with the foreman. The latter tells him: "You're the first Jew I've ever really talked to. I'm pleased to know you." The viewer shares these sentiments.

In this particular episode the Jewish grandparents are not only comfortable in Jewish observances and beliefs, but their rootedness in tradition and its teachings enables them to offer perspective and comfort to others. Thus, when Rebeccah and her grandparents meet her boyfriend's angry wife (!) the grandparents are able to get their moral convictions across to Rebeccah without hysterics. Grandma's words are well-chosen. When Dr. Buck James faces a tragedy in his own family, he finds comfort in being invited to a Shabbat dinner presided over by Rebeccah's grandparents in her apartment. One feels the transformation of the apartment from a place to flop down after a grueling hospital schedule and from a hideaway for secret rendezvous into a home where the holiness of Shabbat is felt. It is clear that Rebeccah is sufficiently comfortable and proficient in the blessings and traditions to effect that transformation on her own, were she so inclined.

The episode ends with one of television's most significant discussions of Jews and Judaism. Rebeccah's grandmother tells her that while she has passion and fun right now, ten years down the line he may want to take the children to Christmas mass. Rebeccah responds: "Grandma, it's none of your business. What's so terrible about Christmas? It's a national holiday. People give gifts to one another."

It's clear from Rebeccah's tone, however (and Alberta Watson does an excellent job of delivering the lines), that Rebeccah is trying to persuade herself more than she is trying to convince her grandmother. Grandma therefore seizes the opportunity and observes, "Rivkele, you're a Jew in your heart, a Jew in your soul. And no matter what you do or who[m] you marry, that won't change."

"You're wrong, Grandma," Rebeccah responds, again trying to convince herself. "We don't live in a *shtetl* any longer. These are the 1980s in America, not Poland in the 1940s. A person is a person. We go to the same schools, we live in the same neighborhoods, we're not that different."

To which Grandma simply responds with a simple but effective: "Aren't we?" She speaks her mind without nagging.

Rebeccah tells her grandmother that her boyfriend will not be at the Shabbat dinner. Rebeccah had expressed to him her concern that he'll go back to his wife or that his little boy will hate her. (Of course, it reflects badly on Rebeccah's character that she was content to make peace with these issues before and raises them now because her grandmother has awakened other strong feelings in her. Is one's "Jewish-consciousness" to be distinct from one's morality?) Rebeccah tells her grandmother that she and her boyfriend are going to take some time and think things through. Grandma responds with sensitivity, saying, "I'm sorry." When Rebeccah says, "I thought you'd be elated, Grandma," she is told: "To see you unhappy for whatever reason doesn't elate me. I may not always react as you want and say the right things, and I *can* be foolish, but I do love you."

The episode is effective and thought-provoking (for the viewer as well as for Rebeccah) but it does leave us with some questions that the writers of this series and of future series with Jewish characters will have to consider. Where were Rebeccah's parents? Does TV intend to communicate that only grandparents care about religious tradition and loyalty? Does this not subtly (or perhaps not so subtly) suggest that such concerns are old-fashioned or at least fated to skip a generation or two? Would Rebeccah have stuck to her decision on both moral and religious grounds, and hopefully have noted a correlation between the two? Or were the writing staff setting the viewers up for the old "love conquers all" scenario, that would have undermined all of the thoughtful dialogue in this episode? Lastly, if the *Buck James* writers were so intent on contrasting "North" and "South," why not show that there is a Jewish "South" as well by letting Rebeccah find romance and a worthy sparring partner with a Texas Jewish man?

Jewish Divorce—Tragedy And Comedy:
"L.A. Law," "Hester Street"

By the spring of 1993, *L.A. Law* had degenerated into a parody of itself, combining the worst elements of screwball comedies and slasher flicks. Many of the fall episodes exploited shamelessly the L.A. riots, using them as a background for amateur family therapy, psychology, and social commentary. At that time, the series mounted a major promotion campaign, promising to clean up its act, deliver thoughtful scripts, and return to the kind of product that audiences once esteemed. After all, the program still boasted a fine cast, with the addition of impressive performers like A. Martinez.

As the quality of the show fluctuated, so did its depiction of Jews. For several weeks Arnie Becker (Corbin Bernsen), always charmingly opportunistic, was playing up to an aging Jewish film mogul, Ben Flicker (Shelley Berman) with hopes of landing a cushy executive job in the movie industry. Ben Flicker, true to Hollywood's depiction of Jewish moguls, uses Yiddish expressions freely, and especially likes the term, *hondling* (bargaining). His biggest fear, however, is that the studio's books will be audited. His major request of Arnie Becker is that the latter help him to placate his sister in case of any stock battles—by sleeping with her! So with the degradation of *L.A. Law* came as vulgar and embarrassing a Jewish stereotype as you can find.

Things improved, however, in the depiction of Jewish themes with an April 22, 1993 episode that dealt with the theme of Jewish divorce. It even had Arnie Becker on his best behavior.

At a divorce settlement session, a Jewish woman, represented by a female attorney, requests a *get* from her husband, whose lawyer is Arnie. Her soon-to-be-ex taunts her with the question, "Reclaiming your faith, Alison?" When Arnie asks what a *get* is, he receives a correct answer, "It's a document that makes the divorce official in the Jewish religion."

Alison says that she wants the *get* because her future husband, Jonah, "is a spiritual man. He is a devout Jew and I intend to share his devotion." Her soon-to-be-ex is obviously none too spiritual; his first question is how much the *get* will cost him. Alison informs him, "It's not going to cost you anything. You just have to come with me to a rabbi and participate in the ceremony."

While meeting Jonah after the session, Alison's estranged husband sarcastically states that he wonders what the Talmud says about stealing another man's wife. "I met Alison a long time after you and your wife were separated," Jonah replies, "I know that we all have to answer for what we do." Alison's estranged husband retorts, "God's not going to cut him any slack because he's wearing a *yarmulke.*"

This dialogue is indeed interesting, for Jonah *has*, after all, been dating another man's wife. Often *get* disputes come up after a civil divorce has been in process for a while, or even when it is completed, and a traditional wedding ceremony is on the horizon. But here we *do* have a case of adultery, according to Jewish Law and American mores. Could it be that while our writers want to treat a traditional Jew sympathetically, they must do so within certain parameters of soap opera genre? Or do they want to make him more sympathetic, more easily identified with, by giving him weaknesses and imperfections? The dialogue offers no room to explore such issues, in that it culminates in a simple "I'm there for you" resolution. Jonah says, "I know that my being here is painful to you, but Alison asked me to come here." Alison chimes in, also addressing her estranged husband, "I need all the emotional support I can get."

The next *get*-related scene takes place at an unseemly meeting that the estranged husband holds with his partners in the advertising agency in which he has poured all his time and concern, to the detriment of his marriage. His partners exhort him to do anything and everything to keep his wife from getting hold of any agency documents. One says he sued for child custody which he didn't want, but used this for leverage since his wife had just been to the Betty Ford clinic. Their fear is that even rumors of the opening of agency information to a third party, especially a scorned wife, could destroy the confidence of clients forever.

Given this background, we know exactly what to expect next. Arnie has done his homework, and knows that Alison can't get a *get*, a Jewish divorce document, without her husband's issuing it. So they tell her that she must give up her share in the agency, and take only 20% of her portion of a Martha's Vineyard home, if she wants the *get*. Alison capitulates, and her husband agrees to go to the synagogue for the *get* ceremony. Once there, however, he demands even more, their local home. Even Arnie, who is more often than not without scruples, is appalled at this wholesale abuse of religion to cheat a wife in divorce, and says that *he* won't go back on a previous agreement, that he never has.

At the *Bet Din* (Rabbinic Court), a rabbi with a flowing beard tells the estranged husband a parable whose moral, translated from the Hebrew is, "If you ask too much you may end up with nothing." Sure enough, this remarkable morality play ends up with the husband, who is too bitter and materialistic to understand the parable, beginning to realize that there is some kind of Divine justice in this world, one way or another.

This episode by William Finkelstein, Peter Schneider, and Roger Lowenstein was creditable. One wishes, however, that it had spelled out more the purpose of the *get*, namely to protect the wife, and had underlined the irony of its creating the possibility of the husband's perverting Jewish Law and ethics. One gets the impression that an important opportunity, achievable with a few more lines of dialogue, was missed.[1]

This episode of *L.A. Law* reminded me of the 1975 film, *Hester Street*, which becomes more and more impressive each time it is seen. Its locus is the immigration experience of the late nineteenth/early twentieth centuries, which it describes vividly, movingly and with marvelous simplicity.

Can a "greenhorn" woman, Gitl (Carol Kane), who comes over with her little boy, adjust to her "Americanized" husband's abuse or to his girl-friend? Can she stay with a father who has assimilated the worst aspects of life in a strange new land, when she still respects the piety and learning of the ghetto? While pondering these heartfelt questions, the viewer marvels at how the cast, some of them non-Jewish, mastered the Yiddish language.

At the time of the film's release, some critics complained that it was *too* simplistic, that it suggested that one had to choose between tradition and acculturation without offering any golden mean. The beauty of *Hester Street*, however, is precisely that it depicts the tragedy of many Jews who, for lack of time or willpower or both, could never enjoy their Jewish heritage (including the Yiddish language), and could not transmit it with dignity and grace, so forcing subsequent generations to discover it either by chance or through great struggle. Joan Micklin Silver wrote and directed a classic.

Hester Street culminates in a traditional Jewish divorce ceremony, which, like the scene much later in *L.A. Law*, points to the tragedy of Jews unable or unwilling to abide by the moral principles of their faith.

---

1.   See Elliot B. Gertel, "Jewish Views on Divorce," in *The Jewish Family and Jewish Continuity*, ed. Steven Bayme and Gladys Rosen (Hoboken, N. J.: Ktav Publishing House, 1994).

13

CONVERSION

ℰᏋᏓ

Thoughtful Conversion:
"Sisters"

In an absorbing and well-written 1992 episode of the NBC series, *Sisters*, Frankie (Julianne Phillips) accompanies husband Mitch Margolis (Ed Marinaro) to his nephew's bar mitzvah and finds that she enjoys the ceremony and likes Mitch's family and wants to see them more often. "Maybe if you saw them more often," quips Mitch, "you wouldn't like them." Yet Frankie, a successful young professional awaiting her first child, is not easily discouraged. She tells Mitch that they should make a point of visiting his family "so [that] our son can know both sides. Maybe he'll learn something about your religion, your tradition, culture."

This sets Mitch to thinking, immediately striking a nerve and eliciting from him a gut reaction: "Yeah, I wish I knew more myself. But over the years [I've] kinda forgotten it all. But being here and seeing this all again makes me remember all I've missed." With just one additional, very simple comment by Frankie, "It's not too late to get it back," Mitch articulates what script and excellent actor's delivery reveal to be a deep-seated primal desire: "I can't help but imagine what it would be like standing up there with my son, giving him what my parents gave me. Frankie, how would you feel about raising our son as a Jew?"

Shortly after this point, Frankie and Mitch are joined by Mitch's sister, the mother of the bar mitzvah. (Interestingly, Mitch's mother, who in an episode the previous season lamented his loss to Judaism and gave Frankie Sabbath candles for sentimental reasons, is kept completely out of the dialogue in this episode.) Mitch's sister takes time from *kvelling* over her son's fine job to learn about Frankie's willingness that her future child learn about Judaism. Yet Frankie is flustered by not being knowledgeable enough to ask questions, and doesn't even understand a reference to the "four questions." Her sister-in-law reassures her, "We'll teach you the questions and answers." She welcomes Frankie's interest, but does not push her or proselytize her. Frankie admits that she does feel like an outsider: "I feel like you guys are in a club, and I don't know the secret handshake." Mitch's sister responds, "In our club you'll always be a welcome guest."

For the moment it seems that the writer presents Judaism as a closed club which no one can enter, even through conversion. Yet it soon becomes clear that Frankie (and the writer) realize that there is a way to enter the "club," to be more than a guest. Frankie says that she wants to be able to answer the questions, to be part of the celebration, rather than just an outsider looking in. She tells Mitch that she wants to convert.

The conversion theme is developed throughout the episode. Frankie shares her intentions with her sisters, and she discusses them with her mother. Just before Frankie joins her sisters, they are happily chatting about the family christening gown in anticipation of Frankie's baby (who is, by the way, being carried by another sister, Georgie, who is acting as a surrogate mother!). Her sister, Teddi (Sela Ward), upon hearing the news, asks her: "Do you have to go to school, take a test, get a diploma?" But it is with Georgie (Patricia Kalember) that she has the most meaningful and touching conversation. Georgie asks if she'll still visit for Christmas and Easter. Frankie responds in general terms, "I'll always be a part of us—no matter where I am, no matter what I am." In prefacing this conversation and foreshadowing later scenes, Georgie warns Frankie, "Mom's not a Jewish mother. She's never going to be."

Sure enough, Mom (Elizabeth Hoffman) is very upset, far more violently upset than Frankie had anticipated. "One of the things your father and I gave you girls was our faith," Mom insists. "It's who we are, it's who you are. By turning your back on that, you're not just denying you religion, you're denying us." Even on television where problems must be neatly cast about and wrapped up at the end of an hour, such a statement requires another scene to be resolved. In that last, climactic scene, Frankie makes the ultimate pitch to her mother for a change of faith. She asks her mother if she looks any different because of her decision, and then tells her mother that it was she, Mother, who made "each of us strong, to make our own decision, to do what we think is right."

The scenes are touching and, I believe, true to life, given what I have been told about the experiences of converts or would-be converts to Judaism. There is a realism, too, in the treatment of Mitch's responses—blurting out his deepest desires right after Frankie makes the slightest overtures toward Judaism, and then unable to contain his disappointment when Frankie expresses some doubts in between conversations with her mother. In one scene, Mitch says that her expressed desire to convert was his "glimmer of hope that I was important to you as your family. I want this, Frankie, and you said that you wanted it, too."

Now in this 1992 episode of *Sisters*, the theme of conversion to Judaism is better delineated than in any other TV treatment I had seen up to that point. That is not saying much, however, given the poor handling of the theme previously. The series that broke the ground, *A Year In The Life* (1986), would not tell us at first whether or not the conversion had taken place, maintaining a deliberate ambiguity (see above). A year after this *Sisters* episode, in 1993, the theme would also be treated impressively by *Homefront* (see below).

Here, conversion is discussed from both the Jewish and Gentile points of view. What is interesting here, however, is that a Jewish parental view is purposely ignored. It is the Jewish sibling whose encouragement is sought, the sister. While this may be appropriate for a program called *Sisters*, it is important to note that on Frankie's side, both her mother and sisters are consulted. Her "liberal" and hip eldest sister, who loves Freud and Jewish artists, is particularly delighted. Were we beginning to see a trend in television, where the Jewish mother and father are bypassed altogether, and where siblings (or sometimes, as in the past, grandparents) come to represent Jewish family?

Also to be considered are Mitch's expressed reasons for wanting Frankie to convert—namely, to show that she regards him as "family." Shouldn't some representative of Judaism point out to them that that is not sufficient, or perhaps even fair, reason?

As for Mitch himself, the "Jewish husband" on *Sisters* had been depicted as the stud who married two sisters, who showed more ego-gratification than responsibility, who utterly alienated his mother-in-law, and whose own mother said that he doesn't care about Judaism. We never did see enough transformation in him to match his strong feelings about Judaism. Still, the script by Lisa Melamed enabled *Sisters* to make the best beginning on TV in exploring the issue of conversion to Judaism.

Tough Conversion:
"Homefront"

The landmark TV series, *Homefront* (1991 - 1993), about life in a small Ohio town after the end of World War II, was a masterpiece in character-ization and social commentary. Produced with great care, thoughtfulness and artistry by Bernard Lechowick and Lynn Marie Latham, it succeeded at recreating an era, and did so with fine writing as well as period pieces. The show had a knowing humor, persona who changed and grew and an excellent cast that made the characters real and alive.

There was amazing change and growth, as well, in the show's treatment of Jews and of Judaism. By the last episode, in May 1993, *Homefront* had achieved a remarkable balance and sensitivity in its Jewish themes which was not apparent during the first several episodes, but which was most pronounced and touching at the end.

Until the last episode, the writers could not decide whether to present Gina (Giuliana Santini) as an Italian, or as a Jewish survivor of the Holo-caust. That dichotomy in characterization was brought home in a dialogue between Gina's WASP in-laws, Mike and Ruth Sloan (Ken Jenkins and Mimi Kennedy). Protesting Gina's methods of rearing their granddaughter, Ruth complains: "Where is this vaunted Jewish brainpower? If they're all so smart where did she come from?" To which her husband responds: "Don't forget. She's also Italian."

Yet by the last episode, written by James Stanley and Dianne Massock, Gina had decided that her boyfriend, Charlie Hailey (Harry O'Reilly), the boyhood buddy of her husband who was killed returning from World War Two, would have to convert to Judaism before she could marry him. At the beginning of that last episode, Gina's mother-in-law drew her into a typical Ruth Sloan conversation. Mrs. Sloan tells Gina that it would be better for baby Emma if people did not know she was half Jewish; there would be no discrimination. Gina tells Ruth that her baby is not "half-Jewish," but fully Jewish, because, in Jewish Law, that is determined by the mother. "Not by my religion," says Ruth.

Gina responds thoughtfully to Ruth's bigoted and insensitive proposals, observing that she cannot herself understand her own "stubbornness," her zeal for her Jewish heritage. She says that she wasn't religious before the war, but the Nazis regarded her as Jewish. When Ruth Sloan replies, "You don't want the Nazis to define you," Gina says that she doesn't want to give the Nazis even a small victory. (These lines of dialogue echo Emil Fackenheim, the noted Jewish theologian.) Ruth becomes concerned that Gina wants to emigrate to Palestine, but Gina reassures her mother-in-law that she considers Emma "100% American and 100% Jewish."

When Gina's boyfriend, Charlie, invites her out to a movie on Friday night, an "old American custom," Gina replies, "I also have a custom. I want you to be with us when I light the Sabbath candles." As she guides him through the Friday night rituals, she says, "There's more to the Sabbath evening, but we'll do more when I understand more." The writers thus make it clear that Gina's religious awakening is very recent and spontaneous. Gina shows Charlie the *Kiddush* cup and says that Emma's father will use it. (*Kiddush* is the Blessing of Sanctification that inaugurates the Sabbath Day and sets it apart as holy.)

Gina then tells Charlie, in a very direct and considerate way, that she does not think that Emma should see her father wearing a St. Christopher medal. That is her way of telling Charlie that they must break their relationship and that Gina must find a Jewish husband. Needless to say, this was a unique, milestone scenario for television, perhaps the only time this has happened in a TV drama, at least in recent memory (except for *Ivanhoe* remakes). Charlie is undeterred from his pursuit of Gina. He removes the medal. Gina tells him that she does not want him to violate his religion. But Charlie responds that he only wears the medal because it helps him to remember his mother, but he can remember her in other ways.

Still, Gina is determined to break the relationship, especially after she and Charlie see newsreels of the concentration camps at the movies. She says she is sorry, she loves him, but she can't marry him because he is a Gentile. When he points out that her first husband was not Jewish, Gina replies that at that time in her life, she was glad just to be alive. Now that she has a daughter, she wants her to learn the traditions and Festivals from her father. Charlie asks, "You'll marry some guy you don't love, just because he's Jewish?" (Charlie reminds her that her children would be Jewish regardless of her husband's religion.) "No," Gina responds, "I would have to love him. But he would have to be Jewish to understand my culture, my history."

At this point, Charlie tells Gina that he'll raise the children as Jews, he'll learn Hebrew. "You want a Jewish father to make a 100% Jewish home. I'll convert." It's amazing how many times in this episode the only acceptable percentage was given as 100%. But it was also very refreshing—and very touching—to viewers who care about Judaism that it is a 100% Jewish identity that is repeatedly affirmed and encouraged in the Gina-Charles segments.

True to their characteristic wit and humor and eye for historical-sociological detail, the writers brought the viewer along as Charlie seeks out a rabbi for his conversion, and is repeatedly discouraged. One rabbi tells him that his motivation for conversion can never be pure because he is studying Judaism only to marry Gina. Charlie responds, "With all due respect, Rabbi, it sounds like a lot of legal mumbo-jumbo." Charlie protests: "If being Jewish made Gina the woman I fell in love with, then maybe being Jewish is something worth looking into....Even if I look into Judaism for the wrong reason, what's to prevent me from converting for the right reason, when all is said and done?"

Charlie must battle not only the skepticism and obstacles of the rabbis, but Gina's uncertainty, too. "It's not my fault that I was born a gentile, Gina," he feels he has to say at one point. Charlie tries holding back with the next rabbi, saying that he wants to convert because he has a "Jewish friend" he "admires," But that rabbi won't take his interest in converting seriously because Charlie has "so little knowledge of Judaism." We sympathize with Charlie when he sighs, "I'm finding it next to impossible to choose to be one of the chosen." He asks, "With all the Jews killed in the last war, how come you people aren't looking for a few replacements?" The question reminds me of a book, *Hope Is My House*, published in 1966 by Deborah Wigoder, a woman born Irish Catholic, who describes her desire to become a Jew in the 1940s initially because she wanted to take the place of a martyred Jew.

Finally, Charlie is able to spin his own Talmudic logic, and to convince a rabbi that God might have had him fall in love with a beautiful Jewish woman just so he might look into Judaism. "Maybe," he adds, "whoever is keeping me from Judaism is denying God's will." Charlie convinces this third rabbi that he wants to become a Jew, knowing full well that Jews have been persecuted. After all, Charlie says, he used to be "a part of that"—that is, he used to insult Jews.

Lechowick, who wrote this episode, captures well an era and a mindset in which conversion was discouraged, and probably too much. Most rabbis today would be very happy to embrace a bright and interested convert like Charlie, and would not put any stumbling blocks before anyone's desire just to *learn* about Judaism. Alarming statistics about intermarriage, encouraging statistics regarding the Jewish identity of the children of sincere converts, and fewer inhibitions about letting Judaism compete in the market of ideas, have rendered the rabbinic approaches here anachronistic and counterproductive.

I mentioned that the writers achieved a balance, and so they have. As much as Gina is returning to her Jewish heritage, that is how much Al Kahn (John Slattery), the union leader branded Communist, is moving away from his heritage, to the point of no return. Latham penned the realistic scene where Al and Ann (Wendy Phillips), a local widowed matriarch, a Roman Catholic, are expecting a child together. They discuss, under a big crucifix on Ann's wall, possible names for the baby. "We don't have Juniors," Al tells Ann. "It's tradition." Yet it is clear from that conversation and many before that Al doesn't defer to traditions. He can joke about the name "Christopher Kahn" being an oxymoron, or about Ann trying to name the as yet unborn baby after Catholic saints when it might suit everyone better to name him after a Jewish saint. Al had become both apostle and symbol of the "social gospel" of labor.

Just before telling Charlie about her intention to establish a Jewish home for her child, Gina asks Al whether it bothers him to live in a house in which there are so many statues and crosses and Christian symbols. She asks Al what his son will think. Al says that he will tell his son about Jewish traditions—"just the part I agree with." When Gina presses Al to tell her what it is he doesn't like about Judaism, Al responds., "I'm not picking on Judaism *per se*. I have an equal affection for all religions. None."

Gina asks Al how he can think it's possible to turn his back on so many hundreds of years of tradition. Al replies, "How can you think it is *not* possible?" So, in this conversation, unique in the annals of prime time TV because one Jew actually takes another Jew to task for assimilation and, even more unusual, for complacency, we find the writers noting, and not without an underlying sadness, that Al's decision to abandon traditions will probably be the last Jewish decision in his family tree. In the shared context of the story about Gina and Charlie, and Al's story, we find a TV drama which consciously and sincerely and explicitly contrasts an abandonment with an awakening of Jewishness. My only regret is that, along the way, the drama did not foreshadow or initiate such a contrast. It would have added more dimension to the Gina and Al characters, and to their interaction.

The last scene of the series, *Homefront*, is a Shabbat dinner at Gina's apartment, with Charlie present. It would have been unthinkable even a half-decade before that a TV series would have ended with Shabbat. The series based on Herman Wouk's *Winds Of War* (1983), about a Jewish heroine caught in Europe during the Nazi era, offered a Sabbath dinner in Italy solely to indicate that her one hope of rescue was her husband's influential Gentile family. Gina was not rescued by her first marriage, though it is clear that she needed someone at that time in her life, and responded to the kindness and affection of an American soldier. Now, widowed, and a mother, she is thinking about her heritage and about her child's identity.

Homefront will be remembered in the annals of television history for dealing seriously with the issues of Jewish continuity and of conversion to Judaism—and with the thoughtfulness, wit, humor and warmth that always characterize a fine series. It was a program of 100% quality that ultimately yielded 100% regard for Jewish concerns and commitments.

Hostility to Converts: "Seinfeld"

A 1997 episode of *Seinfeld*, written by Peter Mehlman and Jill Franklyn, was a turning point of sorts in that series' treatment of "Jewish" subject matter. Jerry's dentist tells him that he is now a Jew, having finished converting only a couple of days before. Jerry's immediate response is to politely and sincerely say, "Welcome aboard."

Yet as time passes and Jerry has further contact with his dentist, he finds himself reacting strongly and negatively to the conversion. When Jerry comments that his dentist did not seem to spend too much time at the health club, the latter quips: "I didn't do much. I just sat in the sauna....It was more like a Jewish workout." That is the last straw for Jerry, who soon complains to his friend Elaine, "The guy's Jewish two days. He's already making Jewish jokes....I believe that....[he] converted to Judaism just for the jokes."

The writers are on to something here. There is some distrust of converts and their motives in the Jewish community, and perhaps some wariness in Jewish teachings and observances as well. After all, the belief in Judaism is that you don't have to be Jewish to be regarded as a good person or as worthy of salvation. God cares about all people, and entered into a covenant with them through Noah. The whole purpose of God's covenant with Israel is to safeguard Divine teachings for all humanity.

Conversion is often a challenge to Jews, especially if they don't do much about being Jewish. It shakes up the sense of security of some Jews in their own Jewish authenticity. Many Jews, when so challenged, fall back either into a sense of ethnic noblesse oblige, clannishness, or what they regard as their inalienable right to determine Jewish folk culture. There are Jews who hold certain foods or inflections or even kinds of humor as more sacred than the Torah and the traditions by which Torah is interpreted or lived.

Something rings true here. A comedian is always on guard against possible usurpers of his repertoire of jokes. There are Jewish comedians, I am sure, who would resent "outsiders" who now appropriate Jewish humor, especially if those "outsiders" are now "practicing Jews" in a fuller sense, in both learning and commitment, identification and observance, than the "natives."

The writers have presented a good opportunity for some humorous reflection on a theme that entails some self-scrutiny on the part of their lead character as on the part of all Jews. Suddenly the theme and plot take a sharp turn, or perhaps detour, into a rather contrived theory regarding Jerry's hostility. We are told that Jerry's real problem is a prejudice against dentists, that he is, in effect, and "anti-dentite." That is not, however, the issue with which our writers began. They started out with some real gut issues about self-confidence and self-assurance as a Jew. One wishes that they had seen *those* subjects through in the same effectively humorous way with which they raised them.

14

POSITIVE HEREAFTER

೫⊃ೞ

The Afterlife Respected:
"The Cemetery Club"

C*emetery Club* (1992) is a film of paradoxes. Upon hearing its title, one could conclude that it is morbid. Actually, it is a vital, heartwarming and amusing movie. It is by far one of the most "Jewish" films in recent years: it offers a rare look at Jewish ethnic and social life among middle-aged women in the semi-suburbs (in this case, of Pittsburgh). Yet it is by far the most interesting and universally appealing glimpse not only into Jewish 60-something (or late 50-something), but into that age group in general, especially as it focuses on the ordeal of widowhood.

One cannot emphasize enough the charm and uniqueness of *Cemetery Club*, due in no small measure to Ivan Menchell's script based on his stage play. The performances by Ellen Burstyn, Olympia Dukakis, Diane Ladd, Danny Aiello and Lainie Kazan, along with all the other performances, are fine and memorable. This movie is more than special. It is a surprise, and on many levels.

First, the film focuses on details of Jewish observance and custom. It highlights everything from a *mezuzah* on the door to the washing of the hands upon returning from the cemetery.[1]

It allows the characters to sound off a little about Jewish customs, but never to mock those traditions. Indeed, more often than not it demonstrates their therapeutic or spiritual value. When Burstyn's character protests that she doesn't like the covered mirrors,[2] one of her friends observes, "It's *shiva.* You're not supposed to like it." Some of the best scenes, when characters truly open up, are at *shiva* (the seven-day home mourning observance).

Secondly, *Cemetery Club* shatters the widely-accepted myth, even among Jews, that Jews do not believe in life after death. Not so. It is Judaism that gave that belief to both Christianity and Islam. In *Cemetery Club*, three widowed friends share a time-honored Jewish custom of visiting the cemetery, and they even make a bit of a ceremony of it on special *yahrzeits* (anniversaries of deaths). While one wishes that some attention were given to the custom of attending the *minyan* (prayer quorum)

---

1.   Ritual washing after leaving the cemetery has its origin in biblical commandments regarding the purification of those who had come in contact with the dead. (See Numbers 19) Biblical law regarded death as generating ritual impurity that was a challenge to the holiness of the community. The differentiation between death and holiness was, most likely, an effort to wean the Israelites away from the death-centered religions around them, that they might affirm their covenant with God which required that they live lives of holy deeds. Jacob Milgrom regards the biblical laws as an effective program to free the ancient Israelites of fears of demons associated in ancient times with the cemetery and with death. See Jacob Milgrom, "The Paradox of the Red Cow" (Excursus 48), *The JPS Torah Commentary—Numbers*, commentary by Jacob Milgrom (Philadelphia: The Jewish Publication Society, 1990), p. 438; and Dr. Milgrom's more detailed essay by the same name in *Vetus Testamentum* 31 (1981), 67-72, reprinted in Milgrom, *Studies in Cultic Theology and Terminology* (Leiden: E. J. Brill, 1983).

2.   The covering of mirrors came to symbolize the mourner's turning from thoughts of personal vanity. See Rabbi Isaac Klein, *A Guide to Jewish Religious Practice* (N.Y. The Jewish Theological Seminary of America, 1979), p. 286. The custom may have originated in superstitions about mirrors being receptacles for demons at the time of a death, but, in keeping with the thrust of biblical law, obsessing on demons or spirits and ghosts was prohibited. (See Deut. 18:10-12)

and saying the Kaddish (affirming God before a living congregation as one's source of comfort and strength), a practice that is more and more followed by women as well as men, this film does make the point, both subtly and loudly that Jews believe that something endures beyond death.

The film is not without its cemetery humor, but it is genuinely pious humor, rare in films with a Jewish theme. Here, a grieving widow can say to her friends that she has not made a double tombstone so as not to spook her granddaughter with a "coming soon" sign next to the place where her beloved grandfather is buried. Only in a film where people still care about the dead can widow Moskowitz, played by Burstyn, and widower Katz, played by Aiello, meet at the most unlikely of places, a cemetery. And only in a film with a pious heart can the most mocked of characters, Kazan's much-wed divorcée, who ends up doing the unthinkable, get some sympathy.

Cemetery Club is unique, finally, because it's the only film I know that makes fun of mixed marriage. Not of the traditional Jewish response to mixed marriage, mind you. There are plenty of films that do *that* in the name of "love conquers all" or "Jewish families stifle all." This film actually has the guts and audacity to suggest that at a mixed marriage, the slightest disturbance, provoked by totally unrelated factors, can lead to "ninety-four people beginning to argue about who killed Christ."

Whereas the film *Used People* (1992) got some cheap laughs with references to Italian-kosher mixed marriage cuisine and romanticized mixed marriage among seniors as the spice of variety in life which keeps one youthful and kicking, *Cemetery Club* makes fun of that very stance. It mercilessly mocks interfaith marriage ceremonies. (*Used People* mocked the clergy, but still glorified the ceremony as an obstacle surmounted.) Both *Used People* and *Cemetery Club* introduce sour-faced Italian relatives-to-be who don't relish having Jewish relatives (and it's amazing that such stereotypes should appear in two independently and simultaneously produced movies), but it is clear, upon comparison, that in the former that type is seen as an anachronism and in the second as a complication. In *Used People* the romantic figure is an Italian admirer from outside; in *Cemetery Club* it is a retired Jewish policeman from the periphery of community standards of social status and responsibility. What other film suggests how Jews in the mainstream can bring those on the periphery into some kind of normalcy as people and as Jews? Off hand, the only other examples I can think of are *Mermaids* (1990) and *The Plot Against Harry* (see above).

The portrayal of Burstyn's Jewish granddaughter as sensitive, together, talented, sweet and pretty is a rather novel look at a female Jewish child, especially when you consider that the contemporaneous TV series *Brooklyn Bridge* all but suggested that there was not a lass in all of Brooklyn who could be a worthy girlfriend to young Alan except for fair and bright Katie Monihan of the nearby Catholic school.

My only problem with *Cemetery Club* was with the ending, which was a bit cutesy, but perhaps not improbable given the characters involved. Still, this is a positive depiction of Jews and Judaism, in which non-Jewish actors portrayed well a variety of interesting Jewish types. Indeed, the most beloved and sympathetic character is played by Olympia Dukakis, who is the voice of traditional gut Jewish responses. That is the most unique thing of all in this film. The character mocked in the Sixties and still trotted out for cheap laughs in the Nineties, ends up with the last laugh here, and earns the most heartfelt tears.

INDEX

E

E. R. (1994-95), 55–57, 77, 152
Edelstein, Lisa, 170, 251
Education of Max Bickford, The (2001-
    02), 41–44
Edwards, Anthony, 55
Elfman, Jenna, 46, 115
Elijah's chair, 53
Embarrassment, 178–179
Emunah (faith, faithfulness), 91, 134
Englee, Charles H., 3
Epstein, Pierre, 74
Erev (day before Yom Kippur), 227
Esformes, Nathan, 222, 224, 225–226
Estrin, Allen, 140, 217
Ethical will, 77–78
Ethnicity, 130
Euthanasia, 79–80
Evangelical Christianity, 79
Exodus
    (12:49), 234
    (21:7), 195
    (22:12), 212
Exploitation/transformation of Judaism
    by the media, 9
Ezekiel, 121

F

Fackenheim, Emil, 269
Faith, 117–118, 145
False witness, 119
Fame, 30
Family Affair, 184
Family Channel, 246
Family Law episode (2001), 170–174
Family Of Cops, 65–67
    and "Jewish" themes, 66–67
Family Ties, 133
Fanaticism, 72–73
Fantana, Tom, 147, 237
Farrakhan, Louis, 154
Fasting, 227
Fay, Meagan, 169
Fear as redemption, 132–133
Feldshuh, Tovah, 83

Fiddler On The Roof, 58, 102
Fight For Life (1987), 239–242
    Haftarah (prophetic reading) and,
        240–241
    teaching of Jewish concepts, 240
Final Judgment, 52
Fine, Fran, 149
Fink, Mark, 215
Finkel, Fyvush, 101, 175, 177, 178
Finkelstein, M., 3
Finkelstein, William, 264
Five Mrs. Buchanans, The (1994-95),
    59–61
Fleet, Jo Van, 44
Fleming, Ian, 89
Flint, Carol, 55
Florek, Dann, 119
Ford, Faith, 91
Foreman, Milos, 116
Forer, David H., 140
Forgiveness, 19, 158, 159, 164
Foster, Don, 47
"Four Questions", 19, 266
Fox Network, 72, 104, 151
Fox, Terry Curtis, 48
Frank's Place, 137–139
Franz, Dennis, 202, 203
Frazer, Dan, 85
Fressing (stuffing of food), 16, 114
Friday The Rabbi Slept Late (1964),
    176
Friedman, Peter, 133
Frolov, Diane, 231

G

Gallagher, David, 161
Gammill, Tom, 21
Gandolfini, James, 7
Ganz, Lowell, 62
Garbe, Josh, 87
Gefilte fish, 90, 91, 102
Genesis, 108
Gentile
    in *Apprenticeship of Duddy Kravitz*
        (1974), 113
    bar/bat mitzvah and, 215

in *Family Law* episode (2001), 172
in *Gideon's Crossing*, 164, 166
in *Good Advice* (1993-94), 39–40
in *Homicide* episode (1997), 235, 237
Jewish relations, 258
in *Living in Captivity* (1999), 108
in *Naked City* (1958-63), 223–227, 224
in *Nanny, The* (1993-1999), 150
in *Picket Fences* (1994), 179
prophet, 231, 258
Seinfeld and, 23, 24
in *Sofie* (1993), 129
State and Main (2000) and, 71
stereotypes of, 235
in *Stranger Among Us, A* (1992), 233
in *Thirtysomething* episode (1990-1991 season), 125
viewer, 2
in *Way We Were, The* (1973), 2
woman, 116, 164
in *A Year In The Life* (1986), 95
A Year In The Life (1986), 97
Gerard, Danny, 133
Get (divorce document), 8, 262, 263, 264
Gets, Malcolm, 40
Gibson, Channy, 3
Gibson, Thomas, 46
Gideon's Crossing, 164–167
Gilford, Jack, 185
Gilliland, Eric, 15
Glass Menagerie, The, 137
Glass, Ned, 242
Glatstein, Jacob, 174
Gleason, Jackie, 136
Gless, Sharon, 243
God, 170–171, 242
    acknowledgement of, 142
    affirmation of, 86
    anger, frustration with, 204–205, 239
    aversion to, 163
    belief/existence of, 25, 26, 27, 31, 42, 43, 85, 103, 145, 170, 187

chutzpah with, 241
honoring of, 212
human humility before, 219
Jewish arguing with, 218
and Judaism, 128
justice of, 264
love of, 180
loyalty to, 85
miraculous deliverance, 249
peace and, 123
People of Israel and, 214
personal action and, 178
prayer to, 56, 168, 218
presence of, 36, 85
shame and, 74
at Sinai, 171
sovereignty of, 106
teachings about, 108
teachings of, 90
will of, 165
"God of pathos", 28
God's Grace, Malamud, Bernard (1982), 145
Goldberg, Barry, 259
Goldberg, Eric Ian, 42
Goldberg, Gary David, 133, 135
Goldbergs, The See Molly
Goldblum, Jeff, 131
Golden Girls, The, 60
Goldstein, Ron, 235
Golem, 8–9, 59
Good Advice (1993-94), 38–40
Goodbye Columbus, 16, 37, 216
Goodfellas (1990), 9
Goodman, John, 15
Goodman, Percival, 236
Goodman, Robert, 251, 252
Goodstein, Debbie, 83
Gordon, Barry, 40
Gordon, James, 32
Gordon, Susan, 31
Gorman, Robert, 168
Gould, Mortimer, 79
Graduate (1967), 45
Grammer, Kelsey, 13
Greeks, ancient, 258
Greene, Mark, 56
Griffith, Melanie, 232

L

L.A. Law, 4–5, 181, 182, 262–264
Laborteaux, Matthew, 199
Ladd, Diane, 275
Lahti, Christine, 76
LaMond, Bill, 216
LaMond, Jo, 216
Land of the Giants, 205
Landon, Michael, 200, 201
Last Best Hope, The Tauber, Peter, 221
Latham, Lynn Marie, 268
Latkes (a Chanukah food), 62, 189
Latner, Helen, 15
Law and Order–Special Victims Unit,
        118–119
Lawyer, Jewish, 176
Lazer, Charles, 88
Lear, Norman, 52, 215
Lechowick, Bernard, 268, 270
Lee, Thelma, 259
Leifer, Carol, 23
Leonard, Herbert B., 30, 222, 224, 225
Levi Yitzhak of Berditchev, 204
Levinson, Barry, 45, 63, 235
Levites, 72
Leviticus
        (12:2-3), 152
        (16), 227
        (19:18), 130
        (19:28), 149
Lewis, Jerry, 239, 241
Lewis, Richard, 53, 62, 160
Lidz, Franz, 144
Lieberman, Joseph, 173
Life Goes On, 201
Lilith, 13
Linden, Hal, 4
Linklater, Hamish, 164
Lippman, Amy, 105
Lise-Mynster, Karen, 129
Little House On the Prairie, 199–201,
        228, 240
        insight into the Jewish soul, 199
Living in Captivity (1999), 106–109
Locatell, Carol, 40, 143
Lombardi, Frank, 17
Long, Breckenridge, 42

Long, Shelley, 38
Lorre, Chuck, 47, 48
Louis-Dreyfus, Julia, 20
Love and War, 107
Love Boat, 216
Love relationships, 184
Lowe, Rob, 192
Lowenstein, Roger, 264
Lucas, Caryn, 149
Lucas, John Meredyth, 204, 242
Lumet, Sydney, 232
Lynn, Meredith Scott, 140

M

Maccabees, 248
MacDowell, Andie, 144
MacNicol, Peter, 76
Mad Adventures of "Rabbi" Jacob, The
        (France, 1974), 4, 232
Madame X, 31
Madison, Sarah Danielle, 160
Magid (storyteller), 201
Maharis, George, 24
Malcolm X, 154
Malden, Karl, 194
Mamet, David, 69, 234
Mandel, Babaloo, 62
Mandel, Howie, 147
Manheim, Camryn, 181
Mann, Barry, 251
Mann, Ted, 201
Margulies, David, 140, 142
Marie Rose, 208
Marinaro, Ed, 265
Markinson, Brian, 203
Marshall, Don, 205
Martin, Julie, 235
Martinez, A., 262
Masada, 8
Masius, John, 136
Massock, Dianne, 268
Mathers, Jerry, 133
Matlin, Marlee, 74
Matzah (unleavened bread), 53, 54, 70
Max Glick, 87–90
Mayron, Melanie, 185

Elliot B. Gertel has been Rabbi of Congregation Rodfei Zedek in Chicago since 1988 and media critic for *The Jewish Post and Opinion* (Indianapolis) since 1979. His previous book, *What Jews Know About Salvation* (2002) convinced the Library of Congress to recognize "salvation" as a subject heading under Judaism.